# THE AMERICAN COLONIZATION SOCIETY

# THE AMERICAN COLONIZATION SOCIETY

## AND THE FOUNDING OF THE FIRST AFRICAN REPUBLIC

A History of the Private Enterprise That Made Uneasy Peace With Slavery to Rescue Free Africans and Transplant Them on the West Coast of Africa

JOHN SEH DAVID

iUniverse LLC
Bloomington

**THE AMERICAN COLONIZATION SOCIETY**
**And The Founding Of The First African Republic**

iUniverse books may be ordered through booksellers or by contacting:

iUniverse LLC
1663 Liberty Drive
Bloomington, IN 47403
www.iuniverse.com
1-800-Authors (1-800-288-4677)

ISBN: 978-1-4917-3423-0 (sc)
ISBN: 978-1-4917-3424-7 (e)

Library of Congress Control Number: 2014908747

Printed in the United States of America.

iUniverse rev. date: 06/10/2014

# CONTENTS

Acknowledgements .................................................................................... xi
Introduction ........................................................................................... xiii

Chapter I. *Africans in Mesoamerica* ........................................................ 1
- African Presence in Mesoamerica .................................................. 1
- Early African Voyages ..................................................................... 4
- The Olmec Colossal Heads ............................................................. 5

Chapter II. *Decline of Africa's Civilizations* ........................................ 10
- Indentured Africans ...................................................................... 12
- Attempts to Abolish Slavery ......................................................... 15
- Blacks Fight for White Freedom .................................................. 16

Chapter III. *Freedmen: Neither Slave nor Free* ................................... 17
- The Dilemma of Freedmen ........................................................... 17
- Blacks Break Away From White Churches ................................... 20
- Dred Scott Case: Controversy For Citizenship ............................ 22

Chapter IV. *The Founding Fathers and The Saga of Slavery* ................. 24
- George Washington Grapples With Slavery .................................. 28
- John Adams' Denouncement of Slavery ........................................ 32
- Thomas Jefferson Embraces Slavery ............................................. 33
- Edward Coles' Plea to End Slavery ............................................... 38
- John Randolph's Regret About Slavery .......................................... 39
- James Madison's Ambivalence on Slavery ..................................... 39
- The Constitution's Silence on Slavery .......................................... 41

Chapter V. *The Binary Role of Slave Women* ....................................... 44
- Slave Narratives ............................................................................ 45
- Family Life in Slavery ................................................................... 53

Chapter VI. *The Revolutionary Brothers and Slave Women* ..................... 56
- The Washington—Venus Affair ..............................................57
- Jefferson-Hemings Affair ................................................ 60
- Jefferson's Silence .......................................................62
- Jefferson's Culpability ...................................................63

Chapter VII. *Slave Revolt in the United States* ...............................67
- The Haitian Experience ................................................. 68
- Slaves Insurrection  .....................................................69

Chapter VIII. *Formation of the American Colonization Society* ...............73
- Rationale for Repatriation ............................................. 80

Chapter IX. *The American Colonization in West Africa* .......................85
- Criticism of the ACS .................................................... 88
- Why the Outcry? ......................................................... 90
- William Lloyd Garrison: "All on Fire" .................................94

Chapter X. *Back-to-Africa Conspiracy Theory* .............................98

Chapter XI. *The Anathema: Colonization or Emigration* .......................102
- Delany's Emigration Initiatives .......................................106

Chapter XII. *The Grain Coast Before 1800* ................................ 111
- European Explorers in Africa ..........................................112

Chapter XIII. *Peopling of the Grain Coast* ................................ 116

Chapter XIV. *The Liberian Colony* .................................... 120
- The Colonial Period: 1822-1839 .......................................131
- Battles with the Chiefs ...............................................133
- Unrest in the Colony ..................................................136
- First Constitution .....................................................146
- Commonwealth Period: 1839-1847 .......................................151

Chapter XV. *Native-Settler Conflicts* ....................................153
- Poro-Sande Governance  ................................................156
- Origin of the Sande and Poro .........................................158
- Religious Differences .................................................162
- Racism in the Colony ..................................................163
- Border Disputes .......................................................165
- Antislavery Campaigns .................................................166

Chapter XVI. *Declaration of Independence* ..................................................171
- The Lone Star ..................................................................................178
- Pledge of Allegiance ........................................................................179
- Description of the Flag ....................................................................179
- Description of the Seal ....................................................................179
- National Anthem .............................................................................180
- Liberia College ...............................................................................181
- U.S. Recognizes Liberia ...................................................................183
- Mysterious Death of Edward J. Roye ..............................................186

Chapter XVII. *Final Thoughts: Slavery and Africa's Culpability* ............189
- Dark Side of Domestic Slavery ........................................................196
- Africa's Liability .............................................................................197

Select Bibliography .......................................................................................201
Select Index ..................................................................................................215

*For The Youth of Liberia*

# Acknowledgements

The French philosopher Bernard of Chartres noted that "Dwarfs perched on the shoulders of giants." Indeed, I am indebted to many academic giants for the vast amount of resources available to conduct scholarly inquiries. I am especially grateful to the following historians and scholars for their invaluable historical records that helped with my study on the American Colonization Society, chattel slavery in the United States, and domestic slavery in Africa.

Allen C Guelzo, *Lincoln's Emancipation Proclamation:*
   *The end of Slavery in America*
Amos Beyan, *African American Settlements in West Africa*
David B. Davis, *Inhuman Bondage: The Rise and*
   *Fall of Slavery in the New World*
Elizabeth Ischei, *A History of The Igbo People*
John H. Franklin, *The Free Negro in North Carolina*
Hollis Lynch, *Edward Blyden: Pan-Negro Patriot: 1832-1912*
Ivan V. Sertima, *They Came Before Columbus*
J. Gus. Liebenow, *The Evolution of Privilege*
Ralph Randolph Gurley, *Life of Jehudi Ashmun,*
   *Late Colonial Agent of Liberia*
Thomas Jefferson, *Notes on the State of Virginia*

I want to thank the University of Texas Library staff at Arlington for providing me access to the Library large collection of books and articles on Africa. They were immensely resourceful.

Meanwhile, I select three educators, out of many, whose influence in my life is indelible. First, missionary Else J. Lund of the Fassama United Pentecostal Mission School in rural Liberia for the nurture she provided in my formative years. It still amazes me how she was able to combine two grades, at a time, in the same class, yet, we completed all textbooks before the year ended, and best of all, Fassama always had perfect scores in the National Examination, while she was a teaching principal at the school.

I also extend my hearty gratitude to the late Professor Ermel Stepp at Marshall University in West Virginia. He inspired me in graduate school to pursue post graduate studies in higher education. And finally, Professor John Eddy at the University of North Texas was a dear friend to me and many African students at the University. He always seemed to understand the plight of foreign students and did what he could to help.

I also want to thank Dianne Kortu of Euless, Texas, for reviewing and making helpful comments on sections of my draft work. And on the personal side, I thank my family for the moral support I received.

# INTRODUCTION

In the summer of 1986, I was invited to speak to a group of students and faculty at a mission station in Mississippi. I had a life-changing experience that weekend. A group of students surrounded me after the assembly, asking questions about what life was like in Africa and whether I spoke *African*. Before uttering a word, someone asked, "Well, how do you say hello in African? And tell us stories about lions and elephants."

I responded the best way I could to satisfy the curiosity of the youngsters, but one of the school administrators stepped in and urged the children to take a break. It was lunchtime.

Toward nightfall, two African American boys who had said nothing to me previously decided to introduce themselves. They commended me for my talk in the chapel and expressed the fact that I was the first African speaker to ever be invited to their school. Indeed, the boys did not like the line of questioning from their schoolmates after the assembly. "All they want to hear is about lions and elephants and stupid stuff so they can make fun."

That "so they can make fun" got me thinking about the fact that I may have missed something. As one of the boys (whom I call Jerry) added the missing pieces later, a real picture started to emerge. As he vented his frustration, the young man made me understand that some of his classmates often teased him and other African American students about the jungle of Africa where black people allegedly came from, and that their ancestors lived in trees and caves. The other young boy (whom I call Perry) talked about how the teachers would bring films in class about Tarzan, the Ape Man, who was raised in the African jungle. "When that show is on, some of the white children turn and look at us and laugh. Some of the black children go under their tables and so did I. They just want to embarrass black people. Are there ape people in Africa, Mr. David?" Then Jerry interjected, "Yes, and what about all that monkey business, that black people came from . . . ?

I interrupted Jerry before he could end his sentence. "If I tell you the truth, would you believe me?" He answered enthusiastically, "Yes!"

I proceeded: "First, the Tarzan story is not true and never took place in Africa. The story is a mere fiction. Edgar Burroughs created the Tarzan story in the early 1900s to demonstrate the life of a man who accepted civilization and then rejected it later. Although the Ape Man, Tarzan, was white, the setting of the series is in the African jungle. Many people feel it sends the wrong message about African people. And that monkey thing, it is not true. So spread the word to your friends, and let them know that Tarzan is a fiction and black people did not come from apes."

As I ended my visit and headed back to Marshall University in West Virginia where I was pursuing a graduate degree in education, I decided to do something about disinformation and misinformation in black history.

Back then, it was not unusual to talk to Americans who thought Africa was a country, instead of a continent. They wanted to know about people who spoke a language called "African."

Others believed Africans were tree dwellers or cave men, who never ventured beyond their own tribal regions.

Equally astonishing was how much a large number of critics lacked knowledge about African civilizations, except for Timbuktu, which they associated with abundant gold. The Everly Brothers even recorded one of their famous songs, "Take a Message to Mary," in 1959, and they wrote about going to Timbuktu "searching for gold."

Most Americans only talk about Africa in the context of slavery. Such limited knowledge leads many to conclude that Africa had never made any meaningful contribution to world civilization, apart from the pyramids of Egypt. But even with that said, some scholars claim that culturally, Egypt was a nation of Caucasian-Hamitic people who are not a part of Africa.

My experience in Mississippi has inspired the writing of this first Chapter. It emphasizes the fact that Africans did not first come to the Americas as slaves. Though they did not discover America or create the great civilizations of Mesoamerica, there is evidence that black people first arrived and lived in the New World before Christopher Columbus in 1492. While scholars are still arguing who is responsible for the creation of the first civilization in the Americas, there is evidence that Africans were present when the first civilizations of the Americas evolved.

The Africans experience in the New World may be likened to Swiss cheese. It is held together by fillings that are littered with holes. This has been the case, because most textbooks in the United States narrate the black experience largely from the perspective of slavery. There is a virtual silence about Africa's contributions before descending into captivity. The lack of details and negative depiction of black people have led to the belief that Africa is inconsequential, when it comes to the development of world civilizations. According to some historians, whatever technological development had occurred on the continent had been influenced by Europeans. However, archeological findings and study of artifacts reveal that the impact of African civilization on the world extends much farther than the pyramids of Egypt

*   *   *

After demonstrating that there is more to African history than the experience of slavery, I set out to discuss the key problem that gave rise to the founding of the Republic of Liberia, and that was slavery. *The American Colonization Society and the Found of the First African Republic* demonstrates how the Founding Fathers conspired with slaveholders to subjugate Africans. Once forced labor became the way of life for plutocrats, most states passed laws to endorse the horrid and willful torture of blacks in captivity. As a result, no sustained political efforts were mounted by states government to demolish the peculiar institution of slavery.

The entrenched Anglo contemptuousness toward blacks, on one hand, and the panting of slaves for vengeance, on the other hand, made the prospect of racial integration in America improbable, unpractical, and ill-advisable at that time. Most people in antebellum America thought that way.

Private philanthropic and religious individuals organized themselves to take on the challenge of finding practical solutions to end slavery. Their organization became known as the American Colonization Society or ACS. Its prime goal was to establish a homeland for blacks somewhere outside of the United States and then persuade emancipated slaves to repatriate. However, the Society's precarious mission was disparaged and rebuked by critics who charged the ACS of having a secret motive of sustaining slavery in the United States. The way to accomplish that was to unite with slaveholders and forcibly remove freed blacks, while leaving the slaves behind to fight for their own survival.

For nearly two centuries, news about the ACS clandestine activities has attracted opponents and supporters on both sides of the argument. However, my endeavor has been to demonstrate that the ACS had a humanitarian agenda, and it managed to remain largely true to its code mission of urging freed blacks to repatriate to Africa. Eventually it succeeded in establishing the Republic of Liberia in West Africa.

*   *   *

The founding of Liberia created a new set of problems, which remained controversial among contemporary historians. The conflicts that arose between the indigenous people and black Americans have been attributed to disagreements over unjust land acquisition by the settlers. Certainly, the controversies over land and settlements cannot be overlooked, when considering the natives and settlers ominous relationship. But more importantly, the slave trade in West Africa and conflicting traditions were the main sources of tension in colonial Liberia. The demolishment of slave warehouses and the sharing of cultural values helped to solidify relations, built trust, and minimize ethnic conflicts. Liberia struggled to establish a separate identity. At the end, it was neither wholly African nor American. Rather, Liberia turned out to be a hybrid nation, with both American and African influences and values, as demonstrated in the narratives that follow.

Undoubtedly, some readers will want to know why so much emphasis on slavery and the Founding Fathers, if the book is about the ACS and its founding of Liberia? The highlighting of slavery in the United States serves two purposes. First, it is important to understand that the history of Liberia is deeply rooted in American slavery. The colonizers of the African nation, with the help of the American Colonization Society, were former slaves mostly from the United States. It is vital to have a background information about the brutality, suffering, and impoverishment caused by slavery. The dilemma was that neither the states nor federal government had the political will to free the forced laborers. It took a private enterprise to legally remove some liberated slaves and repatriate them to Africa as an act of humanitarian imperative. The second reason for recounting the narratives or atrocities of slavery and highlighting the abuse of slave women by white masters is to vindicate the American Colonization Society for its steadfast endeavor to remove blacks from among whites, which at the time, seemed to be the most practical thing to do. The vagrant disposition of freed slaves in North America was disparaging, and therefore the colonization initiative seemed more humane at the time than the alternative of permanent enslavement.

-Dr. John S. David

# CHAPTER I

# AFRICANS IN MESOAMERICA

The impact of African history on world civilizations is a trivia tale to some historians. Most educators have questioned claims of African-Mesoamerican contacts before 1492. But the travesty is largely based on the teaching of black history from the perspective of chattel slavery. As a result, students adopt the prevailing belief that black history began in 1619. That was the year the first slave ship from Africa landed in Jamestown, Virginia. Basing on this distortion of historical facts, students in the United States are led to believe or infer that Africa has not made any meaningful contributions to science, technology, or world civilizations.

## African Presence in Mesoamerica

Despite the misinformation and, sometimes, disinformation, it is arguable that Africans had a long abiding presence in the Americas before Christopher Columbus arrived in 1492.[1] Many historical accounts and archeological artifacts point to blacks' presence before the emergence of civilization in the Americas, which flourished 1200 BC to 400 BC.

European explorers acknowledged African activities in South America. According to King John II of Portugal (1455-1495), reports of foreign commercial activities in South America had stated that "canoes had been found which set out from the coast of Guinea (West Africa) and sailed to the west with merchandise."[2] Bartolomé de las Casas, editor of Columbus' travel notes, said inhabitants of Hispaniola (now Haiti) told Columbus that "from the south and the southeast had come black people whose spears were made of a metal called guanín . . . from which it was

---

[1]    Sabas Whittaker, *Africans in the Americas Our Journey Throughout the World* (NE: iUniverse, 2003), 50.

[2]    Joan Baxter (13 December 2000). *Africas Greatest Eexplorer, BBC News*. http://news.bbc.co.uk/2/hi/africa/ 1068950.stm, accessed July 1, 2013.

found that of 32 parts: 18 were gold, 6 were silver, and 8 copper."[3] The elements were said to be from Guinea, West Africa.

Interestingly, Columbus himself sent a sample of the spears to metallurgists in Spain to determine the composition. However, the clarification made by the metallurgists did not satisfy some historians who held the view that Africans did not have the skills to build sturdy and durable ships that could navigate the Atlantic Ocean and reach the Americas, before European explorers became fully aware of the American continents.

Opponents have expressed doubts about the navigability of North African sailors to venture across the Atlantic Ocean. One critic, Historian Washington Irving and author of *A History of the Life and Voyages of Christopher Columbus*, writes:

> These black people may have come from the Canaries or the western coast of Africa and been driven by tempest to the shores of Hispaniola. It is probable however that Columbus had been misinformed as to their colour or had misunderstood his informants. It is difficult to believe that the natives of Africa or the Canaries could have survived a voyage of such magnitude in the frail and scantily provided barks they were accustomed to use.[4]

As Irving claims, it was unlikely for Africans to make the trips across the Atlantic Ocean. However, there are ample reasons to argue otherwise, and it is conceivable that African sailors could have made the voyage. The possibility lies in the fact that Africa has the Nile River, the longest river in the world.[5] The 4,130-mile waterway is shared by eleven countries: Tanzania, Uganda, Rwanda, Burundi, Democratic Republic of the Congo, Kenya, Ethiopia, Eritrea, South Sudan, Sudan, and Egypt.[6] For centuries, the Nile has been the lifeline for most of these countries, especially as an irrigation source for agriculture and means of transportation. Large ships

---

[3]  John Boyd Thatcher, *Christopher Columbus, His Life, His Work, His Remains,* (NY: Putnam's Sons, 1903), 380.

[4]  Washington Irving, *A History of the Life and Voyages of Christopher Columbus,* Vol. 2 (NY: G & C CARVILL, 1828), 153.

[5]  Pamela Crossley, Daniel R. Headrick, Steven Hirsch, Lyman Johnson, *The Earth and Its Peoples: A Global History: to 1550* (MA: Houghton Mifflin, 2009).

[6]  Adams Oloo, *The Quest for Cooperation in the Nile Water Conflicts: The Case of Eritrea.* http://www.codesria.org/IMG/pdf/07_Oloo.pdf (accessed May 8, 2013).

coupld travel up to 2600 miles up the River.[7] Many of the ships carried a large number of people and huge animals like elephants, among other goods. Given that the closest point between America and Africa is only about 1500 miles, traversing the Atlantic was probable.[8]

As Bartolomé indicated, Africans were trading in the Americas and Columbus knew of their presence. He stated:

> Certain principal inhabitants of the island of Santiago came to see him, and they said that to the south-west of the island of Huego, which is one of the Cape Verde, distant twelve league from this, may be seen an island, and that the King Don Juan was greatly inclined to send to make discoveries to the south-west and that canoes had been found which start from the coasts of Guinea and navigate to the west with merchandise.[9]

Although it has been alleged for decades that black people accompanied Columbus to the New World, doubts have lingered in the mind of Mesoamericanist historians. However, modern technology has made it possible to conduct DNA testing of bones from the first Mesoamerican colonial town of La Isabella in 2009. The test reviews that some of the skeletons in the graveyard were bones of Africans.[10] Dr. Hannes Schroeder of the Centre for GeoGenetics at the University of Copenhagen, Denmark did the DNA analysis. With the collaboration of archeologist Douglas Price from the University of Wisconsin, Madison, the scientists declared, that "up to seven of the 49 skeletons exhumed from La Isabela's 15th-century graveyard had belonged to Africans."[11]

Western and Islamic historians knew for centuries about Africans' navigation across the Atlantic Ocean. Sometimes the accounts were ignored, disparaged, or the records mysteriously disappeared from public view. For example, two historic expeditions from West Africa occurred in 1311 and 1312 AD. The voyages included a large number of men and

---

[7]  William Marder, *Indians in the Americas: The Unknown Story* (CA: Book Tree, 2005), 40.

[8]  Ibid, 40.

[9]  Abdullah Hakim Quick, *The African, and Muslim, Discovery of America—Before Columbus*.http://historyofislam.com/contents/the-classical-period/the-african-and-muslim-discovery-of-america-before-columbus/ (accessed April 25, 2013).

[10]  *Graveyard DNA Rewrites African American history*, http://www. Newscientist.com/article/dn19455-graveyard-dna-rewrites-african-american-history.html (accessed May 4, 2013).

[11]  Ibid.

women and Columbus may have encountered some of them at various points on his three-year voyage along the Mesoamerican coast.

## Early African Voyages

The first voyage occurred in 1311. In that year, King Abubakari II of Mali commissioned thousands of military men to explore regions beyond the Atlantic Ocean with 400 ships.[12] The vessels contained women, gold, livestock, foodstuffs, and drinking water to last one year. The soldiers ventured to explore "fabled lands far across the waters," as instructed by the King. However, with the exception of one ship, which did not complete the journey, none of the other ships and soldiers ever returned to Mali. It is believed that strong currents and waves caused the ships to drift, and they ended up on the coast of South America. One year later, Abubakari II decided to sail across the Atlantic Ocean in an exploratory spirit. Before leaving, he turned over the kingship to his brother, Musa, and then organized another expedition in 1312 with 2000 ships.[13] A large contingent of military men, women, gold, and livestock made the voyage. After their departure, the adventurers were never heard from again, but it was later discovered that Abubakari II and some of his followers ended up in Recife, Brazil.[14] Among other evidences, archeologists have found many inscriptions on rocks and burial grounds along the coast of South America and other places, which attested to the African presence in the region.

An inquirer once confronted King Musa about his ascendency to power, and he said:

> The ruler who preceded me would not believe that it was impossible to discover the limits of the neighboring sea. He wanted to find out and persisted in his pan. He had two hundred ships equipped and filled with men, and others in the same number filled with gold, water, and supplies in sufficient quantity to last for years. He told those who commanded them: "Return only when you have reached the extremity of the ocean, or when you have exhausted your food and water."

---

[12] David Imhotep, *The First Americans Were Africans: Documented Evidence* (IN: Authorship. 2012), 100.

[13] Molefi Kete Asante, *The History of Africa: The Quest for Eternal Harmony* (NY: Routledge, 2007), 131.

[14] *Expressions of Africa in Los Angeles Public Performance, 1781-1994* (MI: ProQuest and Learning Company, 2008), 57.

They went away, their absence was long, before any of them returned. Finally, a sole ship reappeared. We asked the captain about their adventures. "Prince", he replied, "We sailed a long time, up to the moment when we encountered in mid-ocean something like a river with a violent current. My ship was last. The others sailed on, and gradually as each one entered the place, they disappeared and did not come back. We did not know what had happened to them. As for me, I returned to where I was and did not enter the current." "But the emperor did not want to believe him. He equipped two thousand vessels, a thousand for himself and the men who accompanied him and a thousand for water and supplies. He conferred power on me and left with his companions on the ocean. This was the last time that I saw him and the others, and I remained the absolute master of the empire."[15]

Much earlier, about 1000 years before the Malian expedition to discover "lands across the waters," the Egyptians landed in Mexico. The reputable Indian historian, R.A. Jairazbhoy, declared that Ancient Egyptians were among the earliest pioneers of the Americas. According to him, "The black began his career in America not as slave but as master."[16] The exact year of arrival varies among scholars. However, it seems probable that cultural diffusion from Africa to South America occurred.

## The Olmec Colossal Heads

In 1873, historian Herr Remisch, a Viennese and Egyptologist, astonished European educators when he declared that Egyptians had an African origin. He added, "The human races of the ancient world, of Europe, Asia, and Africa, are descended from a single family, whose original seat was on the shores of Equatorial Africa."[17]

The Egyptian civilization, among the oldest in the world, has continued to enjoy a position of eminence among scholars, but not

---

[15]   Mandinka (Mandidng) Voyages and Exploration. http://historyofislam.com / contents/the-classical-period/the-african-and-muslim-discovery-of-america-before-columbus/(accessed March 10, 2013).

[16]   Ivan V. Sertima, *African presence in early America*, Journal of African Civilizations, Volume 8, Issue 2 (1992), 80.

[17]   Gabriel Kingsley Osei, *African Contributions to Civilizations* (MD: Black Classic Press, 1999), 11.

without detaching it from Africa by critics.[18] According to opponents, Egyptians are not Africans. They argue that the advanced Nile valley culture was developed by people with European lineage. Later, the diffusion continued from Egypt, where the inhabitants were light-skinned.[19] It spread to other parts of the continent where the inhabitants were darker in complexion. The darker Africans were less enlightened and, therefore, they borrowed heavily from the anglicized Egyptians.

The belief that Africa has not made any meaningful scientific contributions to world civilizations is now facing some of its greatest challenges. The claim that major technological developments in Africa, such as agriculture, artworks, and smelting of iron have been handled down by Caucasians or their lineage is incorrect.

One of the few Mesoamerican books that was not destroyed by rampaging soldiers is the *Popol Vuh*. The book states that the black people, who arrived in the Americas came "from the land of the sunrise."[20] Mayan colored murals from Bonompak and Chichen Itza in Mexico show black and light-skinned warriors together.

European military leaders who conquered the Americas told stories of sighting small settlements of black people among tribesmen and villages throughout the New World. There existed "colonies of blacks in Northern Brazil called the Chares. Others are found at Saint Vincent on the Gulf of Mexico, where black Caribs clustered around the mouth of the Orinoco River in present-day Venezuela."[21]

*San Lorenzo Colossal Heads*

---

[18]  Ibid, 16.
[19]  Ibid.
[20]  Marder, *Indians in the Americas*.
[21]  *Blacks in the New World*. http://ftp.wi.net/~census/lesson32.html (accessed January 4, 2013).

Huge African-like head images have been found in various regions of Mexico. In 1869, the earliest account of a colossal head was reported in South America by Mexican Explorer José Maria Melgar y Serrano.[22] The head with African features was found by a farmer in Hueyapan, Veracruz. Since then, seventeen images have been found on other sites in Mexico, each weighing from five to fifty tons and dating as far back as 5000 to1000 BC.[23]

Dr. Andrzej Wiercinski discovered three African skulls at separate Olmec sites, including Tlatilco, Cerro de las Mesas and Monte Alban.[24] As one of the distinguished experts on skulls analysis, he declared in 1974 at the 41st Congress of Americanists in Mexico that "13.5 percent of the skeletons from Tlatilco and 4.5 percent of the skeletons from Cerro de las Mesas were Africoid."[25]

The probability of Africans' influence in establishing the first Mesoamerican civilization of Olmec, Mexico, is attracting global reviews from optimists and skeptics. Notwithstanding, opponents have vehemently, and sometimes angrily, attacked the claim that the first Africans in the Americas were not slaves but traders and explorers.

In 1997, for example, a forum of critics assembled on the theme, *Robbing Native American Cultures* and assailed the concept of Africans being major players in world civilizations. Gabriel Haslip-Viera, Bernard Ortiz de Montellano, and Warren Barbour—authors of *CA Forum on Anthropology* in *Public: Robbing Native American Cultures: Van Sertima's Afrocentricity and the Omecs*—dismissed any accounts of blacks' influence in America before Columbus as a mere Afrocentric ideology.[26] They claim that blacks came to America as slaves, "Whereas the slave ancestors of African-Americans came primarily from tropical West Africa."[27]

---

[22]    *Early Reports on the Olmec*.http://anthropology.si.edu/olmec/english/introduction/ earlyReports /melgar.htm(accessed March 23, 2013).

[23]    Marder, *Indians*, 14.

[24]    Paul Ifayomi, *Grant, Blue Skies for Afrikans* (United Kingdom: Navig8or Press, 2005), 263.*The Cross, the Rabbi & The Skin Walker: Part 2*.http://open.salon.com/ blog/jack heart/2011/11/06/the _cross the_rabbi_ the_skin_walkerpart_2 (accessed May 3, 2023).

[25]    Ibid.

[26]    Gabriel Haslip-Viera, Bernard Ortiz de Montellano, and Warren Barbor, "*CA Forum on Anthropology in Public: Robbing Native American Cultures: Van Sertima's Afrocentricity and the Omecs*." *Current Anthropology*, Vol. 38, No. 3 (June, 1997), 419-422.

[27]    Ibid, 422.

The CA Forum invited scholars who were known to express strong anti-Sertima sentiments.[28] Dr. Sertima, who was the object of the academic scourging, was not invited. However, the presenters charged him of making pseudoscientific claims during the forum. They disregarded the enormous records from other anthropologists, archeologists, historians, and linguists who promote the view of African presence in pre-Columbian America. Historians like Bartolomé de las Casas, an associate of Christopher Columbus, Dr. Leo Wiener, author of *Africa and the Discovery of America*, Indian historian Rafique Jairazbhoy, anthropologist Ivan Van Sertima, author of *They Came Before Columbus*, Dr. Carter Woodson,[29] Father of Black History, and a host of other academic personalities have presented indisputable evidence of the presence of Africans in Mesoamerica before Columbus.

Europeans called Africa the Dark Continent. The term was first published by explorer Henry Stanley, author of *Through the Dark Continent*.[30] Proponents of the African inferiority complex theory argue that, through diffusion, Africa had borrowed most of its technology from foreigners. Allegedly, artworks, agriculture, astronomy, and navigational techniques are few of the contributions made to Africa by white people.[31]

Eurocentric scholars have the tendency to denigrate theories about African engagements in the Americas before Columbus. For them, no evidence is valid and no proof is adequate. As a matter of facts, claims of African presence are viewed by some scholars as an attempt to rob Native Americans of their heritage.[32] The theories are described as speculative, unfounded, or a form of ethnocentric racism.[33]

However, the mounting evidence suggests strongly that Africans were in Latin America before 1492. Also, a number of black people accompanied Columbus on his voyages. Native Indians told him African

---

[28] Martin Bernal, *Geography of a Life* (Xlibris Corporation, Jul 3, 2012), 369.

[29] In 1936, Dr. Woodson published *The African Background Outline*. He claimed that many scholars in history also believed that Africans discovered America before Columbus.

[30] Henry M. Stanley, *Through the Dark Continent: Or, the Sources of the Nile, around the Great Lakes of Equatorial Africa and down the Livingstone River to the Atlantic Ocean* (NY: Harper and Brothers Publishers, 1878).

[31] Osei, 7.

[32] Gerald Jackson—2005—Preview "Robbing Native American cultures Van Sertima's Afrocentricity and the Olmecs." *Current Anthropology*, 38, (3), 419-431. 358 (October 26, 1999).

[33] Ibid.

traders had visited Native American villages and towns, and now, the Colossal African Heads of the Olmec era tell nations of the world that Africans were in America when the Mesoamerican civilizations began, at least 1200 years before Christ.

# CHAPTER II

# DECLINE OF AFRICA'S CIVILIZATIONS

Mounting scientific evidence points to Africa as the original home of the human race. It is also one of early cradles of civilization. Africa's evolutionary cradles of civilization rose to eminence in art, trade, and commerce.

The three major West African empires were Ancient Ghana, Mali, and Songhai. They flourished from about 700 AD to 1591.[1] Ghana thrived from 700 AD to 1076, before Mail conquered and incorporated the first Empire by the 1100s. Mali ruled for about 300 years, and it eventually fell to Songhai. From about 1468 to 1591 Songhai was at the top of its power, but the third kingdom also disintegrated after 1591. All these empires excelled in "art, religion, science, education, trade, government, and warfare."[2] More is now known about the Malian ancient city of Timbuktu and Alexandria in Egypt. They developed great institutions of learning and served as commercial centers for commerce and trade.

Historian Mauren Jame, author of *Thomas Clark and the Abolition of Slavery*, wrote:

> In the fifteenth and sixteenth centuries, parts of West Africa, particularly the Songhay city of Empire, were as advanced as Europe . . . Industrial innovations had taken place quite early in the region, iron smelting had been carried out since the 2nd century AD. Copper working had reached the high level shown by the Benin Bronzes and gold mining was a function of the economy. Studies of the Benin show that they were also highly skilled in ivory carving, pottery (from clay), beeswax, rope

---

[1]    Mary Quigley, *Ancient West African Kingdoms: Ghana, Mali, & Songhai* (IL: Feed Educational Professional Publisher, 2002).

[2]    Ibid, 5.

and gum production. There was a plentiful supply of wood for building houses and canoes.[3]

Slavery ruined Africa. First, there was the domestic and trans-Sahara slave trade, before the trans-Atlantic slavery trade. By the time the Kingdom of Songhai finally went under Moroccan rule in 1591, slave trade was already in full swing.[4] While Arab and Muslim traders traversed the continent between the 7th and 20th centuries, eighteen million slaves crossed the Sahara Desert and Indian Ocean to various destinations in the Middle East and Europe.[5] Beginning in the 15th century, for five hundred years, nearly twelve million Africans were herded along the Atlantic slave routes to the New World.[6] From the early 1600s, British North America began experimenting with slavery.

> The economies of all thirteen British colonies in North America depended on slavery. By the 1620s, the labor-intensive cultivation of tobacco for European markets was established in Virginia, with white indentured servants performing most of the heavy labor. Before 1660 only a fraction of Virginia planters held slaves. By 1675 slavery was well established, and by 1700 slaves had almost entirely replaced indentured servants. With plentiful land and slave labor available to grow a lucrative crop, southern planters prospered, and family-based tobacco plantations became the economic and social norm.[7]

Before 1776, most colonies had already instituted slavery as an economic imperative. The plutocrats argued that human servitude was an economic necessity, and nearly 20 percent of the American population had African ancestry.[8]

---

3    Mauren James, *Thomas Clark And The Abolition Of Slavery* http://www.thomasclarkson.org/ resources/ clarkson1.pdf (accessed, June 5, 2013).
4    Paul E Lovejoy, *Transformations in slavery: a history of slavery in Africa* (UK: Cambridge University Press, 2000).
5    *Historical survey: Slave-owning societies*, http://www.britannica.com/ blackhistory/ article-24156 (accessed May 29, 2013).
6    *Focus on the slave trade*, http://news.bbc.co.uk/2/hi/africa/1523100.stm (accessed May 28, 2013).
7    *African Slavery in Colonial British North America*, http://www.monticello.org/ slavery-at-monticello/african-slavery-british-north-america (accessed January 2, 2012).
8    *Introduction to African American Life,* http://www.history.org/almanack /people / african/aaintro.cfm (accessed September 5, 2011).

Slave labor in colonial America started in Virgin. In 1619, the first Africans landed at Port Comfort near the Chesapeake Bay, which was then part of the Colony of Virginia. This was the beginning of chattel slavery in the thirteen original colonies.

## Indentured Africans

The first Africans arrived from the kingdom of Ndongo in Angola and included 350 adults and children.[9] They were captured by Portuguese and African invaders. While sailing from Angola under the command of Manuel Mundes da Cunha, pirates ambushed the ship (the *São João Bautista*), assuming the vessel was loaded with gold.[10] Instead, the captains of the two pirate ships found a large number of enslaved Africans in transit to Vera Cruz, Mexico. The bandits shared the slaves and parted ways. Captain John Colyn Jope of the *White Lion*took his share of plunders to Point Comfort, on the James River, and sold them in exchange for food.[11] From Point Comfort, some of the slaves were transported to Jamestown, Virginia, and resold as farm walkers.[12] However, the other pirate, Captain Daniel Elfrith of the *Treasurer*, also arrived in Jamestown a few days later, but did not succeed to sell any slaves in Virginia.[13]

According to John Rolfe, the colonial secretary of Virginia, more than twenty Africans landed in Virginia. In a letter to John Smith in January of 1620, Rolfe reported that in the later part of August 1619, "20 and Odd Negroes arrived on board a "Dutch Man of War" at Point Comfort.[14] Smith's reply quoted "20 Africans."[15] In 2000, another report emerged

---

[9]    Peter C. Mancall, *The Atlantic World and Virginia, 1550-1624* (NC: University of North Carolina Press, 2007), 225.

[10]   Tim Hashaw, *The First Africans: A group of enslaved Africans changed Jamestown and the future of a nation*, in USNews & World Report, http://www.usnews.com/ usnews/news /articles /070121 /29african.htm, January 21, 2007 (accessed September 5, 2011)Hashaw, *The First Africans*.

[11]   Martha McCartney, *Virginia's First Africans*. http://www.encyclopediavirginia.org/ Virginias_First_Africans (Accessed January 8, 2013).

[12]   Charles C. Mann, *1493: Uncovering the New World Columbus Created* (NY: Alfred A. Knopf, 2011), 67.

[13]   The *Treasurer* originated from Virginia. Its piracy mission was partly financed by former Virginia Governor Samuel Argall. Three months before the Africans arrived Samuel Argall lost his position as governor for piracy.

[14]   The Thomas Jefferson Papers Series 8. Virginia Records Manuscripts: 1606-1737. http://hdl.loc.gov/ loc.mss/mtj.mtjbib026605 (Accessed January 10, 2013).

[15]   Randall M. Miller and John David Smith, *Dictionary of Afro-American Slavery* (CT: Greenwood Press, 1997), 781. Ibid, 781.

stating 32 captives, including 15 men and 17 women, instead of twenty as previously reported.[16]

The first Africans may have been indentured servants. This is inconclusive because the word "slave" did not appear in the Virginian records until 1656. Before then, "servant" was used, which could mean a slave or indentured laborer,[17] and some historians view the "20 and Odd" as referring to indentured servants and not slaves.[18]

The status of Africans remained vague until the 1660s when the slave codes emerged. In 1662, Virginia enacted a law, which recognized the children of slave mothers as slaves.[19] The codes disregarded the status of the fathers in the designation. Therefore, even if the fathers were free, their children were considered slaves if the mothers were slaves. The law was designed to benefit slaveholders because it ensured the increase of slaves through procreation with slave women.

Planters and other farmers had relied on indentured servants from Europe for cultivation, planting, and harvesting. This situation changed during the second half of the 1600s when indentured labor became more costly, and it made economic sense to obtain free slave labor. Indentured white servants could become citizens, lawyers, plantation and landowners, community leaders or slave owners after gaining their freedom; blacks could not. By 1773, slaves were supplying most of the cheap labor for Virginia.

Africans were more preferable to white servants due to the obvious difference in color. The masters were white and slaves were black. Moreover, the Africans served for life. During their time of service, they could be bought, mortgaged, pawned, rented, sold, traded, or forced to procreate to increase the masters' labor force and wealth. They could be held perpetually as sex slaves. Slaves were barred by law from making civil rights claims or enjoy legal protection under the law.

Virginia became the model for the codification of slavery. In *White Over Black*, historian Winthrop Jordan states that "the legal enactment of Negro slavery followed the social practice, rather than vice versa."[20]Thus, from 1662 Virginia lawmakers codified slavery. These slave codes provided the framework for slave laws in British North America. Thus:

---

[16]   Ibid.

[17]   Robert McColley in *Dictionary of Afro-American Slavery*, Randall M. Miller and John David Smith, eds. (CT: Greenwood Press, 1988), 281.

[18]   Kevin Schultz, *America Unbound: A U. S. History* (Clark Baxter and Susanne Jeans, 2010), 51.

[19]   Randall M. Miller and John David Smith, *Dictionary of Afro-American Slavery* (CT: Greewood Press, 1997), 393.

[20]   Winthrop D. Jordan, The *White Man's Burden : Historical Origins of Racism in the United States* (London: Oxford University Press, 1974), 45.

1662—Children born to Negro women were free or bonded according to the condition of the mother. 1667—The baptism of slaves as Christians did not alter their status as slaves. 1669—A master who killed a disobedient slave could not be accused of a felony. 1670—Free Negroes and Indians were prohibited from buying Christian indentured servants. 1680—Slaves were prohibited from carrying weapons and leaving their owner's plantations without a pass. 1682—No master or overseer could permit a slave to remain on his plantation for longer than four hours without the permission of the slave's owner. 1691—Any white man or woman who married a Negro, mulatto, or Indian was banished from Virginia. 1705—All servants not Christians in their native countries (except for Turks, Moors, and others who could prove they were free in England or another Christian country) and imported to Virginia were slaves. Slaves remained slaves even if they traveled to England.[21]

Massachusetts became the first colony to legalize slavery in 1641.[22] The lawful practice of subjugating blacks spread to all colonies. During the Revolutionary years, a higher proportion of blacks lived in Virginia and Maryland with the highest concentration in the Chesapeake Bay area where blacks made up more than 50 percent of the population.

In 1691, Jamestown revoked the right of owners to free slaves. When blacks became slaves, they served for life in a phenomenon known as chattel slavery. Miscegenation codes forbade Anglo women from marrying Negroes or mulattoes.[23]White women that violated the law could legally be expelled from Virginia.

Free slaves could not legally live in Virginia; they had to leave. Blacks lost the privilege to move freely or protect themselves against brutalities. Other Southern colonies also prohibited emancipation and the free movement of blacks. The practice of allowing slaves to raise crops and cattle to purchase their own freedom in Virginia became illegal in 1705. In less than a century, slavery developed into a legally entrenched and powerful institution in most of the American colonies.

---

[21]   *A Selection of Virginia Slave Laws, 1662-1705*. July 9, 2013. **http://www.vahistorical. org/ sva2003/ slavelaws.htm.**

[22]   Clint Johnson, *The politically incorrect guide to the South: and why it will rise again* (Washington: Regnery Publishing, 2006), 124.

[23]   *Virginia Slave Law and Record*, http://www.slaveryinamerica.org /geography /slave_ laws_ VA.htm, (access November 2, 2011).

## Attempts to Abolish Slavery

In the North, individuals and religious groups attempted to fight against human servitude. The inhabitants of Ipswich, Massachusetts Bay took a stand to outlaw slavery:

> There shall never be any bond-slavery . . . or captivity among us, unless it be lawful captives taken in just wars, and such strangers as willingly sell themselves or are sold to us. And these shall have all the liberties and Christian usages which the law of God established in Israel concerning such persons doth morally require.[24]

A Quaker named Richard Saltonstall went to court and testified against Captain James of the *Rainbow* slave ship. The vessel landed in Boston in 1645 with slaves from the Guinea coast. Saltonstall demanded their release and return at the public expense.[25]

A petition was presented to a Pennsylvanian assembly in 1688 to urge the colony to enact some basic human rights principles based on rule of the Bible, "Do unto others as you would have them do unto you."[26] The German-Dutch settlers in Germantown sought to eradicate slavery in their colony. They argued that humankind had rights that should not be violated by anyone, including the government, irrespective of color, creed, or ethnic background. Though largely ignored by the pro-slavery leaders, it became one of the earliest documented pleas for equal rights for all Americans. It called for the extension of human rights to every human being and set the stage for a standard of fairness in America. Proponents of the natural rights, including John Adams and Thomas Jefferson, referenced this sentiment from time to time.

The Society of Friends was a Protestant religious sect which denounced slavery. The group, with large presence in Massachusetts, Rode Island, and Pennsylvania, amplified the horror of slavery. Its members were able to galvanize enough support to present a petition to the Pennsylvania Assembly in 1773. It called for a "ban on the entire British slave trade, not merely on imports to . . . North America."[27]

---

24    Thomas Franklin Waters, *Ipswich in the Massachusetts Bay Colony, Vol. 2* (Boston: Ipswich Historical Society, 1917), 210.

25    Waters, 210.

26    David B. Davis, *The Problem of Slavery in Western Society* (New York: Cornell University Press, 1966), 213.

27    Christopher L. Brown, *Moral Capital: Foundations of British Abolitionism* (NC: University of North America Press, 2006), 140.

## Blacks Fight for White Freedom

At the outbreak of the Revolutionary War, there were many voices, mainly from Christian communities, calling for the abolition of slavery. Slaves constituted one-fifth of the population of the nation.[28] Nearly 5,000 blacks saw the war as an opportunity to justify their worthiness and plea for freedom as patriotic warriors. Motivated by the thought of freedom, some blacks enlisted as minutemen in militia groups. They fought bravely in battles, including the Battle of Bunker Hill and the Siege of Yorktown.

Slaveholders opposed blacks in the army for fear of an uprising against slave owners.[29] George Washington, commander of the Continental Army, yielded and banned blacks from enlisting in a fighting force.[30] Meanwhile, an estimated 20,000 blacks enlisted with the British in exchange for freedom after the war. Washington reversed course and accepted black enlistees. Restrictions against them were either ignored or not enforced.

While the war continued, the United States declared its independence in 1776. The Declaration of Independence envisioned a country where all men were treated equally, but a contradiction loomed. Justifying the enslavement of other human beings who helped secure liberty for the country that enslaved them became a menacing oddity for the Revolutionary Fathers. It was a moral evil, an affront to the idea of democracy, and the belief in the basic natural rights of man.

The decades following the Revolution proved critical to the idea of balancing socioeconomic interest and the morality of human servitude. Americans were warming up to the view that slavery was evil. With this new awaking, they blamed the British for imposing slavery on the colonies in the first place. Others argued that slavery was an unavoidable evil, because cheap labor was needed to keep up with the increasing demand for farm workers. Once planted in the colonies, the institution of slavery became addictive and rose to become the most powerful institution in antebellum America.

---

[28]  Gordon Wood, *The American Revolution: A History* (New York: Modern Library, 2002) 55.

[29]  Martha S. Putney, *Blacks in the United states Army* (NC: McFarland, 2003),

[30]  *The Revolutionary War.* http://www.pbs.org/wgbh /aia/ part2/2narr4.html (accessed May 25, 2013).

# CHAPTER III

# FREEDMEN:
# NEITHER SLAVE NOR FREE

Slave narratives often describe the horror of subjugation, with chilling effects. Equally appalling are the numbing accounts of free blacks, a large number of whom became drifters without a country.

Various historical accounts affirm that the status of freedmen was generally indistinguishable from slaves. Liberated blacks roamed from one state to another for security and in search of jobs. Most states had residency requirements for non-white workers. Free Africans were denied citizenship and some residential permits were only seasonal. Once free, however, the laws required them to leave town within a year or risk arrest and re-enslavement.

## The Dilemma of Freedmen

At the beginning of the Republic, whites had entertained the belief that blacks were inferior beings and mentally challenged. Most Americans held the view that Africans were genetically endowed with the natural tendency to commit crimes, regardless of their sociopolitical status. With this mindset, states enacted laws to constrain the lifestyles of freed blacks. Racial lines were drawn to segregate the races, which eventually led to the deportation laws against free slaves. Supporters believed segregation was the cure for pauperism among jobless Africans, and a panacea against amalgamation.

By 1700, Virginia had laws that prohibited emancipation, unless the emancipator was willing to pay fees to transport their former slaves out of the colony within six months.[1] In 1723, the legislation stated that "a slave could not be freed unless the slave owner guaranteed a security bond for the education, livelihood, and support of the freed slave."[2]

South Carolina had more slaves than whites at one point, and stringent laws controlled their movement. Manumitted slaves were required to leave the colony within six months or be captured and resold. By 1820, enslaved African Americans could only be freed by a legislative act, and free blacks from out of state were prohibited from entering South Carolina.[3]

By 1790, the number of free blacks was on the rise also in Northern states. The Census Bureau listed 13,059 freedmen in New England, with another 13,975 in New York, New Jersey, and Pennsylvania.

Freedom did not necessarily change the sociopolitical and economic dispositions of blacks. This was not the case for most white indentured servants from Europe. Once free, they had the opportunity to become respectable citizens and contribute to their community. Free slaves lived merely as "common laborers and washerwomen, living separately in ghettoes and other segregated communities."[4]

The Ohio constitution abolished slavery throughout the state in 1802, but that did not necessarily make life easy for blacks. They continued to endure constant harassment, with strict residency and immigration requirements. An instance of this was the refusal of the state to allow John Randolph of Virginia to settle 518 emancipated slaves in southern Ohio. An Ohio lawmaker cautioned that settling the free blacks in the region could result in bloodshed: "The banks of the Ohio . . . would be lined with men with muskets on their shoulders to keep off the emancipated slaves."[5]

Northern freemen, like bondsmen, had to carry permits in some states. They could not own property in other parts. New England restricted voting rights for all blacks, though freedmen were required to pay taxes. At the discretion of local officials, free blacks had a duty to

---

[1]  W. O. Blake, *The History of Slavery and the Slave Trade; Ancient and Modern. The Forms of Slavery that Prevailed in Ancient Nations, Particularly in Greece and Rome. The African Slave Trade and the Political History of Slavery in the United States* (Ohio: J. & H. Miller, 1857), 381.

[2]  Ibid.

[3]  Judith Kelleher Schafer, *Becoming Free, Remaining Free: Manumission and Enslavement in New Orleans: 1846-1862* (Louisiana: Louisiana University Press, 2003).

[4]  *Slavery In The North,* http://www.slavenorth.com/exclusion.htm (accessed February 12, 2012).

[5]  Paul Kalra, *Slave to Untouchable: Lincoln's Solution* (CA: Antenna Publishing Company, 2011), 135.

do compulsory work on public roads in Massachusetts. In Rhode Island, freemen could not own horses or sheep in some towns. In Boston, it was against the law for them to carry a cane, except in the case of disability.[6] However, despite these disadvantages, the northern state of Pennsylvania held high the banner of hope for racial egalitarianism when it passed its antislavery constitution in 1780.[7]The document provided a framework for blacks to obtain freedom and equality. Instead of segregation and deportation of freedmen, freedom-minded whites planned to engage blacks to advance anti-slavery sentiments and create opportunities for former slaves to assimilate into the dominant culture.

The spirit of optimism towards a slave-free society soared in several colonies. The spotlight was on Philadelphia, where manumission societies continued to increase. Abolitionists pushed to end the importation of Africans as slaves and mandated the advancement of a scheme to gradually end domestic servitude. It was in Philadelphia that the first concept for gradual emancipation was constitutionalized. Two years earlier, Rhode Island offered freedom to Africans who fought in the Revolutionary War. By1796, all but three states granted voting rights to free African Americans, without granting citizenship. A 1790 Federal law granted naturalization rights to White immigrants only, effectively excluding blacks from becoming citizens.[8]

As the drumbeat of freedom echoed in every American Colony, Dr. Benjamin Rush, an ally of the anti-slave movement, wrote: "For God's sake, do not exhibit a new spectacle to the world, of men just emerging from a war in favor of liberty, with clothes not yet washed from the blood which was shed in copious and William streams in its defense, fighting our vessels to import their fellow creatures from Africa, to reduce afterwards to slavery".[9]

Rush did not support immediate emancipation. He believed it would harm the slaves and society but wanted "slavery to be made as comfortable as possible where it existed, without importing more slaves."

In 1786, New Jersey started on the path of gradual emancipation by outlawing the importation of slaves. Fourteen years later, the legislature passed laws to end slavery gradually. The plan called for a mass education

---

[6]   John Chester Miller, *This New Man, the American: Beginnings of the American People* (NY: Oxford University Press, 1974), 345.

[7]   An Act for the Gradual Abolition of Slavery: 1780. http://www.ushistory.org/ presidentshouse/ history/ gradual.htm (February 1, 2012).

[8]   Michael Leyman, Elliott R. Barkan, *U.S. Immigration and Naturalization Laws and Issues: A Documentary History* (CT: Greenwood Publishing Group, 1999).

[9]   Kristen Forster, *Moral Visions and Material Ambition: Philadelphia Struggles to Define the Republic 1776-1836* (Lexington Books, 2004), 166.

of blacks to learn the responsibilities of freedom, and in the process, female and male slaves were to serve their masters for 21 and 25 years respectively, then emancipated. This legislation was also intended to enlist the support of slaveholders. Designers of the scheme argued that a practical approach had a better chance of succeeding "than a more radical plan for immediate and total abolition." The 1804 ruling included an "abandonment clause" to guarantee compensation of slave owners for relinquishing their "property" in human chattel slavery.

Africans were mindful of the marginal prods toward liberty, but the concept of gradual emancipation was a non-starter for them. It was branded as a precarious tantalizer and a moving target that might never be reached. Besides, abolitionists soon admitted that the goodwill claims were not translating to economic gains for blacks. The dream of racial harmony was becoming a nightmare, since there was no clear path to achieve economic equality in a racially divided society of "haves and have-nots".

## Blacks Break Away From White Churches

Two black Christian ministers, Absalom Jones (1746-1818) and Richard Allen (1760-1831) were optimistically cautious of the prospect of having one nation without prejudice or racial segregation. They called on blacks to assimilate on the basis of economic, religious, and political values of the dominant white cultures. "Racial assimilation," according to them, "offered black Americans their best hope for racial betterment."

The hope was short lived. In 1786, Jones and Allen were members of the integrated St. George's Methodist Episcopal in Philadelphia. That year, the white membership decided, in an exclusive meeting, to ban all blacks from sitting with whites in the church. They had to sit in the balcony. Without being informed, while praying in church the following Sunday morning, Allen was interrupted and asked to leave his seat to sit in the balcony. He and other blacks walked out of the church and eventually led to the establishment of the first black denomination (African Methodist Episcopal Church) in 1816.

Seven years after the split, Jones still believed that racial harmony was possible. On August 22, 1793, he and other black leaders hosted a lavish banquet in Philadelphia and whites were invited. The festivity was successful. First, the whites were seated and served by their African hosts. Later, the whites rose from their seats and humbly proceeded to serve the blacks. Dr. Benjamin Rush could not hold back the warm emotion he felt at the occasion, as stated in this letter to his wife Julia:

> This day agreeably to invitation I dined a mile from town, under the shade of several large trees, with about an hundred carpenters and others who met to celebrate the raising of the roof of the African Church. They forced me to take the head of the table much against my inclinations. The dinner was plentiful—the liquors were of the first quality—and the dessert, which consisted only of melons, was very good. We were waited upon by nearly an equal number of black people. I gave them the two following toasts: "Peace on earth and good will to men," and "May African churches everywhere soon succeed to African bondage." After which we rose, and the black people (men and women) took our seats. Six of the most respectable of the white company waited upon them, while Mr. Nicholson, myself, and two others were requested to set down with them, which we did, much to the satisfaction of the poor blacks. Never did I witness such a scene of innocent—nay more—such virtuous and philanthropic joy.[10]

However, blacks in white churches remained second-class worshippers on back pews. Eventually, resistance mounted against the white clergy. This led to the formation of the African Methodist Episcopal Church of New York in 1796. The AMEC and AMEZ were formed at different times under different leaderships, but racial prejudice caused the breakup of both groups from white churches.[11]

There was a reversal in earlier political gains and optimism plummeted. Many lawmakers passed inadmissible laws that kept free blacks from some states. Delaware banned free Negroes in 1811 from living within its borders. In other jurisdictions like the District of Columbia and Ohio, legal restrictions forced emancipated slaves to carry certificates of freedom at all times. Other states required bonds up to $1000.00 for residency. For most blacks, the fees effectively barred them from obtaining the necessary permits. They could not work because

---

[10]   Rush's letter to Julia Rush, http://www.pbs.org/wgbh/aia/part3/3h459t.html (accessed, July 3, 2012).

[11]   http://www.missionstclare.com/english/people/feb13.html (accessed July 5, 2011).

hiring undocumented Negroes carried the risk of jail time, fines, or both.[12]

The status of Africans in the colonies had remained in limbo since the first slaves landed in Jamestown, Virginia, in 1619. The federal Constitution of 1787 made an uneasy peace with slavery by leaving the issue unresolved. It succeeded, however, in banning the trans-Atlantic Slave Trade at a feature date in 1808.

Abolitionists were disappointed that the constitution did not abolish slavery outright. Inter-states slave trade remained vibrant and unrestricted by the federal government. The decision to define blacks' political status was left to individual states. The federal government made no constitutional provision for manumission, black citizenship, integration, assimilation, or colonization of freedmen.

## Dred Scott Case: Controversy For Citizenship

The question of black citizenship reached a defining moment in the Dred Scott case of 1857. Chief Justice Roger B. Taney (1777-1864) conveyed the opinion of the court in defense of slavery as a legal institution.[13] The ruling was a political dragnet as it succinctly stated, "Neither slaves nor free blacks were citizens of the United States. At the time the Constitution was adopted," according to the Chief Justice, "blacks had been regarded as beings of an inferior order no rights which the white man was bound to respect."

Most Americans did regard blacks as "beings of an inferior order" and, although the U.S. Constitution recorded nothing directly about enslaved Africans in the country, the Immigration and Naturalization Laws of 1790 granted naturalization privileges to "free white persons of good character."

Freedmen did not have special legal protection against violence from slaveholders or even from poor whites who made complexion a basis for white superiority. The systematic abuse and denial of citizenship resulted in increased criminal activities and deadly violence against whites.

The justice system often failed to link abuses and impoverishment to antisocial behaviors among Africans. Medical officers alleged black misconducts were linked to curable Negro diseases. In a highly publicized

---

12      John Bach McMaster, *A History of the United States, From Revolution to Civil War* (New York: D. Appleton and Company, 1922).

13      Jeffrey A. Segaland Harold J. Spaeth, *The Supreme Court and the Attitudinal Model Revisited* (UK: Cambridge University Press, 2002).

document, *Diseases and Peculiarities of the Negro Race*, Dr. Samuel Cartwright, a reputable physician from the University of Louisiana, claimed that there were diseases, which exclusively affected African Americans. He called one *Drapetomania*; it excited slaves to run away. He identified another as *Dysaethesia Aethiopica*. It caused "trickery, dishonesty, or slipperiness" in African Americans.[14] Dr. Cartwright concluded that, "With the advantages of proper medical advice, strictly followed, this troublesome practice that many negroes have of running away, can be almost entirely prevented, although the slaves be located on the borders of a free state, within a stone's throw of the abolitionists."[15]

The predicament continued. Many Southern states forbade free persons of color from becoming preachers, selling certain goods, tending bar, flirting with whites, staying out past a certain time at night, or owning dogs, among other restrictions.

---

[14]    Paul F. Paskoff and Daniel J. Wilson, ed. *The Cause of the South: Selections from De Bow's Review, 1846-1867* (Louisiana: Louisiana State University Press, 1982).

[15]    James W. Loewen, Edward H. Sebesta, *The Confederate and Neo-Confederate Reader: The Great Truth About the Lost Cause* (MS: University Press of Mississippi, 2010), 67.

# CHAPTER IV

# THE FOUNDING FATHERS
# AND THE SAGA OF SLAVERY

The role of the Revolutionary Fathers to end slavery continues to be a controversial subject among historians. Prior to 1776, abolitionism was not a dramatic concept in the American colonies. Although antislavery sentiments existed, slaveholders generally ignored sentimental expressions against slavery, and their impact was generally inconsequential.

Ending slavery proved to be more daunting and problematic than most Americans envisaged. In retrospect, winning the Revolutionary War was relatively easier than eradicating slavery in the United States. The Founding Fathers could have inscribed this view, as an epitaph on their tombstones.

The War lasted less than a decade; slavery lasted nearly 300 years. The roots of the peculiar institution extended deep in the socioeconomic system and Christianity in a way that made its eradication nearly impossible, without war or consent of slaveholders.

The Founding Fathers justified enslavement of Africans by blaming the British. They argued that slavery was introduced against the will of the colonies. Thomas Jefferson vented his frustration in a series of grievances against King George III:

> He (King George III) has waged cruel war against human nature itself, violating its most sacred rights of life and liberty in the persons of a distant people which never offended him, captivating and carrying them into slavery in another hemisphere, or to incur miserable death in their transportation thither. This piratical warfare, the opprobrium (disgrace) of infidel powers, is the warfare of the Christian King of Great Britain. He has prostituted his negative for suppressing every legislative attempt to prohibit or to restrain an execrable

commerce (that is, the King would not support efforts to abolish slavery, but rather insist on sustaining it).[1]

However, it is unconscionable that Virginia petitioned the colonial power to end slavery, but once the state achieved freedom, it recoiled and turned slavery into an empire. The colonies called for an end to slavery when they were not in charge of their own political affairs. After securing freedom from Britain, they created draconian laws to protect the nefarious enterprise of slavery. The deprivation of blacks continued, under the supervision of unfeeling slave masters who were no longer British but Americans. Had the Founding Fathers treated their zeal for freedom from Britain as they did to end slavery, the American Revolution would not have happened at the time it did.

Some contemporary historians defend the Founding Brothers against complacency for slavery. Defenders go on a literary fishing expedition to highlight favorable speeches made or point out failed legislative proposals to liberalize slave codes. However, disregarding the fact that political leaders said one thing while doing another is indefensible.

The American public acknowledged that slavery was immoral. Due to its depravity and propensity for cruelty, reputable men like President John Adams and Andrew Coles, among others, refused to associate with the despicable enterprise.

Nearly all the Revolutionary Founders acknowledged that slavery was evil and some even expressed fear that God would judge the nation for indulging in such a hideous crime against humanity. Thomas Jefferson bemoaned the effect in his *Notes on the State of Virginia* (1781) and declared:

> The whole commerce between master and slave is a perpetual exercise of the most boisterous passions, the most unremitting despotism on the one part, and degrading submissions on the other. Our children see this and learn to imitate it; for man is an imitative animal. This quality is the germ of all education in him. From his cradle to his grave he is learning to do what he sees others do. If a parent could find no motive either in his philanthropy or his self-love for restraining the intemperance of passion towards his slave, it should always be a sufficient one that his child is present. But generally it is not sufficient . . . .

---

[1]   Baron H. B. Brougham and Vaux, *Historical Sketches of Statesmen Who Flourished In The Time of George III* (London and Glasgow: Richard Griffin and Company, 1861), 284.

The man must be a prodigy who can retain his manners and morals undepraved by such circumstances. And with what execration should the statesman be loaded who permits one half the citizens thus to trample on the rights of the other . . . . And can the liberties of a nation be thought secure when we have removed their only firm basis, a conviction in the minds of the people that these liberties are of the gift of God? That they are not to be violated but with his wrath? Indeed, I tremble for my country when I reflect that God is just; that His justice cannot sleep for ever . . . . The Almighty has no attribute which can take side with us in such a contest . . . . [T]he way, I hone [is] preparing under the auspices of Heaven for a total emancipation.[2]

With this understanding, what prevented slaves manumission? Both Washington and Jefferson blamed the slave codes of 1723, which prohibited emancipation of slaves. However, in 1782, the restrictions were liberalized to allow manumission by deed or will.[3] Washington did not take advantage of this window of opportunity to free his slaves. The "unprofitable half" of the slaves that he did not need could have been emancipated. Instead, the President waited until 1799 to set the slaves free in his will.[4] However, Washington's action was more humane in comparison to the architect of civil liberty in the United States, Thomas Jefferson. Jefferson never set any of his slaves free during his lifetime or in his will, with the exception of the seven mulattoes belonging to his alleged black concubine, Sally Hemings.

In an attempt to vindicate the Founding Fathers from the charge of culpability for slavery, the American evangelical Christian minister David Barton, has advanced the argument that, "Though the issue of slavery is often raised as a discrediting charge against the Founding Fathers, the historical fact is that slavery was not the product of, nor was it an evil introduced by, the Founding Fathers; slavery had been introduced to America nearly two centuries before the Founders."[5] But, the "discrediting charge" Barton writes about does not address the fact that

[2] Thomas Jefferson, *Notes on the State of Virginia*, 2nd ed. (New York: M. L. & W. A. Davis, 1794), 240-242, Query XVIII.

[3] George M. Stroud, *A Sketch of the Laws Relating to Slavery in the Several States of the United States of America* (Philadelphia: Henry Longstreth, 1856), 236-237.

[4] Don Higginbotham, *George Washington Reconsidered* (VA: University Press of Virginia, 2001).

[5] David Barton, *Original Intent: The Courts, the Constitution, and Religion* (TX: Wallbuilder, 2008), 289.

the American patriots knowingly participated in slave trade, supported, and sustained slavery by laws and actions, all while denouncing the evil institution. They passed laws to protect slavocracy and plutocrats, while calling slavery evil. As Barton observes, the President of Congress, Henry Laurens declared:

> I abhor slavery. I was born in a country where slavery had been established by British Kings and Parliaments as well as by the laws of the country ages before my existence . . . . In former days there was no combating the prejudices of men supported by interest; the day, I hope, is approaching when, from principles of gratitude as well as justice, every man will strive to be foremost in showing his readiness to comply with the Golden Rule.[6]

Laurens expressed a passionate abhorrence against slavery, but he had the largest slave-trading house in North America. His enterprise sold nearly 8,000 slaves in the 1750s.[7] It is difficult not to see his rhetoric as a mere travesty for someone who claimed to "abhor slavery."

The fault is not merely the ownership of slaves at one time or another. The crime of the Founders is, after recognizing that it was immoral and a blot on the American character, they continued buying, selling, and treating Africans as farm animals. They enacted draconian laws, which gave them the right to enslave the indigents. They destroyed black families by creating an environment to rape black women and men with impunity. They forced blacks to produce bastards for sale like animals in slave markets. Slave laws denied black people primary education in some states, thus forcing them into poverty and crime. Blacks were denied education and jobs, but the slave masters accused them of ignorance and indolence. This is the crime of the Founding Founders. They found it easier to sustain slavery than end it.

The disparagement of blacks was aided and sustained by most U.S. presidents in Antebellum America. Of the first sixteen presidents, six did not own slaves, including John Adams, John Quincy Adams, Millard Fillmore, Franklin Pierce, James Buchanan, and Abraham Lincoln.[8]

---

[6]  Scott J. Hammond, Kevin R. Hardwick, Howard Leslie Lubert, ed., *Classics of American Political and Constitutional Thought: Origins Through The Civil War* (ID: Hackett Publishing Company, 2007), 317.

[7]  *Slavery and Justice*, http://www.brown.edu/Research/Slavery_Justice/documents/SlaveryAndJustice.pdf (accessed January 1, 2012).

[8]  *Which U.S. Presidents Owned Slaves?*http://home.nas.com/lopresti/ps.htm (accessed May 22, 2013).

# George Washington Grapples With Slavery

George Washington (1732-1799), first president of the United States, inherited slaves from his father when he was eleven years old. Later, he added fifty more slaves before the Revolutionary War. After the War, he vowed never again to buy or sell another human being: "I never mean . . . to possess another slave by purchase; it being among my first wishes to see some plan adopted by which slavery in this country may be abolished by slow, sure, and imperceptible degrees."[9]However, the first President had about 316 slaves at Mount Vernon and leased others from neighboring plantations to work his enormous land. His wife Martha Custis owned 153 from her former husband, Daniel Parke Custis. Her slaves became known as the "dower slaves."

Washington had owned slaves since he was eleven years old. After the United States' Independence, he gave financial and military aid to French in Haiti to suppress the Haitian uprising.[10] President Washington agreed with slave catchers and signed into law the Fugitive Act of 1793, which authorized slave owners to capture runaway slaves.[11] He was also willing to grant U.S. citizenship to whites only and made laws for blacks to serve white people freely. The President approved the *Northwest Territory Act* of 1789 that prohibited slavery in the Northwest Territory, while he preserved the right to secure his own slaves in his southern territory.

There were times when Washington expressed the desire to set all his slaves free but blamed the slave codes for prohibiting emancipation. The only option was to sell those he did not need and he was not going to do that as a matter of principle, as he claimed. Nevertheless, in 1786 he accepted five slaves as payment for a debt owed him.[12]Another time he requested Henry Lee to buy a slave for him because he needed a bricklayer and he was too busy to do the work himself. Certainly, Washington could afford to pay a fair wage for a bricklayer, as most Americans at the time did. However, he chose slave labor.

---

[9]    Frank E. Grizzard, *George! A Guide to All Things Washington* (Mariner Publishing, 2005), 285.

[10]   Elbridge Streeter Brooks, *The True Story of George Washington: Called The Father Of His Country* (Lothrop Publishing, 1895), 19.

[11]   Leslie M. Alexander and Walter C. Rucker, Eds. *Encyclopedia of African American History 3 Volume* (CA: ABC-CLIO, LLC, 2010).

[12]   Don Higginbotham, *George Washington Reconsidered* (Virginia: The University of Virginia, 2001), 127-28.

The first President set his slaves free in his will after the death of his wife.[13] Mary Custis was troubled with the assignment. If the plan was to emancipate all the slaves after her death, she feared they might kill her sooner to gain their freedom. Consequently, barely a year after Washington's death, she set all of his slaves free on January 1, 1801. The Daniel Custis' heirs inherited the dower slaves when Martha died in 1802 as a matter of law.[14]

Washington was not vocal against slavery after the Revolutionary War. He served as chair of the Constitutional Convention but failed to express any views on slavery during the entire debate. Historian Dorothy Twohig argues that Washington "did not speak out publicly against slavery because he did not want to risk splitting the young republic over what was already a sensitive and divisive issue."[15]

Washington took office with an overwhelming mandate from the Electoral College.[16] It would seem that, if there was ever an opportunity to formulate a national policy to dismantle the peculiar institution, whether gradually or immediately, it was during the presidency of George Washington. By failing to rise to that challenge, Washington did a disservice to his own legacy.

Gouverneur Morris, who was credited for writing the preamble to the United States Constitution, also felt Washington had a political capital to achieve what no other man could. He wrote in 1788 that, "I have ever thought, and have ever said, that you must be the president; no other man can fill that office. No other man can draw forth the abilities of our country into the various departments of civil life. You alone can awe the insolence of opposing factions, and the greater insolence of assuming adherents."[17]Unfortunately, Washington never sought to rise to the occasion of conquering the greatest affront to civil liberty—the inhumane subjugation of Africans in the grip of tyrants in the United States.

Heroes are praised or eulogized for deeds, not words alone. Against slavery and the magnitude of its effects, Washington's utterances were few and far apart, and scarcely after assuming the presidency. He retired

13    Jesse J. Holland, *Discovering African-American History In and Around Washington, D.C.* (Connecticut: The Globe Pequet Press, 2007), 165.

14    Holland, 165.

15    Higginbotham, "That Species of Property", 127-28.

16    Fritz Hirschfeld, *George Washington And Slavery: A Documentary Portray* (Missouri: University of Missouri Press, 1997).

17    John Marshall and Bushrod Washington, *Life of George Washington: Commander in Chief of the American Forces and First president of the United States.* (PA: C.P. Wayne, 1806), 134.

peacefully at Mount Vernon and quietly but conditionally set his slaves free in his will, when he could no longer benefit from their free services.

The Marquis de Lafayette travelled from France to America to participate in the American Revolutionary War. He pointed out the paradox of liberty and slavery by declaring: "I would have never drawn my sword in the cause of America, if I could have conceived that thereby I was founding a land of slavery."[18] The French General was disappointed with the American government, but even more so in his friend, George Washington, for not standing up against slavery.

In February 1783, while writing to Washington to inform him of the preliminary treaty of peace approval, Lafayette also proposed a scheme whereby the two men would purchase an estate and free Washington's slaves, using them as tenants:

> Now, my dear General, that you are going to enjoy some ease and quiet, permit me to propose a plan to you, which might become greatly beneficial to the black part of mankind. Let us unite in purchasing a small estate, where we may try the experiment to free the Negroes, and use them only as tenants. Such an example as yours might render it a general practice; and if we succeed in America, I will cheerfully devote a part of my time to render the method fashionable in the West Indies. If it be a wild scheme, I had rather be mad this way, than to be thought wise in the other task.[19]

Washington put off any action, although he seemed to have shown interested in Lafayette's experiment. In 1785, Lafayette purchased 125,000 acres of land in Cayenne, a plantation that came with slaves. He did not immediately free his slaves but did paid them for their work and provided some education. However, the venture only lasted a few years. In 1791, the Jacobins imprisoned Lafayette and confiscated his property for giving an order to fire on demonstrators.

Samuel Johnson asked, "How is it we hear the loudest yelps for liberty from the drivers of Negroes?" Did Washington ever want to end slavery? May be, according to the yelping, but not by what he did, although he said:

> I can only say that there is not a man living who wishes more sincerely than I do to see a plan adopted for the abolition of

---

[18]    Bruce Chadwick, *The Forging of A Revolutionary Leader and the Making of the Presidency: George Washington* (Ill: Sourcebooks, 2004) 412.
[19]    Hirschfeld, 123.

it [slavery]; but there is only one proper and effectual mode by which it can be accomplished, and that is by Legislative authority; and this, as far as my suffrage [vote and support] will go, shall never be wanting [lacking].[20]

In March of 1791, the President relocated to Philadelphia, with his slaves. By then, the state had passed a law to free slaves after six months of residency. The possibility of losing his slaves disturbed Washington greatly. He instructed Tobias Lear, his secretary, to determine whether the law would apply to his presidential household in Pennsylvania. If it did, and if there were reasons to believe some of the slaves would seek freedom under the Pennsylvania law, the President instructed for an arrangement to be made to send his slaves back to Mount Vernon. "If upon taking good advice it is found expedient to send them back to Virginia, I wish to have it accomplished under pretext that may deceive both them and the Public."[21]

Again, when one of Washington's slaves ran away in 1795, he carefully instructed his overseer to take precaution but apprehend the fugitive. He cautioned, "I would not have my name appear in any advertisement, or other measure, leading to it."[22]

Washington indicated that he did not need all of his slaves and he could do with about half of them and still do well. "It is demonstratively clear that on this Estate I have more working Negroes by a full [half] than can be employed to any advantage in the farming system," he added, "to sell the over plus I cannot, because I am principled against this kind of traffic in the human species. To hire them out is almost as bad because they could not be disposed of in families to any advantage, and to disperse the families I have an aversion." If this had been Washington's conviction about slavery, it is difficult to understand why he was so troubled about the possibility of his slaves declaring their freedom in Pennsylvania, if that was what they wanted. Why did he want to go after a fugitive slave?

Paradoxically, the President turned against buying or selling slaves, by his account. He would not rent out his slaves but he rented other masters' slaves to work on his plantation, instead of hiring freemen or other paid

---

[20] John C. Fitzpatrick, ed. *George Washington, The Writings of George Washington*, (Washington, D. C.: United States Government Printing Office, 1936), Vol. 38, 408, to Robert Morris on April 12, 1786.

[21] Henry Wiencek, *Imperfect God: George Washington, His Slaves, and the Creation of America* (New York: Farrar, Straus and Girous, 2004), 134.

[22] Dorothy Twohig Tobias, *That Species of Property: Washington's Role in the Controversy Over Slavery.* http://gwpapers.virginia.edu/articles/twohig_2.html (accessed 2 Marcn 2012).

labor. At the time of his death, he owned 123 slaves and 40 others he rented from his neighbors.[23] If Washington did not need half his slaves, why was he renting his neighbors' slaves, instead of contracting freedmen for pay?

## John Adams' Denouncement of Slavery

John Adams (1735-1826) was the second President of the United States. Like Jefferson and Madison after him, he was a lawyer, diplomat, and political theorist. He helped Jefferson draft the Declaration of Independence, although Jefferson disputed the role Adams played in the formulation of that historic document. Unlike George Washington and Jefferson, Adams never owned slaves and complained that he had to pay full price for hired labor, while others benefited from free services from slaves. His wife, Abigail Adams, preferred hiring freemen for paid labor than use her father's slaves for free. But Adams wrote:

> I have, through my whole life, held the practice of slavery in such abhorrence, that I have never owned a negro or any other slave; though I have lived for many years in times when the practice was not disgraceful; when the best men in my vicinity thought it not inconsistent with their character; and when it has cost me thousands of dollars of the labor and subsistence of free men, which I might have saved by the purchase of negroes at times when they were very cheap.[24]

In 1776, while discussing trade resolutions before the continental congress, Adams said, "There is one resolution I will not omit. Resolved that no slaves be imported into any of the thirteen colonies." In a letter to his wife in 1819, Adams wrote, "Negro Slavery is an evil of colossal magnitude;"[25] then in 1820, he made the following statement, "There is one resolution I will not omit. Resolved that no slaves be imported into any of the thirteen colonies."

In a letter to his wife in 1819, Adam wrote, "Negro Slavery is an evil of colossal magnitude;"[26] then in 1820, he made the following statement:

---

[23]   Holland, 165.
[24]   Charles M. Christian, *Black Saga: The African American Experience: a Chronology* (Boston: Houghton Mifflin, 1995), 89.
[25]   David McCullough, *John Adams* (NY: Simon & Schuster, 2001), 134.
[26]   Ibid.

I shudder when I think of the calamities which slavery is likely to produce in this country. You would think me mad if I were to describe my anticipations . . . If the gangrene is not stopped I can see nothing but insurrection of the blacks against the whites . . . till at last the whites will be exasperated by madness—shall be wicked enough to exterminate the Negroes as the English did the Rohillas.[27]

Individuals like John Adams did not fall prey to the indignant evil empire of slavery. He rose above the plague of his time, unlike Washington, Jefferson, and Madison.

## Thomas Jefferson Embraces Slavery

"We hold these truths to be self-evident, that all men are created equal, that they are endowed, by their Creator, with certain unalienable Rights, that among these are Life, Liberty, and the pursuit of Happiness." These immortal words were coined by Thomas Jefferson, the author of the Declaration of Independence. But as the patriarch demonstrated throughout his live, "all men" did not include black people or men of other races. He and his rival co-author, John Adams, took two different paths. Adams denounced slavery and never owned a slave. Jefferson denounced slavery but was a slave trader.

Thomas Jefferson (1743-1826) was the third President of the United States and an illustrious political philosophy. On his epitaph, he wrote, "Here is Buried Thomas Jefferson, Author of the Declaration of Independence, of the Statue of Virginia for Religious Freedom, and Father of the University of Virginia." He considered these three accomplishments as his life's crowning achievements.

One subject that buffeted Jefferson was the slave controversy. On September 23, 1800, he sent the following letter to Dr. Benjamin Rush: "I have sworn upon the altar of God, eternal hostility against every form of tyranny over the mind of man."

Before his retirement from public service, Jefferson wrote more persuasively and passionately about the evil of human bondage than most of his compatriots. "In 1769," he stated, "I became a member of the legislature . . . I made one effort in that body for the permission of the emancipation of slaves, which was rejected." Then in 1784, he proposed

---

27    Paul Kalra, *From Slave To Untouchable: Lincoln's Solution* (CA: Antenna Publishing, 2011), 173.

a law in the national Continental Congress to end slavery in America. His proposal stated: "After the year 1800 of the Christian era, there shall be neither slavery nor involuntary servitude in any of the said States, otherwise than in punishment of crimes, whereof the party shall have been duly convicted to have been personally guilty."[28]However, the proposal failed by one vote. Before his death, Jefferson admitted that ending slavery became more daunting than he had envisioned.

The former President disparaged blacks and traced their origin to a subhuman species in a different category from whites. The only book he ever published, *Notes on the State of Virginia*, claims that blacks "are inferior to the whites in endowments both of body and mind; this inferiority is not the effect merely of their condition of life." Jefferson insisted that black people, unlike whites, smell and emit bad odor due to a gland in their skin. They have feeble minds and are incapable of understanding mathematics or science. However, they have endurance for pain and afflictions and easily forget tortures.

As a scholar of letters, it is not clear why Jefferson showed such willful contempt or blatant ignorance in judgment about Africa. However, his polygenic argument was not particularly unusual. Most white people at the time shared similar sentiments. They developed a false sense of superiority complex over the impoverished blacks, who, held against their will, were stripped of basic human rights, without access to education. Further, Jefferson accused blacks of intellectual inferiority based on a faulty generalization.

Among the worst physical qualities for Africans, according to Jefferson, were the black skin, which lacked beauty, unlike white skin; short kinky hair which was unlike "flowing hair, a more elegant symmetry of form."[29] Jefferson added that black men preferred white women as chimpanzees (oranoontan) preferred black women, over their own kind. He added:

> The circumstance of superior beauty, is thought worthy attention in the propagation of our horses, dogs, and other domestic animals; why not in that of man? Besides those of colour, figure, and hair, there are other physical distinctions proving a difference of race. They have less hair on the face and body. They secrete less by the kidnies, and more by the glands

---

[28]  *Journals of the Continental Congress,* Volume XXVI, pp. 118-119, Monday, March 1, 1784.

[29]  Norm Ledgin, Diagnosing Jefferson: Evidence of a Condition That Guided His Beliefs, Behavior and Personal Associations (Arlington: future Horizon, 2000), 74.

of the skin, which gives them a very strong and disagreeable odour. This greater degree of transpiration renders them more tolerant of heat, and less so of cold, than the whites . . . They seem to require less sleep. A black, after hard labour through the day, will be induced by the slightest amusements to sit up till midnight, or later, though knowing he must be out with the first dawn of the morning. They are at least as brave, and more adventuresome. But this may perhaps proceed from a want of forethought, which prevents their seeing a danger till it be present . . . They are more ardent after their female: but love seems with them to be more an eager desire, than a tender delicate mixture of sentiment and sensation.[30]

After the publication of the *Notes on the State of Virginia*, a French antislavery opponent and priest, Henri-Baptiste Grégoire (Abbé Grégoire), challenged the inferiority claim and sent Jefferson a copy of his book, *An Enquiry Concerning the Intellectual and Moral Faculties and Literature of Negroes*. He repudiated the President's inferiority arguments and demonstrated that African societies developed "advanced civilizations and were intellectually competent."[31]

In February 25, 1809, Jefferson responded to Grégoire's rebuke:

Sir, I have received the favor of your letter of August 17th, and with it the volume you were so kind as to send me on the "Literature of Negroes." Be assured that no person living wishes more sincerely than I do, to see a complete refutation of the doubts I have myself entertained and expressed on the grade of understanding allotted to them by nature, and to find that in this respect they are on a par with ourselves. My doubts were the result of personal observation on the limited sphere of my own State, where the opportunities for the development of their genius were not favorable, and those of exercising it still less so. I expressed them therefore with great hesitation; but whatever be their degree of talent it is no measure of their rights. Because Sir Isaac Newton was superior to others in understanding, he was not therefore lord of the person or property of others. On this subject they are gaining daily in the opinions of nations, and hopeful advances are making

<hr>

[30]     Ibid, 74-75.
[31]     Thomas Jefferson, William Peden. ed. *Notes on the State of* Virginia (NC: University of North Carolina Press, 1955), 139-142.

towards their re-establishment on an equal footing with the other colors of the human family. I pray you therefore to accept my thanks for the many instances you have enabled me to observe of respectable intelligence in that race of men, which cannot fail to have effect in hastening the day of their relief; and to be assured of the sentiments of high and just esteem and consideration which I tender to yourself with all sincerity.

Despite the pseudo contrition, Jefferson did not change his racist views about blacks. He still believed that whites were superior to Africans, although he knew very little about African literature and culture. He had only known most blacks as slaves and cheap sex objects for their white owners, like Jefferson himself.

Another rebuttal came from Benjamin Banneker,[32] a black mathematician. In 1791, he produced and published a commended almanac. He sent a copy with a twelve-page letter challenging Jefferson's racist sentiments and asking him to show kindness to the unfortunate Africans who suddenly found themselves in a condition they did not create. Jefferson again replied politely:

I thank you sincerely for your letter . . . and for the almanac it contained. Nobody wishes more than I do to see such proofs as you exhibit, that nature has given to our black brethren talents equal to those of the other colors of men . . . . I have taken the liberty of sending your almanac to Monsieur de Condorcet, Secretary of the Academy of Sciences at Paris, and member of the Philanthropic Society, because I considered it as a document to which your color had a right for their justification against the doubts which have been entertained of them.[33]

Jefferson forwarded Banneker's almanac to the Academy of Sciences in Paris, with a glowing acknowledgement and introduction of the black scholar. This was a challenge for him because Banneker's work unequivocally debunked the kind of pervasive racial sentiments the polygenist held.

Jefferson developed a different set of racist arguments to describe the black mathematician's ingenuity. According to him, Banneker's

---

[32]  Benjamin Banneker was one of the surveyors who laid out the city of Washington, D.C.

[33]  *Jefferson, Writings* (1903), Vol. VIII, pp. 241-242, to Benjamin Banneker on August 30, 1791.

intelligence was an exception among blacks, but Jefferson did not believe his theory about black inferiority was essentially flawed. He clarified his view in a letter to an American poet and politician, Joel Barlow, three years after the death of the black scientist in 1806. The President derided him and contended that he could not have made the calculations contained in the almanac without the help of a white colleague.[34]Therefore, what he saw as evidence of blacks' intelligence, according to Jefferson, "was not real."

If there is any redeeming quality in Jefferson in relation to slavery, it was his role in writing the Declaration of Independence. The document immortalized the this universal sentiment, "We hold these truths to be self-evident, that all men are created equal, that they are endowed by their Creator with certain unalienable Rights, that among these are Life, Liberty and the pursuit of Happiness." Although the phrase is incidental to the fight for equality around the world, the words have been a source of inspiration and hope for the pursuit of civil liberty for all races.

Jefferson, as a prolific writer, expressed feelings on paper more skillfully than many of his compatriots. His philosophical views about the subhuman nature of black people were merely a cover to justify his enslavement and ill-treatment of blacks as animals.

Jefferson was a plutocrat, a careered slave master who bought, bred, flogged, and sold slaves during most of his adult life. He freed only two slaves during his lifetime, and both were related to the slave woman he was accused of sexually seducing, Sally Hemings. Besides her family, he never freed another slave, even in his will. After his death, 130 of Jefferson's captives were auctioned to pay for his lavish aristocratic lifestyle, which landed him in massive unpaid debt.

Supporters of Jefferson argue that he could not free his slaves because it was against the law in Virginia to do so. While the slave codes had undergone several revisions by 1800, some forms of emancipation existed. In 1782, a revised version of the laws allowed emancipation by deed or will. Among other requirements, the slave had to be sound and of good character, between18 (females) or 21 (males) to 45 years.[35]Since at any given year, Monticello had nearly two hundred slaves, it is difficult to argue that no slaves were qualified under the law. He set Robert Hemings and James Hemings free in 1794 and 1796 respectively, both being Sally Hemings' brothers. If Jefferson had been a strong opponent of slavery

---

[34]   Silvio Bedini, *The Life of Benjamin Banneker: The First African-American Man of Science* (The Maryland Historical Society, 1999).

[35]   Philip J. Schwarz, *Slave Laws in Virginia*. (Georgia: University of Georgia Press, 1996).

in words and deeds, as some historians advocate, what kept him from setting the other slaves free? Alternatively, what prevented him from emancipating other slaves, even in his will, besides the Sally Hemings' children and family?

Jefferson was president when the federal government banned the importation of slaves into the country. That really benefitted him even more, as he could sell at higher value to other States without fear of foreign competition. That leads to the troubling conclusion that, even if Jefferson had been granted the right to emancipate or keep his slaves, he would have chosen the latter to keep them in bondage. His lavish aristocratic lifestyle plunged him in debt and he was in danger of losing his own freedom without free slave labor. After his death, the auctioneers sold all but five slaves to pay off creditors. The sale included Monticello, his cherished haven.

## Edward Coles' Plea to End Slavery

Edward Coles (1786-1868) was a Virginian politician and neighbor of Thomas Jefferson. Coles' father died in 1808, leaving his slaves and a 782-acre plantation in Nelson County, Virginia.

The 22-year-old Coles' family was disturbed when he revealed that his inherited slaves would be set free.[36] They objected. He ignored them, and as early as was feasible, he fulfilled his dream in 1819. He sold his estate and moved to the slave free state of Illinois.

Coles transmitted a letter to Jefferson asking him to work aggressively against slavery in Virginia. The former President refused and called on Cole to return to Virginia to defeat slavery there.[37] Jefferson wrote:

> Until more can be done for them, we should endeavor with those whom fortune has thrown on our hands, to feed and clothe them well, protect them from all ill usage, require such reasonable labor only as is performed voluntarily by freemen, and he led by no repugnancies to abdicate them, and our duties to them.[38]

---

[36] Thomas Jefferson to Benjamin Rush, December 5, 1811, in Ford, *Writings of Thomas Jefferson*, 298.

[37] Thomas Jefferson to Edward Coles, August 25, 1814, *E. Coles Papers*, Princeton University Library.

[38] T. Jefferson to Edward Coles, Aug. 25, 1814, Ford, ed., *Works of Thomas Jefferson*, XI, 416.

Coles was disappointed to learn firsthand that the most revered icon of liberty had lost the will to fight for liberty. The young politician moved his slaves to Illinois, set them free, and gave each head of family 160 acres of land.[39]

Edward became the second governor of Illinois. He fought and won against the political machineries in government that intended to adopt a proposal to make Illinois a slave state. [40]

## John Randolph's Regret About Slavery

John Randolph of Roanoke (1773-1833) was a former strong advocate for slaveholders' rights and an influential political leader in the Virginia Assembly. He owned a few plantations in the Tidewater area of Virginia and inherited 400 slaves to work his massive estates of more than 8,000 acres.

Randolph recognized that it was beneficial to society to educate slaves and treat them humanely. First, he decided never again to buy or sell slaves, and devoted personal time to teach the ones he had to read. He also organized them into groups and gave each a separate tract of land to work. This was something most slave owners did not do, not even George Washington or Thomas Jefferson.

Randolph was Thomas Jefferson's representative in the House of Burgesses in Virginia. He broke with the President in 1803. In 1819, the congressional representative manumitted his slaves in his will, and noted, "I give and bequeath to all my slaves their freedom, heartily regretting that I have ever been the owner of one."[41] Randolph provided $8,000.00 for his slaves to resettle in the free state of Ohio. Each black above the age of 40 years was to receive no less than 10 acres of land.

## James Madison's Ambivalence on Slavery

James Madison (1751-1836) was a political theorist. He earned the distinction of being called the "Father of the Constitution" and the principle author of the United States Bill of Rights.

---

[39]   Newton Bateman, Paul Selby, Frances M. Shonkwiler, Henry L Fowkes, *Historical Encyclopedia of Illinois* (Chicago, IL: Munsell Publishing Company, 1908), 259.

[40]   David Ress *Governor Edward Coles and the Vote to Forbid Slavery in Illinois: 1823-1824* (NC: McFarland & Company, 2006).

[41]   Randolph Johnson, *Virginia Reports,* (Charlottesville: The Michie Company Law Publishers. 1902), 24.

Madison was fourteen years old when he saw a spectacle that stayed with him most of his life. The grisly incident occurred June of 1737, when a Negro named Peter received a death sentence for allegedly murdering his owner.[42] The authorities displayed his decapitated head on a pole near a creek, as a reminder to other slaves for violent acts against white people. The creek was renamed *Negrohead Run* and Madison saw the infamous head without a body on the pole whenever he went by the creek. Moreover, in 1748, Madison's uncle, Thomas Chew, Sherriff of Orange County, burned to death a slave girl, Eve, for killing her owner.[43]

It is not certain how much Madison's childhood experience affected his views on slavery, but in general, he viewed slavery as "a blot on our republican character." However, he owned more than 100 slaves at his Montpelier Plantation. The overseers were to treat them as humanely as possible but not to the extent that they forget their status as slaves.

When Madison became president of the American Colonization Society, he took the awkward position of promoting manumission of slaves. He held his own slaves in bondage and did not free them even in his will. As for the free blacks, Madison was of the same mindset as Jefferson and most Americans that emancipated Africans could not peacefully coexist with whites, due to the intense hatred between the two races. Therefore, it was necessary to relocate them away from white society somewhere in the American west or Africa.

When Madison laid on his deathbed in 1836, his bodyguard, a slave named Paul Jennings, was by his side. After Madison's death, his wife sold the 47-year-old Jennings in 1846 to pay off debts. Daniel Webster loaned him money to buy his freedom and repay the amount at $8 a month in service to Webster.[44]From 1847, Jennings lived free in Washington from 1847 until his death in 1870.

Edward Coles, who freed his slaves in 1819, felt betrayed by Madison. According to him, during a short stay at Montpelier, Madison secretly disclosed his intention to free the slaves and even called on Coles to help make it possible.[45] Trusting that Madison would keep the promise of manumission in his will, he was shocked to find out that Madison did not keep the promise.

---

[42]  Ralph Ketcham, *James Madison, A Biography*. (Virginia: The University Press of Virginia, 1990), 12.

[43]  Ketcham, 12.

[44]  *Paul Jennings*, http://www.montpelier.org/research-and-collections/people/african-americans/montpelier-slaves/paul-jennings (accessed May 6, 2011).

[45]  Document: Edward Coles to James Madison, January 8, 1832, folder 30, box 1, E. *Coles Papers*, Princeton University Library.

Madison expressed some of his strongest denouncements against slavery in an underground publication known as the Federalist Paper. He wrote:

> We must not deny the fact, that slaves are considered merely as property, and in no respect whatever as persons. The true state of the case is that they partake of both these qualities: being considered by our laws, in some respects, as persons, and in other respects as property. In being compelled to labor, not for himself, but for a master; in being vendible by one master to another master; and in being subject at all times to be restrained in his liberty and chastised in his body, by the capricious will of another, the slave may appear to be degraded from the human rank, and classed with those irrational animals which fall under the legal denomination of property. In being protected, on the other hand, in his life and in his limbs, against the violence of all others, even the master of his labor and his liberty; and in being punishable himself for all violence committed against others, the slave is no less evidently regarded by the law as a member of the society, not as a part of the irrational creation; as a moral person, not as a mere article of property.[46]

Like Madison, most of the Founding Fathers acknowledged that slavery was a blot on the American character.[47] However, they lacked the political will to dismantle the evil empire.

## The Constitution's Silence on Slavery

When Madison became president of the Constitutional Convention, the subject on every mind, without discussing it, was slavery. It was the untouchable yet unavoidable. After all the tiptoeing, slave states were forbidden to use the slave population to increase their representation in Congress disproportionally.

At the Convention, Governor Edmund Johnson presented what came to be known as the Virginia Plan. Many of the deputies at the Convention were surprised, as they listened to the proposal. Instead of amending the

---

[46] Federalist Paper No. 54.

[47] William Van Deburg, *Slavery and Race in American Popular Culture* (Madison: The University of Wisconsin, 1984), 7.

Articles of Confederation, a new government, with three branches, was proposed.[48]This got two of the New York delegates to leave the meeting in anger. They believed the Convention was making an unconstitutional decision. Creating a new constitution was possibly a surprise to other members of the Convention who only had in mind the mandate to revise the Articles of Confederation.[49]Moreover, Virginia also proposed a bicameral Congress. The citizens were to select members of the Lower House of Representatives, while the Lower House appointed the senators of the Upper House.[50]Members of Congress were to be proportional, according to the population of each State.

Rogers Sherman[51] of Connecticut changed the course of the debate. His plan kept the opposing factions from defecting. Sherman proposed a bicameral Congress, with two chambers: the House of Representatives and Senate. The proposal also included the number of free persons and three-fifths of the number of other persons (slaves) in a given State as the basis for determining the number of representatives. The Senate would have two members from each State, irrespective of size or population, with one representative for every 40,000 people.[52]This was the Great Comprise because it received a general approval from the delegates.

The Sherman's Plan was important because, among other considerations, it addressed the slave problem. Southerners proposed to include slaves as a part of the population. The North objected and called for the abolition of slavery throughout the United States. Sherman was able to get both sides to agree on appropriating representatives in the House, based on three-fifths of slave population in a state. This meant that five slaves equaled three whites, based on what came to be known as the federal ratio.[53]

The three-fifths concept of "all other persons" (indirect reference to slaves) had been discussed prior to the Constitutional Convention in Philadelphia before. In 1783, a group of delegates met to consider some alterations to the Articles of Confederation by specifying how the wealth of a state was to be determined for tax purposes, taking into account its real estate and population.

Finding a formula for proportional taxation became a daunting task. The South instantly opposed the Committee's proposal. The

---

48    Vile, 13.
49    Bardes, 39.
50    Vile, 13.
51    Rogers Sherman never owned slaves.
52    McGeehan, 42.
53    William Jay, *A view of the action of the federal government, in behalf of slaver,* (New York: J.S. Taylor, 1839), 15.

recommendation would have increased the tax base for slaveholding states substantially. Several proposed compromises had failed to gain traction. Congress discussed the inclusion of half of the slave population or three-fourths of "other persons" (slaves).[54]Finally, James Madison broke the deadlock by proposing the three-fifths ratio, which every state supported, excluding New Hampshire and Rode Island. However, a unanimous vote of all the states was required for approval, therefore the amendment failed in Congress.

The Constitutional Convention decided to take up the three-fifths measure again when Roger Sherman proposed it in the Connecticut Plan. Congress passed the measure to read, "Representatives and direct Taxes shall be apportioned among the several States which may be included within this Union, according to their respective Numbers, which shall be determined by adding to the whole Number of free Persons, including those bound to Service for a Term of Years, and excluding Indians not taxed, three fifths of all other Persons."

There was another quasi fix for slavery. The Convention agreed to allow slaves importation until 1808, with an import tax of $10 for a slave brought into the country before that date.[55]The deal was sealed with this clause, "The Migration or Importation of such Persons as any of the States now existing shall think proper to admit shall not be prohibited by the Congress prior to the Year one thousand eight hundred and eight, but a Tax or duty may be imposed on such Importation, not exceeding ten dollars for each Person."[56]

In 1808, the ban on the importation of slaves went into effect. Before the ban, James Madison denounced taxation on slavery as a dishonor to the National character.[57]

---

[54]   *The Three-Fifth Compromise*, http://www.digitalhistory.uh.edu/documents / documents_p2.cfm?doc=306 (accessed October 13, 2010).

[55]   Vile, 725.

[56]   *The Slave Trade and the Constitution*, http://abolition.nypl.org /print/us_ constitution/ (accessed October 15, 2010).

[57]   Vile, 725.

# CHAPTER V

# THE BINARY ROLE OF
# SLAVE WOMEN

Slavery was a demeaning horrid. It amassed absolute power to make and break laws of civility or deny inalienable rights to its victims. The dominant control of masters over slaves led to the debauchment of African people, especially women. Most females experienced horrific tortures as sex slaves. Consequently, black men, as victims of shocking cruelty, proved incapable to protect their women and children from the lewd and lascivious behaviors of slave masters. This incapacitation only helped to weaken the bonds that held black families together.

To treat human beings as creeping things or animals, as slaveholders did, the victims must first be denied human essence and reduced to common brutes. This is what the slave culture did to assert superiority over innocent Africans who had been forcibly removed from their native lands to serve foreign tyrants in colonial America.

To reclaim their humanity and restore whatever dignity left to exhume, many blacks chose to resist their masters. The end result was brutal for slaveholders and slaves. Years of brutal exploitation transformed to an unabated embittered rage against slavocracy and individuals behind the torture of Africans.

Sexual intimidation was a ready apparatus to induce compliance or demand unquestionable loyalty from slave women. As early as 1660, British colonies in North America had laws to encourage sexual tyranny against blacks. This was intended to boost the economic and social gains of owners. Children born in slavery naturally increased the slave populations and holdings of their owners. Black women became human breeding machines for popping out bastards in forced sexual servitude.

Plantation owners often bought young women to serve a binary role. First, they became field hands or housemaids. Most house slaves were light-skinned, mulattos, and served as sexual partners for the masters. House slaves could also be the master's children whose mothers were also slaves. All offspring of slave mothers automatically became slaves, even if the masters were the fathers of the children, because the genealogical line in slavery was matriarchal.[1]

Secondly, slave women served as breeders. They were required to have children—a lot of children, beginning at an early age—or be sold. The intended purpose was to increase the slave populations.

The master often paired women with men of his choice, irrespective of their marital status. Sometimes the men came from other plantations to impregnate the women. The goal was to have robust children to be bred for service or sale.

Sexual relations between masters and slaves could hardly be seen as mutual. There was no choice in bondage, without consent of the masters. Refusing sexual advances could result in severe punishment, such as whipping, even for pregnant women. Most slaves dreaded being sold away from their spouses or children. As a result, though "married," they generally gave in to the sexual demands of their masters. Sex became a coercive force to induce compliance. Slave women were also sexual objects to entertain guests, relatives, friends, or reward plantation overseers and supervisors. In case of pregnancy, paternity was not significant, because a slave child was a commodity for sale, depending on the choice of the master.

Sexual affairs with black concubines were generally ignored by the community. Sometimes wives of the white adulterers looked the other way, although others did result to violence. Infidelity was sometimes seen as a business decision to increase the slave populations, while others were hurt over the affairs. In most cases, the frustration was taken on the maids, though she had no rights to resist.

## Slave Narratives

The following narratives demonstrate the tyranny of slavery. The WPA (Works Progress Administration) Slave Narrative Project did the interview in 1937.[2] It must be understood that the cruelest hardships

---

[1]    Ann Patton Malone, *Sweet Chariot* (NC: The University of North Carolina Press, 1992).

[2]    The Library of Congress has indicated that it "is not aware of any copyright in the documents in this collection. As far as is known, the documents were written by U.S. Government employees. Generally speaking, works created by U.S. Government employees are not eligible for copyright protection in the United States, although they may be under copyright in some foreign countries. The persons interviewed or whose words were transcribed were generally not employees of the U.S. Suggested credit line: Library of Congress, Manuscript Division, WPA Federal Writers' Project Collection".

endured by enslaved Africans was the sexual abuse by slaveholders, overseers, and others whose power to dominate blacks was complete.

Enslaved women were forced to submit to their masters' sexual advances, perhaps bearing children that would engender the rage of a master's wife, and from whom they might be separated forever as a result.[3] Masters forcibly paired "good breeders" to produce strong children they could sell at a high price. Resistance brought severe punishment, an often death.

In his 1857 narratives, according to WPA accounts, William J. Anderson wrote: "I know these facts will seem too awful to relate, as they are some of the real 'dark deeds of American Slavery."[4] The following are testimonies of enslaved women and eyewitnesses to the horror of slavery:[5]

> Plenty of the colored women have children by the white men. She know better than to not do what he say. Didn't have much of that until the men from South Carolina come up here [North Carolina] and settle and bring slaves. Then they take them very same children what have they own blood and make slaves out of them. If the Missus find out she raise revolution. But she hardly find out. The white men not going to tell and the nigger women were always afraid to. So they jes go on hopin' that thing[s] won't be that way always.

> The slave traders would buy young and able farm men and well developed young girls with fine physique to barter and sell. They would bring them to the taverns where there would be the buyers and traders, display them and offer them for sale. At one of these gatherings a colored girl, a mulatto of fine stature and good looks, was put on sale. She was of high spirits and determined disposition. At night she was taken by the trader to his room to satisfy his bestial nature. She could not be coerced or forced, so she was attacked by him. In the struggle she grabbed a knife and with it, she sterilized him and from the result of injury he died the next day. She was charged with murder. Gen. Butler, hearing of it, sent troops to Charles County [Maryland] to protect her, they brought her to

---

3    Claude H. Holen, *African Americans in slavery, Civil War, and Reconstruction*, (McFarland & Company, 2001).

4    http://nationalhumanitiescenter.org/pds/maai/enslavement/ text6/text6read.htm

5    Text is available under the Creative Commons Attribution-ShareAlike License.

Baltimore, later she was taken to Washington where she was set free . . . This attack was the result of being goodlooking, for which many a poor girl in Charles County paid the price. There are several cases I could mention, but they are distasteful to me . . . .

There was a doctor in the neighborhood who bought a girl and installed her on the place for his own use, his wife hearing it severely beat her. One day her little child was playing in the yard. It fell head down in a post hole filled with water and drowned. His wife left him; afterward she said it was an affliction put on her husband for his sins.

*Richard Macks, enslaved in Maryland, interviewed 1937*: One time dey sent me on Ol' man Mack Williams' farm here in Jasper County [Georgia]. Dat man would kill you sho. If dat little branch on his plantation could talk it would tell many a tale 'bout folks bein' knocked in de head. I done seen Mack Williams kill folks an' I done seen 'im have folks killed. One day he tol' me dat if my wife had been good lookin', I never would sleep wid her agin 'cause he'd kill me an' take her an' raise chilluns off'n her. Dey uster [used to] take women away fum dere husbands an' put wid some other man to breed jes' like dey would do cattle. Dey always kept a man penned up an' dey used 'im like a stud hoss.

*William Ward, enslaved in Georgia*: Durin' slavery if one marster had a big boy en 'nuther had a big gal de marsters made dem libe tergedder. Ef'n de 'oman didn't hab any chilluns, she wuz put on de block en sold en 'nuther 'oman bought. You see dey raised de chilluns ter mek money on jes lak we raise pigs ter sell.

*Sylvia Watkins, enslaved in Tennessee*: I 'member he had a real pretty gal on his place . . . One of the overseers was crazy about her, but her mother had told her not to let any of 'em go with her. So this old overseer would stick close 'round her when they was workin', just so he could get a chance to say somethin' to her. He kept followin' this child and followin' this child until she almost went crazy. Way afterwhile she run away and come to our house and and stayed 'bout three days. When my marster found out she was there, he told her she would have to go back, or at least she would have to leave his place. He didn't want no trouble with nobody. When that child left us she stayed in the woods until she got so hungry she just had to go back. This old man was mad with her for leavin', and one day while she was in the field he started at her again and she told him flat footed she warn't goin' with him he took the big end of his cow hide and struck her in the back so hard it knocked her plumb crazy. It was a big lake of water about ten yards in front of 'em, and if her mother hadn't run and caught her she would have walked right in it and drowned.

In them times white men went with colored gals and women bold[ly]. Any time they saw one and wanted her, she had to go with him, and his wife didn't say nothin' 'bout it. Not only the men, but the women went with colored men too. That's why so many women slave owners wouldn't marry, 'cause they was goin' with one of their slaves. These things that's goin' on now ain't new, they been happenin'. That's why I say you just as well leave 'em alone 'cause they gwine [going] to do what they want to anyhow . . . .

. . . Now sometimes, if you was a real pretty young gal, somebody would buy you without knowin' anythin' 'bout you, just for yourself. Before my old marster died, he had a pretty gal he was goin' with and he wouldn't let her work nowhere but in the house, and his wife nor nobody else didn't say nothin' 'bout it; they knowed better. She had three chillun for him and when he died his brother come and got the gal and the chillun.

One white lady that lived near us at McBean slipped in a colored gal's room and cut her baby's head clean off 'cause it belonged to her husband. He beat her 'bout it and started to kill her, but she begged so I reckon he got to feelin' sorry for her. But he kept goin' with the colored gal and they had more chillun.

*Chris Franklin,* enslaved in Louisiana: On this plantation were more than 100 slaves who were mated indiscriminately and without any regard for family unions. If their master thought that a certain man and woman might have strong, healthy offspring, he forced them to have sexual relation, even though they were married to other slaves. If there seemed to be any slight reluctance on the part of either of the unfortunate ones, "Big Jim" would make them consummate this relationship in his presence. He used the same procedure if he thought a certain couple was not producing children fast enough. He enjoyed these orgies very much and often entertained his friends in this manner; quite often he and his guests would engage in these debaucheries, choosing for themselves the prettiest of the young women. Sometimes they forced the unhappy husbands and lovers of their victims to look on.

*Louisa and Sam* were married in a very revolting manner. To quote [Louisa]: Marse Jim called me and Samter him and ordered Sam to pull off his shirt—that was all the McClain niggers wore—and he said to me: Nor, 'do you think you can stand this big nigger?' He had that old bull whip flung acrost his shoulder, and Lawd, that man could hit so hard! So I jes said 'yassur, I guess so,' and tried to hide my face so I couldn't see Sam's nakedness, but he made me look at him anyhow.

"Well, he told us what we must git busy and do it (have sex) in his presence, and we had to do it. After that we were considered man and wife. Mc and Sam was a healthy pair and had fine, big babies, so I never had another man forced on me, thank God. Sam was kind to me and I learnt to love him."

*Sam & Louisa Everett,* enslaved in Virginia: If a hand were noted for raising up strong black bucks, bucks that would never "let the monkey get them" while in the high-noon hoeing, he would be sent out as a species of circuit-rider to the other plantations—to plantations where there was over-plus of "worthless young nigger gals." There he would be "married off" again—time and again. This was thrifty and saved any actual purchase of new stock.

*John Cole,* enslaved in Georgia: He had so many slaves he did not know all their names. His fortune was his slaves. He did not sell slaves and he did not buy many, the last ten years preceding the war. He resorted to raising his own slaves . . . .

*Hilliard Yellerday,* enslaved in North Carolina: Dere am one thing Massa Hawkins does to me what I can't shunt from my mind. I knows he don't do it for meanness, but I allus [always] holds it 'gainst him. What he done am force me to live with dat nigger, Rufus, 'gainst my wants.

*Rose Willaims, enslaved in Texas*: My master often went to the house, got drunk, and then came out to the field to whip, cut, slash, curse, swear, beat and knock down several, for the smallest offense, or nothing at all.

He divested a poor female slave of all wearing apparel, tied her down to stakes, and whipped her with a handsaw until he broke it over her naked body. In process of time he ravished her person and became the father of a child by her. Besides, he always kept a colored Miss in the house with him. This is another curse of Slavery—concubinage and illegitimate connections—which is carried on to an alarming extent in the far South. A poor slave man who lives close by his wife is permitted to visit her but very seldom, and other men, both white and colored, cohabit with her. It is undoubtedly the worst place of incest and bigamy in the world. A white man thinks nothing of putting a colored man out to carry the fore row [front row in field work] and carry on the same sport with the colored man's wife at the same time.

*William J. Anderson, Life and Narrative of William J. Anderson, Twenty-Four Years a Slave, 1857*: I know these facts will seem too awful to relate, but I am constrained to write of such revolting deeds, as they are some of the real "dark deeds of American Slavery." Then, kind reader, pursue my narrative, remembering that I give no fiction in my details of horrid scenes. Nay, believe, with me, that the half can never be told of the misery the poor slaves are still suffering in this so-called land of freedom.

I knew a man at the South who had six children by a colored slave. Then there was a fuss between him and his wife, and he sold all the children but the oldest slave daughter. Afterward, he had a child by this daughter, and sold mother and child before the birth. This was nearly forty years ago. Such things are done frequently in the South. One brother sells the other: I have seen that done.

*Solomon Northup, Twelve Years a Slave:* I was born in North Carolina, in Caswell County, I am not able to tell in what month or year. What I shall now relate is what was told me by my mother and grandmother. A few months before I was born, my father married my mother's young mistress. As soon as my father's wife heard of my birth, she sent one of my mother's sisters to see whether I was white or black, and when my aunt had seen me, she returned back as soon as she could and told her mistress that I was white and resembled Mr. Roper very much. Mr. Roper's wife not being pleased with this report, she got a large club-stick and knife, and hastened to the place in which my mother was confined. She went into my mother's room with a full intention to murder me with her knife and club, but as she was going to stick the knife into me, my grandmother happening to come in, caught the knife and saved my life. But as well as I can recollect from what my mother told me, my father sold her and myself soon after her confinement [period of seclusion after childbirth].

*Henry Bibb, Narratives of the Life and Adventures of Henry Bibb, An American Slave, 1849:* There was a whisper that my master was my father; yet it was only a whisper, and I cannot say that I ever gave it credence. Indeed, I now have reason to think he was not. Nevertheless the fact remains, in all its glaring odiousness that, by the laws of slavery, children in all cases are reduced to the condition of their mothers. This arrangement admits of the greatest license to brutal slaveholders and their profligate sons, brothers, relations and friends, and gives to the pleasure of sin the additional attraction of profit. A whole volume might be written on this single feature of slavery, as I have observed it.

One might imagine that the children of such connections would fare better in the hands of their masters than other slaves. The rule is quite the other way, and a very little reflection will satisfy the reader that such is the case. A man who will enslave his own blood may not be safely relied on for magnanimity. Men do not love those who remind them of their sins—unless they have a mind to repent—and the mulatto child's face is a standing accusation against him who is master and father to the child. What is still worse, perhaps, such a child is a constant offense to the wife. She hates its very presence, and when a slaveholding woman hates, she wants not means [she doesn't lack methods] to give that hate telling effect. Women—white women, I mean—are IDOLS at the south, not WIVES, for the slave women are preferred in many instances; and if these idols but nod or lift a finger, woe to the poor victim: kicks, cuffs, and stripes are sure to follow. Masters are frequently compelled to sell this class of their slaves out of deference to the feelings of their white wives; and shocking and scandalous as it may seem for a man to sell his own blood to the traffickers in human flesh, it is often an act of humanity toward the slave-child to be thus removed from his merciless tormentors.

*Frederick Douglass, My Bondage and My Freedom, 1855*: I was regarded as fair-looking for one of my race, and for four years a white man—I spare the world his name—had base designs upon me. I do not care to dwell upon this subject, for it is one that is fraught with pain. Suffice it to say that he persecuted me for four years, and I—I—became a mother. The child of which he was the father was the only child that I ever brought into the world. If my poor boy ever suffered any humiliating pangs on account of birth, he could not blame his mother, for God knows that she did not wish to give him life. He must blame the edicts of that society which deemed it no crime to undermine the virtue of girls in my then position.

*Elizabeth Keckley,* Behind the Scenes: Or, Thirty Years a Slave, and Four Years in the White House, 1868: But I now entered on my fifteenth year—a sad epoch in the life of a slave girl. My master began to whisper foul words in my ear. Young as I was, I could not remain ignorant of their import [meaning]. I tried to treat them with indifference or contempt . . . He tried his utmost to corrupt the pure principles my grandmother had instilled. He peopled my young mind with unclean images, such as only a vile monster could think of. I turned from him with disgust and hatred. But he was my master. I was compelled to live under the same roof with him— where I saw a man forty years my senior daily violating the most sacred commandments of nature. He told me I was his property that I must be subject to his will in all things. My soul revolted against the mean tyranny. But where could I turn for protection? No matter whether the slave girl be as black as ebony or as fair as her mistress. In either case, there is no shadow of law to protect her from insult, from violence, or even from death; all these are inflicted by friends who bear the shape of men. The mistress, who ought to protect the helpless victim, has no other feelings towards her but those of jealousy and rage. The degradation, the wrongs, the vices that grow out of slavery are more than I can describe. They are greater than you would willingly believe.

*Harriet Jacobs, Incidents* in the Life of a Slave Girl, 1861: You may believe what I say, for I write only that whereof I know. I was twenty-one years in that cage of obscene birds. I can testify from my own experience and observation that slavery is a curse to the whites as well as to the blacks. It makes the white fathers cruel and sensual, the sons violent and licentious. It contaminates the daughters and makes the wives wretched. And as for the colored race, it needs an abler pen than mine to describe the extremity of their sufferings, the depth of their degradation.

Yet few slaveholders seem to be aware of the widespread moral ruin occasioned by this wicked system. Their talk is of blighted cotton crops—not of the blight on their children's souls.

If you want to be fully convinced of the abominations of slavery, go on a southern plantation and call yourself a Negro trader. Then there will be no concealment, and you will see and hear things that will seem to you impossible among human beings with immortal souls.

## Family Life in Slavery

The humiliation and pain of not being able to protect their spouses and children was devastating to black men. Of course, nothing could be done because marriage had no legal status in slavery. The masters reserved the right whether to recognize such unions.[6]

Slaveholders did not only abuse young children. They could take spouses of their slaves and retain them as sex objects for themselves or

---

6    Ibid, 36.

others. Sometimes male slaves were forced to helplessly watch sexual affairs forced on their women or children, with no ability to react.

In 1850, seventy-year old Robert Newsome bought one Celia, and she was about fourteen years old at the time. From the night she was purchased, the girl was brutally raped repeatedly by Newsome. Thereafter, Cilia became an unwilling concubine of her master. Five years later, she was pregnant with their third child. The young mother asked Newsome to stop the molestation and even pleaded with Newsome's two daughters in the house to intervene, but they did not. He reminded the slave girl that she was his personal property and could do with her whatever he desired. One night, the rapist went to her cabinet and demanded sex. A struggle erupted, and she stuck his head with a deadly object, which led to his death. Celia burned corpse in rage and fear.

A white jury was seated and found her guilty of murder. The sexual abuse and repeated rape played no role in the deliberation, because she was a private property. The girl was hanged December 21, 1855.[7]

Slave women naturally bemoaned their inescapable plight, especially when their enslaved spouses could not rescue them. As a result, when running away was not possible, "they employed forms of symbolic resistance such as meandering to end pregnancy, refusing to bring pregnancies to term in other ways, or met violence with violence by killing their rapists."[8]

The breakdown of the African American family is rooted in slavery. Black men had to endure the pain and shame of watching their women forced into sexual relations against their will to preserve their quasi family. Sometimes slave women were taken from men they loved only to be paired with bullies they disdained.

Distinguished white politicians and statesmen were discrete about their sexual orgies for good reasons. From the offset, colonial America attempted to set the races apart by providing a legal framework for defining race. The courts advanced the concept of racial purity and the criminalization of interracial marriage.[9]As such, mixed-race romance was forbidden by law, and it was not politically prudent to publically violate legislative prescriptions against acts deemed immoral for "Christian gentlemen," that is Anglo males. Another problem was the role of mulatto children fathered by whites. A mixed child took on the mother status. If

---

[7]    *Celia, A Slave Girl.* http://law2.umkc.edu/faculty/projects/ftrials/celia/celiaaccount. html (accessed June 13, 2013).

[8]    Deborah Gray White, *Ar'n't I a Woman?: Female Slaves in the Plantation South* (Revised Edition) (NY: Norton & Company, 1999).

[9]    Kevin Johnson, *Mixed Race America and the Law* (NY: New York University Press, 2003).

she was free at the time of birth, then the children were considered free, even if the fathers were slaves. Legally, the white fathers could not claim their children if the mothers were slaves.[10]Most influential and well-connected politicians lived up to that precept. They enslaved their own children or sold them for profit. There were incidents when jealous wives would hurt their husbands' mulatto babies or make life extremely difficult for the slave mistresses.[11] Consequently, white men did not generally acknowledge their mulatto children. They were slaves and were treated as such. Their fathers or representatives sold them when necessary for cash. Thousands of wailing women watched their children herded away like cattle, never to see them again.

---

[10]    Ibid, 13.
[11]    Holen, 38.

# CHAPTER VI

# THE REVOLUTIONARY BROTHERS AND SLAVE WOMEN

President John Adams expressed doubt about the highly publicized claim that his friend, Thomas Jefferson, fathered children by the slave girl called Sally Hemings. However, he admitted that, "There was not a planter in Virginia who could not reckon among his slaves a number of his children."[1] He then pointed out that sexual exploitation of slaves was a "natural and almost unavoidable consequence of that foul contagion in the human character—Negro Slavery."

It is common knowledge that frequent sexual relations occurred between white men and black women, despite anti-miscegenation statues. At the time of the Jefferson's scandal, 20% of divorce cases in Virginia involved adultery with colored people.[2] What is often disputed is whether the Founding Fathers themselves lived up to the anti-amalgamation prohibitions.

Two high-profile allegations of sexual liaisons between enslaved women and two Revolutionary Fathers have persisted into the 21st Century. A lot more is now known about the Jefferson-Hemings years of cohabitation to the extent that most critics are currently muted or subdued. What is hardly ever talked about is another allegation involving the first President of the United States, George Washington, and his brother's slave called Venus. It is alleged that they had one son, the only child Washington ever had. These stories will now be reviewed on their merits, beginning with the Jefferson-Hemings episode.

---

[1] Larry Flynt and David Eisenbach, *One Nation Under Sex* (New York: Polgrave Macmillan, 2011), 25.

[2] Ibid, 25.

# The Washington—Venus Affair

Linda Bryant recalled as a young child what her grandmother often told the children about their bloodline, leading back to George Washington, the first President of the United States. According to the family oral history, Washington went to visit his brother's plantation at Bushfeld, Virginia, and developed a relationship with a slave girl called Venus. According to the account, during his visit, he asked to be "comforted" and his brother John Augustine Washington sent the fifteen years old to "take care" of the man who would become the first President of the United States.

Venus became the regular "care-taker" of Washington whenever he visited the plantation. The relationship seemed to have lasted until he became president five years later. "When he became president, he no longer associated with her," Bryant claims.

In July of 1999, Nicholas Wade of the New York Times broke the following headline: "Descendants of Slave's Son Contend That His Father Was George Washington." According to Wade:

> Three descendants of Venus's son, who was called West Ford, declared that, according to a family tradition two centuries old, George Washington was West Ford's father. They hope to develop DNA evidence from descendants of the Washington family and Washington's hair samples to bolster their case.[3]

George Washington was 26 years old when he married the rich widow Martha Custis. She had four children in her previous marriage but no children with Washington. This has been explained to mean that Washington was sterile and incapable of fathering children. Accordingly, he contracted smallpox in Barbados while he and his brother visited the region, which left the 19-year-old sterile.

Many flagship historians have disputed the West Ford-Washington allegation, and the allegation has not received much publicity. Rather, Bushrod Washington, the President's nephew, is said to have been the father of West Ford. However, there is no evidence to authenticate the claim because Bushrod, like his uncle George, never left any accounts affirming the paternity assertion.

---

[3]   Descendants of Slave's Son Contend That His Father Was George Washington, http://www.nytimes.com/ 1999/07/07/us/descendants-of-slave-s-son-contend-that-his-father-was-george-washington.html?pagewanted= all&src=pm (accessed July 14, 2012).

"When West Ford was a little boy, he heard the slaves talking about how much he looked like George Washington . . . We're the heirs of George Washington on the slave side," Ms. Allen said, "and we can't get a Washington to come forward."[4]

Bryant and her sister Janet Allen, an editor in Peoria, Illinois, have been trying to arrange a DNA test to compare West Ford's descendants with any family member of Washington bloodline without success.

"We were told she was his personal sleep partner and that when it was obvious she was pregnant he no longer slept with her," Bryant said, referring to her great-grandfather's statements about Venus. "When she was asked who fathered her child, she replied George Washington was the father."[5]

"My grandmother used to tell us all the time when we were very young that West Ford was the son of George Washington," she said. "His mother was Venus, daughter of Jenny who was the servant to Hannah Washington, George Washington's sister-in-law."[6]

George Washington's wife, Martha Custis, brought two children into the marriage from her previous husband, Daniel Parke Custis. This is the story of the first President's family life that is often told. However, there is another side of George Washington that historians have ignored until now, and that is his alleged sexual relation with a slave girl named Venus.

From 1783 to 1786, Washington is said to have visited his brother, John Augustine's plantation in Virginia. He had a liaison with Venus, one of his brother's slaves, and she conceived, but the incident never appeared in any of the George Washington's papers. In John Augustine Washington's slaves record of March 3, 1783, there is no mention of West Ford; only his grandparents, Billey and Jenny are listed as slaves, including Venus.[7] However, West's grandparents and Mother are mentioned in Washington's June 11, 1784 will, with instruction for his wife to give them to other relatives.

George Washington had fun with West Ford. They went for horse rides and attended Church together with the family. The lad was baptized in the St. Paul's Episcopal Church, where Washington Attended, and became Washington's personal attendant, as he grew older.[8]

---

4    Ibid.
5    Ibid.
6    Ibid.
7    From J. A. Washington's Ledger C, RM-73, MS-2166), referenced at (http://westfordlegacy.com/ mvmtg/qa.html (accessed May 16, 2012).
8    Linda Allen Bryant, *I Cannot Tell A Lie: The True Story Of George Washington's African American* (NE: iUniverse, 2001), 443.

In the *Wills of George Washington and his immediate ancestors*, edited by Worthington Ford, West Ford is listed as a benefactor in Clause Sixteen. "I give to West Ford the tract of land on Hunting . . . which I purchased from Noblet Herbert deceased, which was conveyed to him by Francis Adams, to him the said West Ford, & his heirs."[9]

This was an extraordinary act of generosity for a slave boy. West Ford was given over one hundred acres of land near Mount Vermont. He later sold the land to buy other property to create a settlement for black people near Mount Vermont called Gum Springs. Indeed, it was not unusual for rich Southern whites to provide for their family's mulattos without ever admitting of the affairs with their slave women.

No doubt, Ford received preferential treatment from all of the Washington's family. He lived in his own home, while other blacks or mulattoes lived in the slave quarters. Ford went to church, hunting, and travelled with the Washington family. His children attended school with the Washington children on the estate, although there was a Virginian law against teaching blacks to read.

The historian Thomas Fleming provides an alibi for the West Ford quandary. He suggests that it is likely that the boy's father was someone else of the Washington bloodline. He singles out Bushrod Washington, nephew of the President. In his book, *The Intimate Lives of Founding Fathers,* Fleming writes: "There would be no doubt that West Ford had Washington blood in his veins. But it was probably inherited from Jack Washington or one of his sons, Bushrod, Corbin, or William Augustine."[10]

Fleming also blamed Venus for the possibility of fabricating the story. He added that slave women were in the habit of telling their mulatto children that "old master" or "someone even more distinguished, rather than an overseer or temporary white workman or some nameless white guest to whom the master had given access to his slaves, in what some considered the great tradition of southern hospitality." Like the Jefferson-Hemings story, only DNA can bring some closure to the Washington-Ford affair.

9    George Washington, *Wills of George Washington and his Immediate Ancestors* (NY: Historical Printing Club, 1891), 161.
10   Ibid.

## Jefferson-Hemings Affair

News about a sexual liaison between President Thomas Jefferson and his slave girl, Sally Hemings, first became public in1802. James Thomas Callender (1758-1803), wrote an article in a Virginian newsmagazine, which declared that Jefferson had several children with one of his slaves in Monticello.[11] The girl was Sally Hemings, a sister of Jefferson's wife.

Sally Hemings' family story had its origin with an Englishman called John Hemings and a slave woman named Susannah.[12] They had a child who they called Betty (Elizabeth) Hemings. While in Virginia, both Betty and her mulatto baby became property of Francis Epps IV in 1746. He passed the two slaves on as a gift to his newlywed daughter, Martha Epps, wife of John Wayles.[13]Martha died in less than three weeks after her daughter was born in 1748. John remarried twice, and both ended in the death of the wives. In 1761, he took his mulatto slave, Betty Hemings, to be his concubine.[14]In twelve years, they had six children, and the youngest of them was Sally Hemings, born February 9, 1773. Sally was light-skinned and beautiful.

Thomas Jefferson met Sally's half-sister, Martha Wayles, and married her in 1772. She became a window when her first husband died in 1768.

John Wayles died in 1777. Jefferson inherited over one hundred of his slaves, including Sally Hemings, who was his wife's sister, and a large plantation.

Jefferson and Martha had six children in ten years. Two survived to become adults. Meanwhile, Martha Jefferson died in 1782. She was known to be in ill health most of her married life. Having many children in a short period helped to further weaken her frail body and may have led to her early death. Jefferson promised Martha on her deathbed that he would never marry another woman again.

In 1784, Jefferson accepted an appointment as ambassador to France. His older daughter, Martha, and Sally's brother, James Hemings, accompanied him. In 1787, he sent for his daughter, Maria (nine years old at the time) to be escorted by fifteen-year-old Sally Hemings.

Jefferson and Sally began an intimate relationship in Paris, and she became pregnant. Ironically, Sally refused to return to the States with Jefferson for undisclosed reasons. It could be that Sally did not want her

---

[11]    http://www.monticello.org/site/plantation-and-slavery/thomas-jefferson-and-sally-hemings-brief-account (accessed December 1, 2012).

[12]    Lucia C. Stanton, Free Some Day: The African American Families of Monticello (NC: University of North Carolina Press, 2000), 103-104.

[13]    Stanton, 103.

[14]    Ibid, 103-104.

child or subsequent children to be born in slavery. She had an opportunity to apply for freedom and live free in France. Knowing the harshness of slavery, it would have been a rational decision to make. Whatever the reason, Jefferson sought to ease the uncertainty by promising to set all Hemings children free.

Once in the States, Jefferson kept his promise by freeing only two slaves in his lifetime: Sally's two brothers, Robert Hemings (freed 1794) and James Hemings (freed 1796). Five of Sally's other family members were freed in Jefferson's will: Joseph (Joe) Fossett (1780-1858), Burwell Colbert (1783-1850), Madison Hemings (1805-1856), John Hemings (1776-1833), and Eston Hemings (1808-1856). He allowed two children to "run away" from Monticello before they were 21 years old, with some monetary assistance from him.[15]Beverly went to Washington D.C. and Harriet headed for Philadelphia. They passed as white people, because they were very pale. Both may have changed their names to fit in their new environment. Most of Sally's children passed as white and she herself was listed in 1830 as a white woman, although listed as "free woman of color in 1826."[16]

Sally remained a slave in Jefferson's will, and no documented justification has been uncovered. What is certain is that she remained his slave and possible mother of his six children, until his death on July 4, 1826. One year later, she was allowed to live free with two of her children in Charlottesville, Virginia.

Sally Hemings' children, like herself, looked white, and some resembled Jefferson. He went to his grave with the secret of not telling anyone whether he fathered six children by a black woman.

Many white plutocrats had black mistresses. Like Jefferson's in-law, John Wayles, they were rarely ever indicted or charged with felony. Incidentally, Jefferson was larger than life. It was unlikely that he could be publicly branded as a hypocrite for violating the anti-interracial law. As for Sally, she remained inconsequential and publically detached from him, though they may have been bedmates for thirty eight years.

Not once did Thomas Jefferson address the Sally affairs publically or privately. His silence was for good reasons. First, his authorship of the Declaration of Independence immortalized his legacy. He was proud of his conservative credentials and sensitive to the planter ethos of Virginia. It was therefore vital for him to play by the rules, especially legislations he

[15]    http://classroom.monticello.org/kids/resources/profile/4/Middle/Sally-Hemings-an-enslaved-house-servant/ (accessed January 4, 2012).

[16]    Ibid.

helped to create, such as anti-amalgamation laws that restricted interracial cohabitation or marriage.

## Jefferson's Silence

Colonial Virginia gave birth to slavery in British North America in 1619. It was the first colony to prohibit interracial marriage. In 1630, Hugh Davis, a white man, was ordered to "be soundly whipped in the assemblage of Negroes and others . . . for lying with a Negro, and in 1662, Virginia enacted laws against interracial marriage.[17] In 1786, Thomas Jefferson proposed a bill, which sought to nullify interracial marriage, even between white and mulatto.[18] It was therefore inconceivable that Jefferson could make any incriminating statements verbally or in writing by which he could be guilty of a felony.

There was another probable reason for ignoring the affair allegation. In the early days of his political career, Jefferson made a conscious decision never to respond to personal attacks against him in newspapers. However, there were instances when he broke his silence under a similar situation. For example, to avoid a duel with John Walker, whose wife accused the president of ten years of sexual harassment and attempted rape, Jefferson wrote a letter of apology and did admit of indecency with the woman.[19] Both men met later at James Madison's house to settle the dispute. John accepted the apology and the duel was averted.

In 1802, Jefferson also broke his silence when he ordered editor Harry Crosswell jailed for libel. Thomas Callender accused the president of fathering children by a slave girl and also of seducing his best friend's wife.

It was also alleged that Jefferson paid editors to smear his political opponents, like his friend John Adams.[20] The President admitted of giving money to Callender but for charitable reasons only. Crosswell called Jefferson a liar and "a dissembling patriot." That was enough to charge the editor with libel.[21]

---

[17]   Werner Sollors, *Interracialism: Black-White Intermarriage in American History, Literature and Laws* (New York: Oxford University Press, 2000).

[18]   Susan D. Gold, *Loving vs. Virginia: Lifting the Ban Against Interracial Marriage* (NY: Michelle Bisson, 2008).

[19]   Jon Kukla, *Mr. Jefferson Women* (New York: Knopf, 2007), 190.

[20]   Flynt and Eisenbach, 22.

[21]   Harry Crosswell, *The Wasp*, quoted in Eric Burns, *Infamous Scribblers: The Founding Fathers and the Rowdy Beginnings of American Journalism* (New York: Public Affairs, 2006), 389.

Crosswell hired Jefferson's political rival, Alexander Hamilton, as defender. Hamilton warned that, "If a newspaper prints the truth, it cannot be guilty of criminal behavior." Apparently, he must have believed the allegations.

Jefferson was very protective of his political life and legacy. During the 1800 presidential run, he was accused of irreligious sentiments, and opponents called him a "howling atheist," a "confirmed infidel," a "liar" and a "hypocrite."[22] Yet, as contentious as that was, Jefferson chose to keep his faith private. Once he wrote to his friend and theologian, Dr. Benjamin Rush, confiding in him, that he was a Christian in the following letter, "To the corruptions of Christianity I am indeed opposed, but not to the genuine precepts of Jesus himself. I am a Christian, in the only sense in which he wished anyone to be . . ."[23]

Dr. Rush fundamentally disagreed with the President's basic philosophy about Christianity. The formal President had serious doubts about the creation story of Adam and Eve, the virgin birth of Jesus, his miracles, divinity, and resurrection. Jefferson blamed the prophets and apostles for distorting biblical truths and the philosophy of Jesus. To correct the "errors" and purify the teachings of Jesus, whom he admired as much as he did Plato, he created a "corrective" version of the four gospels in the New Testament. In his version, which came to be known as the Jefferson Bible, but he called it the "The Life and Morals of Jesus of Nazareth." In the text, Christ was born, performed no miracles but gave parables to simplify the truth, lived as an ordinary philosophy without deity—humble and cared for the downtrodden. Finally, Christ died, was buried, and never rose from the dead. Jefferson claimed not to be an orthodox "Christian or atheist." He never shared his unconventional religious views widely with other people and his bible was only published after his death in 1826. This should prevent the rush to judgment that, because Jefferson chose not to make public statements about allegations against him, did not mean he was innocent.

## Jefferson's Culpability

What to make of the Jefferson-Hemings episode? His defenders claim the incident never took place and the story was made up by political

---

[22] Eve Kornfeld, *Creating an American Culture: 1775-1800, A Brief History with Document* (NT: Pal Grave, 2001).

[23] Matthew A. Misbach, *The Van De Kemp Collection: A Bundle of Thomas Jefferson's Letter* (Misbach Enterprise, 2007).

enemies. Martha Randolph Jefferson claimed her cousins, Peter and Samuel Carr, fathered Sally's mulatto children at Monticello, but none of the men, like Jefferson, even claimed that they did. On the other hand, Sally's children said their mother told them Jefferson was their father. This was probable because Jefferson died in 1826 and Sally passed in 1835. With him dead, what was there to prevent telling her children who their father or fathers were?

For several years after Jefferson's death, The Pike County (Ohio) Republican printed an interview with one of Sally's sons, Madison Hemings. He was sixty eight years old. Madison said his mother was Sally Hemings, and that his father was Thomas Jefferson.[24] He added, "When Mr. Jefferson went to France . . . my mother became Mr. Jefferson's concubine, and when he was called back home, she was enceinte by him . . . She gave birth to four others, and Jefferson was the father of all of them.[25]

Jefferson listed all six of Sally's children in his slave record in Virginia, without stating who their fathers were. Although there were over two hundred slaves at Monticello at one time or another, Sally and her children never worked on the plantation. She worked as a house maid and took care of Jefferson's bed chamber.[26]The children lived near their mother, ran errands, and learned other trades like carpentry and music. Three of Sally's children could play the violin, a musical instrument Jefferson loved to play. Another child was a balloonist. This was something Jefferson also enjoyed doing.

Besides the Hemings' family, no other slaves were free in Jefferson's will. Rather, 130 of them were sold to pay his debts. However, Martha Randolph and her children had denied the concubinary relationship in the Jefferson-Hemings allegation. His grandchildren, Ellen R. Coolidge and Thomas J. Randolph, declared that it was "impossible" for their grandfather to have had a liaison with a slave girl on "both moral and practical grounds." However, as revealed, Jefferson demonstrated high propensity to subdue women, singled or married. It is difficult to find reasons why he would not demand sexual favors from a powerless mulatto slave girl who was beautiful and light-skinned enough to pass for white as most of her children did.

---

[24]   *Sally Hemings and Her Children,* http://www.monticello.org/site/plantation-and-slavery/appendix-h-sally-hemings-and-her-children (accessed August 9, 2011).

[25]   Annette Gordon-Reed, *Thomas Jefferson and Sally Hemings* (Virginia University Press of Virginia, 199), 8.

[26]   *Sally Hemings and Her Children,* http://www.monticello.org/site/plantation-and-slavery/appendix-h-sally-hemings-and-her-children (accessed November 3, 2011).

Jefferson took a diplomatic assignment to France as U.S. Ambassador in 1784, two years after his wife died. He met two women, Maria Cosway, an Englishwoman visiting France with her husband, and an American beauty named Angelica Schuyler Church. Maria was the wife of the renowned artist and musician Richard Cosway. Regardless, both Maria and Jefferson initiated a romantic relationship. They wrote intimate letters to each other when she left with her husband for England in October of 1786.[27] One of the most favorite poems he composed for her survived in a letter called "Head Heart" dialogue, in which his head was telling him one thing and his heart something else about the relationship with the married woman.[28]

In the winter of 1788, as the United States' Ambassador in France, Jefferson developed a sexual relationship with Maria's friend, Angelica Schuyler Church. She was the wife of John Barker Church. Angelica was the sister of Elizabeth Schuyler, wife of Alexander Hamilton.

Jefferson and Hamilton had been political rivals from the revolutionary years of the United States. Despite a personal dislike for each other, both had sexual relationships with Angelica, Hamilton's sister in law. She continued extensive correspondence with both men for many years from England.[29] Jefferson urged Angelica to return to the States with him: "Let's go back together then. You intend it a visit; so do I . . . I will go to see if Monticello remains in the same place, or I will attend you to the falls of Niagara, if you will go with me to the passage of the Potowmac, the Natural Bridge . . ."[30]

Something else happened in 1788 that was astounding. John Walker wrote a private letter to Jefferson in Paris to vent his anger over a confession his wife made that she had been seduced by Jefferson for nearly ten years.[31] According to Walker, Jefferson was a neighbor and friend whom he entrusted with his family when away from home. Walker listed Jefferson as the executor of his will over the objection of his wife, Elizabeth Walker.[32]None of these thoughtful gestures served as a deterrent against Jefferson's lust for Elizabeth.

---

27  John P Kaminski, *The Love Letters of Thomas Jefferson and Maria Cosway* (MD: Rowman & Littlefield Publishers, 1999).

28  http://www.juntosociety.com/i_documents/tjheadheartltr.html (accessed October 8, 2011).

29  http://churchtree.tripod.com/angchurch.html (accessed October 8, 2011).

30  Ibid.

31  Fawn M. Brodie, *Thomas Jefferson, and Intimate History* (W.W. Norton and Company, 1974).

32  Ibid, 77.

Jefferson never made direct public statements about the alleged sexual assaults, as in Sally's case. In 1805, the President sent a personal letter to Secretary of the Navy Robert Smith to acknowledge some responsibility: "You perceive that I plead guilty to one of their charges, that when young and single, I offered love to a handsome lady. I admit its incorrectness."[33]

No one really knows how long the sexual harassment lasted. But Jefferson admitted that other people knew about the affairs, and once, Alexander Hamilton threatened to make the story public.[34] Hamilton himself had been between the anvil and hammer, when he had to pay a $1,000.00 hush money to James Reynolds for having an affair with his wife Maria.[35]

Thomas Paine initially disparaged the rape charge against Jefferson when Walker alleged that the harassment continued for ten years. He wrote this sarcasm: "We have heard of ten years siege of Troy, but whoever heard of ten years siege to seduce."[36]

John Walker challenged the President to a duel if he did not come clean. It was at that point that Jefferson proposed to meet Walker privately and managed to talk him out of the deadly encounter. However, he wrote a private letter of apology, and did admit some guilt.[37]

There appears to be little or no controversy about Jefferson's liaisons with the three white married women. What is highly contested is the possibility of him having sexual relationship with his mulatto slave, over whom he had total control.

Jefferson admirers ignore the not-so-public side of the President. They adore his statesmanship, authorship of the Declaration of Independence, effectuating the Louisiana Purchase, and founding of the University of Virginia. The University was the first institution of higher education without a chapel in the United States.

Jefferson's presumed shyness veiled his wantonness for women, especially married women. His daughter Martha and grandchildren declared that it was impossible for Jefferson to seduce a slave girl on "moral" or "practical" grounds. However, Jefferson's records speak for him. Lasciviousness was certainly not below his dignity.

---

[33]    Jefferson to John Jay, January 11, 1789, Papers, Boyd, XIV, 430
[34]    Brodie, 77.
[35]    Flynt, 28
[36]    Ibid, 26.
[37]    Ibid.

# CHAPTER VII

# SLAVE REVOLT IN THE UNITED STATES

The possibility of slaves' vengeful insurgency had haunted American families, since forced labor became legal in America. Some citizens feared that the slaughter of slaveholders by blacks or God was inevitable.

In 1698, a Pennsylvania Quaker, Robert Pyle, had a dream, after contemplating on purchasing a slave.[1] The following night he dreamed of a vertical ladder extending to heaven. Though he had the desire to claim the ladder, it dawned on him he had a black pot in one hand, and both hands were necessary to ascend the steep incline. Pyle believed the black pot was a symbol of the slave he planned to buy, but God was not pleased. The dream alerted him to the Golden Rule and his sin of owning another human being. After his religious transformation, he turned out to be a strong antislavery advocate. The dream instantly changed his attitude and perspective of the world in which lived.

Professor Benjamin Rush of Philadelphia had a "Paradise of Negro Slaves" dream. He was a member of the Continental Congress and signer of the Declaration of Independence. Though a slave owner himself, he became one of the black community's strongest allies. He also had a dream in 1787 of a ghost walking toward him on a sandy beach, from the gathering of slaves. They talked about the evil slaveholders and the gruesome atrocities of slavery. In the following year, Rush decided to free his slave, William Grubber, and dedicated himself to the cause of abolitionism.

---

[1]  Scott L. Malcomson, *One Drop of Blood: The American Misadventure of Race* (NY: Farrar, Straus, and Girous, 2000), 555.

Evangelist Jonathan Edwards[2] (the younger) reminded whites of their dilemma and proposed a radical solution to slavery. In 1792, he addressed the Connecticut Abolition Society on the future of the United States. He told the assembly that for a shared future with blacks, whites must accept the fact that "their posterity will infallibly be a mongrel breed."[3] Evangelist Edwards acknowledged that sustaining slavery was inconceivable. He said white people had two choices in order to balance their accounts for the injury done to black people: either take the rivalry into infinity by giving them their sons and daughters in marriage, and making them and their posterity heirs, or desert America entirely and leave all their houses, lands, and improvements to the blacks' quiet possessions and dominion.

Because whites had used pigmentation to degrade blacks, the Evangelist suggested that intermarriage between white and black would be a cure. He argued that intermarriage would "raise the Negro's color to a partial whiteness, whereby a part at least of that mark which brings on them so much contempt will be wiped off."[4] Edwards contended that slavery was a horrible sin and it required a drastic response.

## The Haitian Experience

The Haitian Revolution (1791-1804) ended slavery from the French colony of Saint Dominique. It resulted to the establishment of the Haitian nation, the first black Republic in the world. This was especially significant because the American Revolution and the Haitian Revolution, just sixteen years apart, were the two most permanent revolutions achieved in the 1700s in the Americas.

The United States saw the Haitian Revolution as a defining moment in the history of Africans in the Americas. The successful revolt sent shockwaves to slave owners, especially in the South. Fear of slave rebellions quickened American consciousness, as never before the efficacious Haitian Revolution. South Carolina passed a law to disallow any ship from St. Dominique with blacks to discharge its passengers, without armed guards present. "Any vessel . . . from St. Domingo with passengers, Negroes or people of color shall remain under the guns of Ft.

---

2    Evangelist Edwards' father, the revered Rev. Jonathan Edwards, Sr. of the Great Awakening, owned slaves and defended slavery. Edwards, Jr. opposed slavery and often preached against the dehumanization of blacks.

3    Francis D. Adams and Barry Sanders, "Alienable Rights: The Exclusion of African Americans in a White Man's Land." (New York: HarperCollins Publishers, 2003), iv.

4    Ibid, iv.

Johnson till such passengers as the committee many deem improper to admit, and the Negroes and people of color are sent out of the state."[5]

In 1798, news of 5000 black troops from St. Dominique reached the United States Congress. It was alleged that the "forces were within four or five days sail. Not only were they plotting to turn Southern slaves against their masters, but unless the nation raised an effective force to resist the assault whenever wherever it may show its head, the impending alliance between American slaves and French blacks would destroy the country."[6]

The source of the allegation was the U.S. Secretary of State Timothy Pickering. He passed the information on to the House Ways and Means Committee Chairman, General Robert Goodloe Harper, and the news spread through Congress.

After the Revolutionary War, most blacks lurked on the premise of equality assured to all men in the Declaration of Independence: "We hold these truths to be self-evident, that all men are created equal, that they are endowed by their Creator with certain inalienable Rights that among these are Life, Liberty . . ." The misleading declaration from the Founding Fathers about individual freedom renewed the hope of transforming the ethos of disproportionality in slave culture to one of egalitarianism for all Americans. But the spirit of optimism quickly dissipated in view of observable digressions from the principles of racial equality. It became obvious that the tentacles of slavery were deeply entrenched in the economic and sociopolitical life of the nation. It would require the ultimate sacrifice to effectuate its demise.

## Slaves Insurrection

Since the beginning of slavery in colonial North America, the conditions of slaves continued to deteriorate. All appeals for moderation failed. Blacks felt the only alternative was resistance. To some, it was better to die fighting like a man than live as another man's boy.

One of the first cities to experience a strong uprising was New York. It had a large population of slaves by 1712 and most lived in close proximity with freedmen. On April 6, twenty-three blacks rose against the city and killed nine whites. Six others were injured and a building burned down. Afterwards, seventy insurgents were arrested, twenty indicted, and twenty one convicted. All convicts were executed. More restraints were enacted,

---

5    Eric R. Papenfuse, *The Evils of Necessity: Roberty Gooddle Harper and the Moral Dilemma of Slavery* (Philadelphia: American Philosophical Society, 1997), 24.

6    Papenfuse, 24, 29.

and slaves could not assemble in groups of three or more. Offenses such as destruction of property, rape, and plot to murder, were made punishable by death. Freedmen were prohibited from owning land. Slaveholders who decided to emancipate slaves had to pay a tax of £200, a charge much higher than the price of a slave.

Abolitionists appealed for an easing of restrictions. In 1773, slaves in Massachusetts called on the governor and legislature for tolerance. In their complaint, they noted the blatant disregard for their labor and pointed out that "neither they nor their children will ever be able to possess or enjoy anything, including life itself.[7]The appeal was ignored, setting the stage for future violence.

The revolt in Haiti (1791) successfully ended French domination in the Haitian Republic. Nine years later, the United States experienced its first major slave revolt. Twenty-four-year-old Gabriel Prosser gathered nearly 1000 angry slaves to take up arms against slaveholders in what became known as the Gabriel Rebellion. Their motto was engraved on a banner: "Death or Liberty." They planned to kidnap Governor James Monroe for a ransom but not necessarily to kill him. The attack was set for August 30, 1800. It never materialized. Heavy rainfall and severe thunderstorms delayed the plan, and in the process of waiting, two fearful slaves, Tom and Pharaoh, told their master, Mosby Sheppard, about the plot. The authorities were informed in time to abort the scheme. By law, every plotter was to be executed. James Monroe told the Council of State to spare or pardon some of the insurgents, or sell them, instead of hanging or lynching what he called "the fighters for justice." However, 27 plotters were hanged, including Gabriel Prosser. As one historian put it, "Monroe was troubled by the possibility of having to execute many men whose crime was plotting to fight for their freedom."[8]During the trial, he urged the court to show mercy, if there were doubts about any of the insurgents. However, though the plot failed and no person was injured, the authorities' response was swift and brutal, as they usually were in such cases.

One of the men involved in the plot said, "I have nothing more to offer than what General Washington would have had to offer, had he been taken by the British and put to trial by them. I have adventured my life

---

[7]   David B. Davis, *Inhuman Bondage: The Rise and Fall of Slavery in the New World* (New York: Oxford Press, 2006), 146.

[8]   Debbie Levy, "James Monroe" MN. Lerner Publications Company, 2005, 46.

in endeavoring to obtain the liberty of my countrymen, and am a willing sacrifice to their cause."[9]

In 1799, Denmark Vesey bought his freedom for $100, but he was unable to redeem his wife and children. Vesey became extremely angry and committed to destroy slavery. He became a lay preacher in the African Methodist Episcopal Church in 1817, using his home to conduct services for followers on weekdays. While in church, it became customary for security personnel to monitor black services. Members were arrested if their sermons or actions were seen as a threat to the public.

In 1822, Vesey and other church members planned to rebel. The revolt date was set for July 14. Plotters from Charleston and adjacent plantations intended to seize Charleston's arsenals, guardhouses, execute the governor, burn the city, and slaughter every white person they saw. However, other slaves grew weary and leaked the plot to their masters. Vesey was captured on June 22, and on July 2, he and five other men were hanged. Gullah Jack, the mystical East African high priest of the group was executed later, and by August 9, the Charleston authorities executed 35 plotters. Also, the African Church was burned down, followed by a series of prohibitions to further limit slave rights. Notwithstanding, Vesey became a martyr and was extolled as an emblem of resistance for white's cruelty against blacks.

The plutocrats decided to discourage black resistance by making slavery more brutal. Among other things, education for blacks was banned. Piloting boats was prohibited to keep them from learning about the outside world. The harsh retributions only helped to encourage more resistance against slaveholders.

The highest number of white fatalities occurred in a revolt led by Nat Turner in 1831. The Southampton Insurrection took place on August 22, 1831, and about 65 white slaveholders and their families died, including Nat's owner, John Travis.[10] The rebellion was put down within a few days. The insurgents were captured and 56 executed. More than 100 mostly innocent people were also killed by militias and mobs. White resulted to the only remedy they knew: passing new stringent laws prohibiting education to all Africans. White ministers were required to be present at all black worship services, or risked a shutdown of the churches.

John Brown, a native of Connecticut, initiated the first white-led revolt. He and his parents relocated to Ohio at the age of five, and what

---

[9]   Herbert Aptheker, *American Negro Slave Revolts*, new edition (New York: International Publishers, 1974), 219-226.

[10]   Frederic D. Schwarz, *1831: Nat Turner's Rebellion,"* *American Heritage,* August/ September 2006.

he saw in the home of a Michigan family haunted him for the rest of his life. The couple often brutalized their slaves with many lashes, and the wailing cries of the shackled blacks were unforgettable. At the age of twelve, Brown developed a special passion for Africans and intense hatred for slaveholders. From those early days until his death, the white fighter for freedom became a committed abolitionist. He hardly ever missed an opportunity to let slave masters know he was holding them accountable for their atrocities. He called for the abolition of slavery. Brown conducted educational programs for blacks.

One of Brown's first acts of vengeance was demonstrated in 1855. He and five of his ten sons travelled to Kansas where many abolitionists were being killed in a territory divided over slavery. They arrived during a political chaos, which became known as "Bleeding Kansas." Before Brown left Kansas, he and his sons killed five proslavery advocates at Pottawatomie on May 24, 1856.[11] His actions made him a legendary hero, especially to northerners, but southerners put a bounty on his head.

Despite the vigilance of dedicated abolitionists, slavery was not going away, and Brown came to the conclusion that only violence could dismantle the institution. He planned to free slaves by the use of force. Many prosperous abolitionists in the northeast supported his cause with money. He wanted to establish a homeland in the Virginian Mountains as a city of refuge for runaway slaves.[12] With supporters, Brown attacked the federal arsenal at Harper Ferry, Virginia, on October 16, 1859. They took the town and the arsenal quickly but aborted the incursion. The militia, with the help of U.S. marines led by Robert E. Lee, the group was surrendered and captured. Two of his sons died and he himself was hanged in Charleston on December 2, 1859.

Blacks in the United States did not accept their horrifying conditions in slavery passively. When appeals failed, they fought back by using the same weapon whites used against them—violence. While almost all slave related revolts never fully succeeded, they set America on edge and made slavery an albatross in the white psyche.

---

[11] John Brown and the Harpers Ferry Raid, http://www.wvculture.org/history/jnobrown.html (accessed March 8, 2012).

[12] Ibid.

# CHAPTER VIII

# FORMATION OF THE AMERICAN COLONIZATION SOCIETY

Without a doubt, slavery was the most divisive institution ever emerged in the United States. The evil empire made its imprint in the psyche of blacks and abolitionists of all colors and stripes. After nearly three hundred years of dehumanization, blacks had enough and were more determined to resist white slaveholders. However, slave masters demonstrated relentless willingness to crush all insurgencies by all means necessary. The belief that underlined Africans servitude in the United States was always the same: slaves were property, and their status as such required enforcement, even by violence, if it required it.[1]

The American Colonization Society was organized in 1816 to fill in the gap and work toward a legal separation of the races on agreeable terms. This meant removing blacks from among whites to establish a country in the blacks' ancestral homeland of Africa.

As a private enterprise, the ACS undertook the ominous task of ending slavery by offering a legal proposition to remove free slaves from the United States. At the same time, the Society intended to promote compensatory emancipation in order to encourage the gradual fading out of slavery. Of course, this was not the first time a proposal had been made to slaveholders to liberate their slaves for compensation. In 1833, the British Monarchy formulated a policy of compensated Emancipation for its overseas political territories.[2] That decision led to the enactment of similar policies by Denmark and France in 1848, and the Netherlands in 1863.[3]

---

[1]   *Conditions of antebellum slavery.* http://www.pbs.org/wgbh/aia/part4/4p2956.html (accessed June 10, 2013).

[2]   *Slavery in the United States: A Social, Political, and Historical Encyclopedia,* vol. 2 (ABC-CLIO, 2007), 238-9.

[3]   Ibid.

It is also worth mentioning that many South Americans and Caribbean countries emancipated their slaves and got paid for their humanitarian gestures. But the American Colonization Society was the first antislavery organization in the United States to initiate a voluntary removal of free blacks and, at the same time, compensate slave owners who were willing to accept payment to liberate their slaves.

Many political leaders wrote passionately and in graphic details about the inhumanity of slavery, but the rhetoricians were also slave masters who treated blacks as farm animals. Instead of contrition and abdication, they blamed the British for introducing inhuman bondage in the colonies. However, just as much as British America fought against the unjust rules of monarchy in the colonies, it was in the power of the new nation to end the oppression of other races within its borders. Instead, the government recoiled and looked away.

The Constitution of the United States did not end domestic slavery, either. Rather, it eluded the single most important social issue at the time, hoping for posterity to come up with a workable solution.

The Founders settled on a decision of not importing more slaves. But it was not necessary to import more slaves because domestic breeding and forced procreation in the plantations continued to increase the slave population in the states exponentially.

Blacks naturally lost hope for economic or political advancement. African women performed a binary role as plantation workers and sexual slaves. They produced as field hands or housemaids and bred slave children for their masters. Slave owners often denied paternity claims. The mulatto offspring generally ended up on the slave market as bastards, or the lucky ones passed as white.

It was common knowledge that most white people believed that blacks could not remain in the United States, if they could not serve as slaves. States like Virginia had deportation laws for freedmen and freedwomen. Emancipated slaves could not remain in Virginia for more than twelve months or risked re-enslavement.

No ACS members made a stronger case to justify the concept of Colonization than General Goodloe Harper, senator from Maryland. He joined the organization in 1817. His arguments were largely rooted in extreme fear of black rebellions. His solution was to caution against unnecessary provocations, whether directly or indirectly. However, Quakers had problems dealing with Harper's position. They believed "slavery was the Antichrist and the seven-headed dragons of Revelation. The Lord was whetting his glittering sword, and his vengeance was certain unless the new Children of Israel separated themselves from the filthiness of the heathen, and came away from Babylon."[4] Although Harper accepted the fact that their motives and intentions were pure, he urged the preachers to tone the rhetoric down.

General Harper believed that, as bad as slavery was, it had become a "necessary evil" on which the American economy depended. He wanted it to remain that way until the evil could be disposed safely, because immediate emancipation would devastate the economy and even lead to war between black and white. "It would only foster a grim parody of interracial union, the grotesque mingling of blood and bones upon a war-torn battlefield,"[5] he warned.

When the ACS was founded, Harper never looked back again for a solution to the slave problem. For him, colonization was the answer, which he called the "great enterprise." Harper contended that "White racial prejudices created an impassible barrier, which blacks could never hope to overcome."[6]

To make his point of relocating blacks from white America, General Harper drew on Captain Paul Cuffe's awful experience in 1812. After returning from Sierra Leone, his ship was impounded, and he was charged with transporting illegal British cargo.[7] He appealed to President James Madison, a colonization advocate, for recourse. The President did intervene and the ship was ordered released. But when Captain Cuffe went to Boston to take possession of his ship, he was greeted with enmity. Authorities at the Boston Port ignored his presence in the tavern. At dinner time, he was treated as a servant and told to stand behind everyone else in line. After reflecting on the black Captain's episode, Harper argued that no person of color stood a chance to become a respectable citizen of the United States, referencing what happened to Cuffe.

Paul Cuffe had been an iconic personality in most historical narratives about the West African countries of Sierra Leone and Liberia. Moreover, Diasporic Africans embraced his Pan African ideology and first proposed black-led back-to-Africa initiative. Besides, whalers in America took note of his shrewd whaling ventures, which earned him a great fortune.

Cuffe's obsession for trans-Atlantic trade and commerce between Africa and America was not perfunctory or incidental. He had genetic roots on both continents. His father was an Ashanti tribesman from Ghana, West Africa. In 1742, ten years old Kofi was captured and sold

---

4    David Brion Davis, *The problem of slavery in Western culture* (NY: Oxford University Press, 1966), 326.

5    Papenfuse, 32.

6    Ibid, 57.

7    Sidbury, 172.

to Captain Ebenezer Slocum of Dartmouth, Massachusetts.[8] After fifteen years of service, the Captain sold Kofi to his nephew, John Slocum. But as fate would have it, the new owner's Christian value convicted him against owning another human being as slave. Consequently, he set Kofi free in 1745.[9]

Kofi became Cuffe Slocum, no doubt, in keeping with his slave status. Later, in 1746, he married Ruth Moses, a Native American of the Wampanoag Tribe.[10]

The Ghanaian native was a skillful woodworker and farmer. With diligence and perseverance, he achieved his life's greatest ambition, when he taught himself to read and write before his death in 1772.

Paul Cuffe, the seventh of ten children, convinced most of his siblings to drop the Slocum name and retained what seemed to be a variation of their father's first name, Cuffe. The change took place after 1772.

General Harper developed a special appreciation for the black Captain's success and astuteness. After many years of government service, even Harper thought it to be a wishful thinking to hope for racial integration in America.

Unlike Thomas Jefferson, who had argued that blacks were inferior due to genetic defects and could never improve intellectually, even if their social conditions were to change, Harper had a different theory. He argued that it was one thing to be told that you were inferior and another thing to believe and internalize the negative claim. His best example was Paul Cuffe who did not internalize negativism, but rose ahead of the pack, despite what he was told and how he was treated as a black merchant. He did not become a victim of debasement, but other blacks were not like Cuffe. They believed what they had been told and lost the desire to excel and became a "worthless and thievishly race." He made it clear that blacks' inferiority complex or criminal disposition was not innate or genetic but was a result of prolonged deprivation.

The population of the United States was 110,072 in 1800, 186,446 in 1810, and 233,530 in1820.[11] By 1816, African Americans were nearly two million, and two hundred thousand were already liberated. Most Americans believed that free blacks could not assimilate into the majority society due to entrenched prejudice. They claimed blacks had no rights

---

[8]   Brock Cordeiro, *Paul Cuffe: A Study of His Life, and the Status of His Legacy in Old Dartmouth*.(MA thesis, 2004).

[9]   Ibid.

[10]  Lamont D. Thomas, *Paul Cuffee: Black Entrepreneur and Pan-Africanist* (Urbana and Chicago: University of Illinois Press, 1988), 4-5.

[11]  Speech of the Hon. Henry Clay, before the American Colonization Society: In The Hall of The House of Representatives, January 20, 1827

which whites were obliged to respect, and 200 years had demonstrated that Anglo America was becoming more hostile towards non-white peoples.

Historian P.J. Staudenraus contends that the abolitionist advocacy was somehow undermined by a belief in the inevitability of racial prejudice in the United States.[12] Based on that persuasion, most Americans came to the conclusion that blacks' liberty was only possible outside the United States. That conviction led to the formation of the American Colonization Society (ACS) in 1816.

According to historian Bell Wiley:

> The ACS membership . . . included those who believed that slavery was wrong, but that, as Jefferson articulated, living together would be impossible or undesirable; those who believed that African Americans were inferior and a drain on the community; those who believed in the missionary promise of Africa; the anti-slave trade establishment; and those with commercial motives."[13]

The mastermind behind the founding of the American Colonization Society was Rev. Robert Finley (1772-1817). He was a Presbyterian minister and a native of New Jersey, but the idea was not new. Throughout the 1700s, there had been occasions when religious groups and political leaders called for emancipation, to be followed by colonization in North America or Africa. Apparently, there was not sustained opposition to repatriating blacks in those early days, but no serious ventures were ever established.

In 1816, General Charles Fenton Mercer inadvertently discovered the Secret Journals of the Virginia Legislature for the years 1801-5. They had entries regarding an African colonization. He found correspondence between James Monroe and Thomas Jefferson about resolving the slave problem, and often, colonization was seen as one possible way to end it. However, a resolution on the floor of the Legislature failed to support the scheme, and so it ended up in the *Secret Journals*.

When Finley decided to establish a colonization enterprise to return blacks to Africa, public sentiments were already warming up to the idea. Many politicians in the government and some slaveholders were willing

---

[12]   P.J. Staudenraus, *The African Colonization Movement, 1816-1865* (NY: Columbia University Press, 1961), 12.

[13]   Bell Irvin Wiley, *Slaves No More: Letters from Liberia 1833-1869* (Lexington: Kentucky University Press, 1980).

to bring closure to the inhumanity by returning blacks to the continent of their ancestry. It was during this new awakening that Finley took the challenge, although he died a year later in November of 1817.[14]

Robert Finley graduated from Princeton (College of New Jersey) in 1787. He served over twenty years at Basking Ridge, New Jersey, as pastor and principal of a school for boys. He eventually developed interest in African American children when he discovered that many in his neighborhood could not read the Bible. He volunteered to teach them.

In observing their impoverished conditions, Dr. Finley concluded that freedmen could only fulfill their potential as human beings in Africa, the "land of their fathers." Thousands of former slaves were homeless, jobless, and poor. Many turned to crime to survive. There were no comprehensive plans for racial integration on egalitarian basis. States continued to enact laws, which denied blacks civil rights. These legal barriers insured the perpetual servitude of Negros, including freedmen in the Union.

The membership of the American Colonization Society included the following influential politicians: Speaker Henry Clay of Kentucky, author of the *Star Spangled Banner*, Francis Scott Key, Chief Justice John Marshall, statesman John Randolph of Roanoke, Senator Daniel Webster, Reverend Robert Finley, with his brother-in-law Elias B. Caldwell, among others. They gained support from former Presidents Thomas Jefferson and James Madison. Eventually, there were more than 200 local auxiliary chapters, with thousands of supporters nationwide.[15]

The Society had one vice president for each original state in the Union. Caldwell served as the first secretary, and Francis Key became a member of the twelve-man board of managers.

Article II of the 1816 ACS Constitution defined its roles as: "To promote and execute a plan for colonizing (with their consent) the free people of color, residing in our country, in Africa, or such other place as Congress shall deem most expedient. And the Society shall act to affect this object in co-operation with the general government, and such of the states as may adopt regulations upon the subject."[16]

The organization transmitted its objectives to Congress immediately in an attempt to engage the government in the process, but there

---

[14]  Rev. Isaac V. Brown, *Biography of the Rev. Robert Finley of Baskin Ridge N 1, 2nd edition, Enlarged. With An Account of His Agency as The Author of The American Colonization Society; Also a Sketch of The Slave Trade; With An Appendix* (Philadelphia: John W. Moore, 1857).

[15]  http://www.teachushistory.org/second-great-awakening-age-reform/articles / colonization-respectable-way-be-anti-slavery-early-new-en (accessed August 5,2011).

[16]  *The African repository and colonial journal*—Vol. 45, 382.

was no immediate response. The delay was troubling because funds were needed to implement the scheme. Instead of direct response, the government chose to assess public opinion. "Owing to the pressure of business, Congress did not decide on the report, but left it to have its salutary influence on the public mind, without any immediate legislative interference, while the Society felt no small encouragement to go forward in their benevolent purpose."[17]

The ACS structure was complex. It had anti-and-pro-slavery supporters. Representatives of both groups assembled at the first meeting on December 21, 1816, in a Washington, D.C. hotel. In attendance were Speaker Henry Clay and John Randolph. They expressed their pro-slavery view in the gathering: "The proposed institution to colonize blacks should not, in any way, challenge the institution of slavery . . ." Randolph urged other slaveholders to support the association "since many slaveholders believed the presence of free blacks created a dangerous source of discontent among slaves."[18]

Many Americans saw colonization as the solution to the racial "problem." Freedmen were generally blamed for fermenting agitation among slaves. Slaveholders claimed slaves would be happier in their servitude, if freedmen were not present.

The view of the antislavery wing was uncomplimentary as presented by Dr. Elias Caldwell, who invited Clay and Randolph to participate in the venture as a political cover. After listening to Clay, Caldwell said, "America could not continue upholding civil liberties while depriving a part of its population these same liberties."[19] At that meeting and thereafter, the Society never had an official policy to free slaves who chose not to emigrate. It followed the core concept "that there is an utter aversion in the public (white majority) mind, to an amalgamation and equalization of the two races: and that any attempt to press such equalization is not only fruitless, but injurious."[20]

Madison resolved that blacks could not gain equality in America due to white prejudices. He weighed the options whether or not to keep pressing for equality in America or support emigration. He chose emigration but cautioned that slaveholders be compensated for a loss of property. This became the foundational framework of the American

---

[17]  Gardiner Spring, *Memoir of the Rev. Samuel J. Mills: Late Missionary to the South Western United States and Agent of the American Colonization Society* (NY: W Flint, 1820), 113.

[18]  Yarema, 17.

[19]  Ibid.

[20]  Spring, 113.

Colonization Society: no forced removal of people and only freed blacks were to be repatriated.

## Rationale for Repatriation

Slavery in the United States was increasingly becoming untenable, after the Revolutionary War of Independence, but slavocrats contended that it was a "necessary evil." While blacks were considered undesirable nuisance by whites, slaveholders viewed them as a necessary source of free labor.

Most whites dreaded the surge in the number of blacks in the population. Speaker Henry Clay of Kentucky referenced the increase to support the controversial cause of American Colonization. He stated, "The slave population of the United States amounted in 1790, to 697, 697; in 1800, to 896, 849; in 1810, to l91, 364; and in 1820, to 1538.128."[21]

The upsurge was noticeable in the general population. Various arguments were framed to get rid of blacks or reduce their population in certain states. Slaves and freedmen were accused of natural inclination toward criminal behavior, indolence, and feeblemindedness or lack of intelligence to understand democracy. Southerners accused liberated slaves as the mastermind behind uprising and rebellions on the plantations. Most slave owners believed slaves would be happier in their servitude, if free blacks were not around to encourage revolts.

States with a large number of free slaves claimed that the lack of morality among blacks would eventually degrade the white community and plunge it into barbarity. One preventative measure was to illegalize amalgamation between the races. Fear of racial integration was strong enough to motivate a sustained clamor for removal of free slaves from the United States.

Sentiments against the deplorable conditions and dejection of blacks were not uncommon in the white community, even among slaveholders. Speaker Henry Clay of Kentucky, in making the case for colonization, said:

> Here (United States) they (freedmen) are in the lowest state of social gradation-aliens-political moral social aliens, strangers, though natives. There, they would be in the midst of their friends and their kindred, at home, though born in a

---

[21] *Speech of Honorable Henry Clay*, https://archive.org/details/speechofhonhenry1827 (accessed April 20, 2014).

foreign land, and elevated above the natives of the country, as much as they are degraded here below the other classes of the community.[22]

Although the following sentiment was expressed in 1854, individuals could be found throughout the early history of the United States who shared the pity for blacks:

> Abolitionists may talk twaddle till the crack of doom, but after all, Colonization is to be the great cure of Negro slavery in this country, or it remains uncured. You may free the slave in the South, but he is nevertheless a slave North or South. His shackles are only to be cast off by returning to the land of his forefathers. Here he is surrounded by a wall of prejudice as indestructible as the everlasting hills. The fires of the volcano are not more inextinguishable than this prejudice, and we would therefore remove the black man from its influence, instead of encouraging him to break it down by an insolent bearing towards those who are in ninety-nine cases out of a hundred, his intellectual superiors.[23]

In a letter to John Holmes in 1829, Thomas Jefferson noted, "We have the wolf by the ear, and we can neither hold him, nor safely let him go. Justice is in one scale, and self-preservation in the other."[24]

The struggle to achieve amalgamation and racial equality in the United States yielded no useful results in antebellum America. The debauchery of black families by the slave culture gave rise to apparent lawless behavior and perniciousness. An extreme fear of the branded darkies created solidarity among whites to resist or denounce any plan for black citizenship and equal treatment. Hope for egalitarianism became unattainable or illusive. Some abolitionists who had worked for policies that could change the status of blacks for the better began searching for alternatives outside of America.

Historian Douglas A. Egerton saw other reasons for the ACS plan and why some blacks supported it. He concluded that:

---

[22]   Ibid.

[23]   Robert A. Nowlan, The American Presidents, Washington to Tyler: What They Said, What was Said About Them, with Full Source Notes (NC: Farland and Company, 2002), 217.

[24]   Thomas Jefferson to John Holmes, http://www.loc.gov/exhibits/jefferson/159.html (accessed 2014).

Although it's certainly true that the vast majority of black Americans, especially in the northern states, believed that the country of their birth was their country and had no desire to emigrate to Liberia, there were a good number of southern blacks—free blacks, moderately prosperous blacks, barbers, artisans, tavern keepers—who'd simply had enough, and decided to go. They were weary of endless white demands for deference. They were tired of getting off the sidewalk when a white man walked toward them. They decided, as the ante-bellum period dragged on, that America never would give them a even break. And therefore, they decided to leave.[25]

After the founding of Liberia, never again did the ACS actively advocate for legislative efforts to secure civil rights, education, and voting rights for blacks. The Society argued that Liberia was the solution to blacks' alienation. According to its members, the push for racial equality was a tantalizing effort that was designed to tease blacks about something to look forward to but could never achieve. That had been the case for more than 200 years, and it was no use to keep that hope alive. Whites had decided that blacks were inferior beings and could not live with the superior whites amicably. Therefore, giving slaves and freedmen hope of racial equality was injurious and fruitless.

The federal government did not identify with the new enterprise immediately. It was difficult to win Congress over, perhaps in fear of public outcry against the Society. However, an event brought the government around to align with the ACS.

After the Gabriel Rebellion of 1800, The Virginian House of Delegates had a *secret meeting* and declared: "That the Governor . . . correspond with the President of the United States on the subject of purchasing land without the limits of this state, whither persons obnoxious to the laws, or dangerous to the peace of society may be removed." The target was the plotters who had escaped execution due to insufficient evidence against them. They were going to be banished to the West Indies and Santo Domingo. Africa was said to be considered when all else failed.

President Thomas Jefferson had a strong opinion about the resolution. He added: "Africa would offer a last and undoubted resort . . . It is material to observe that they (insurgents) are not felons, or common malefactors, but persons guilty of what the safety of society, under actual

---

[25] *Douglas Egerton on black response to colonization.* http://www.pbs.org/wgbh/aia/part3/3i3135.html (accessed April 2014).

circumstances, obliges us to treat as a crime, but which their feelings may represent in a far different shape."[26]

President James Monroe had wished for the government to assist the colonization endeavor before, but to no avail. There was no plan to use federal funds for a colonization enterprise. But when the door finally swung opened, he leaped through it.

Here is how the political helix unfolded. The government had hundreds of captured slaves who had been brought into the country illegally. What to do with the captives was a menacing nuisance. Some federal leaders sought ways for the country to be put on a path to eradicate domestic slavery, but the infiltration of foreign slaves was making the effort ineffectual. Slavery was breeding in the states and the government did not have the legal authority to halt the underground trade.

The importation of slaves from Africa had been banned; however, no provision was made to prosecute contrabands. As a result, smugglers abounded. The underground trade was encouraged in some states. The statues were designed to benefit the dealers, and thus made the risk of slave trafficking worth taking. In one instance, the State of Georgia put up huge signs advertising captured Africans for sale. Supporters of the American Colonization Society and others became alarmed. General Fenton Mercer, an ACS member, denounced the inconsistency of the slave laws and was so indignant that he introduced a bill into the House of Representatives to "do away with the evil," and the law was enacted on March 3, 1819, to enforce the provision.[27] It provided rigorous clampdown on smugglers and higher rewards for information leading to capture of those who contravened the ban. The prohibition empowered the federal government to take an active role to remove captured slaves from the United States and return them to their homelands, wherever that may be. Alternatively, it could find a secured place where the illegal slaves were to be cared for until they became self-sustaining.[28]

The American government designated $100,000.00 to implement the law against trafficking in slavery, and Congress approved the proposal without dissent. President James Monroe took the opportunity to interpret the provision broadly to mean he was given the right and power to promote any endeavor that provided a secured location for captives.

The migration was largely planned and executed by the American Colonization Society that was instituted in 1816 to repatriate emancipated

---

[26]    Benjamin Brawley, *A Social History of the American Negro* (New: Macmillan Company, 1921), 82.

[27]    Foote, 112.

[28]    Brawley, 175.

slaves to Africa. However, the mission was largely underwritten by the U.S. government, which approved an appropriation of $100,000 in 1819 for a resettlement project. The intended purpose was to use the amount to resettle displaced Africans that were unlawfully transported to the United States after 1808.

# CHAPTER IX

# THE AMERICAN COLONIZATION IN WEST AFRICA

The American Colonization Society did not pioneer the concept of repatriating former slaves from the Americas to Africa. The British had taken the lead and established a successful colony of freed slaves, after the British Empire abolished the slave trade in 1772. In 1787, the government transported 300 freed slaves and seventy white prostitutes to West Africa. They created a settlement on the Sierra Leonean promontory. After two years, most of the settlers died from diseases. Others lost their lives in battles with the local tribesmen, especially the Temne people, who strongly resisted the loss of their land to whites.[1]

The British made another attempt in 1792, and succeeded to settle 1100 freed slaves. The second consignment comprised former British supporters during the American Revolution. But after the war, many blacks protested against their postwar resettlement in Canada. Arrangement was made for their repatriation to Freetown under the leadership of British abolitionist Thomas Clarkson.

Over the years, more emancipated blacks from Canada, the Caribbean islands, and other parts of Africa congregated to a place that became known as Sierra Leone. Thirty three years later, the first blacks under the auspice of the American Colonization Society and the United States arrived in Freetown, the capital of Sierra Leone. They stayed for a while, before leaving to establish a permanent homeland south of Sierra Leone. The country became known as Liberia.

President James Monroe appointed two agents to represent the American government during the expedition. The men included an individual who was already a member of the ACS, Rev. Samuel Bacon. His assistant was John P. Bankson. Dr. Samuel Crozier served as agent for the American Colonization Society. The government gave Bacon

---

[1]    Richard Gott, Britain's Empire: Resistance, Repression and Revolt (UK: Verso, 2011), 94.

$33,000.00, and a ship called the *Elizabeth* was chartered.[2] The *Elizabeth,* or *Mayflower of Liberia*, sailed for Africa on February 6, 1820, with eighty eight immigrants on board (thirty three men, eighteen women, and thirty seven children).[3] The U.S. war ship *Cyane* escorted the vessel.

Departing the United States at the time had its emotional drama. Friends and well-wishers gathered at a black church in New York for the final bon voyage. Outside of the church, however, 3000 indignant protesters gathered and loudly accused the immigrants of "cowardly capitulation." The atmosphere was so tense that "the excited agents removed the immigrants as quickly as possible to the boat and the farewell ceremonies were never held."[4]

Rev. Daniel Coker accepted a request from the ACS to accompany the prospective colony to Africa for moral support. It was good that he was on board, because the distrust of the white agents nearly resulted to a fight with blacks in transit.[5] Some immigrants on board detested the idea that they were returning to Africa under the auspice of white agents, but Coker became a peacemaker and was able to deflect the conflict.

Another conflict arose that even dwarfed the first. An immigrant from Philadelphia named Peter Small had a dog that did not like the other dogs it encountered on the ship. They belonged to the captain of the ship. Hostility fermented and a fight broke out. The owners of the dogs, Small and the Captain, began warming up for their own brawl. The Captain sent for his pistols, but the guns never reached him. Again, Coker was in the middle of another altercation. Eventually, he succeeded to convince Small to apologize to the Captain, because Small's dog was the first to attack the Captain's dogs. Small complied, and the incident was resolved peacefully.

After a few closed calls and edgy encounters, Coker called all the immigrants together and urged them to write their names on a paper, if they still had confidence in the white agents.[6] Eighty six out of eighty eight people signed the first *Liberian Mayflower* or *Elizabeth* Compact to pledge allegiance to the leadership of the agents.

Daniel Coker was born a free man in Baltimore, Maryland. His first name was Isaac Wright. His mother, Susan Coker, was a white indentured servant who married an African slave named Edward Wright.[7]

---

2    Ibid, 175.

3    Ibid.

4    Charles Johnson, *The Story of the Negro Republic* (NJ: Transaction Publishers, 1987), 24.

5    Brawley, 176.

6    Coker, 19.

7    Paul Finkelman, *Encyclopedia of African American history, 1619-1895: From The Colonial Period to the Age of Frederick Douglass,* Vol. 2 (New York: Oxford University Press, 2006), 308.

Whites treated young Wright as a slave. He escaped to New York and changed his name to Daniel Coker. He became a preacher and an antislavery advocate. The AME Church elected him as its first bishop but declined the offer, and Rev. Richard Allan was appointed to the position, instead.[8]

The voyage to Africa had its awkward moments in the ship. For many blacks, the question of repatriation under the leadership of three white agents did not feel right. It felt as though the racist slavocrats had succeeded in rounding up freedmen to be deported from the United States, a country most blacks also claimed as their homeland. Yet, there were immigrants on the first voyage whose excitement to leave America was overwhelmingly emotional and memorable.

Coker wrote that well-wishers assembled at an African Church in New York on January 31, 1820, to "commemorate the first voyage to Africa . . . by the American Colonization Society."[9] At the end of the rushed ceremonies to avoid violence from angry protesters, the attendees joined thousands at the harbor where the *Elizabeth* anchored.

Before sailing, Rev. Samuel Bacon, A Harvard University graduate and principal agent for the American government, read the Bible from Deuteronomy 11: "To go forward fearlessly, obey God's commandments, and teach His laws and the story of their Exodus experience to their children."

The American government attempted to mask its role in the colonization project. Congress did not want to be seen as supporting efforts that might be construed as deportation of blacks, without knowing or getting a decisive clues of how the public felt about the controversial endeavor. Consequently, the U.S. agents were mandated to allow the ACS to lead the enterprise in selecting a location. Of course, the designated spot happened to be the same site the Society had chosen. Despite the government indirect role, its agents were to provide sufficient accommodations and security for three hundred settlers, to include clothing, tools, and food.[10] The United States representatives were expected "to exercise no power founded on the principle of colonization, or other principle than that of performing benevolent offices;" and again,

---

8    Finkelman, 308.

9    Daniel Coker, *Journal Of Daniel Coker, A Descendant of Africa, From The Time of Leaving New York, In The Ship Elizabeth, Captain Sebor, On A Voyage For Sherbro, In Africa In Company With Three Agents, And About Ninety Persons of Colour* (Baltimore: Edward J. Coale, 1820).

10   *Report of Amos Kendall*, Fourth Auditor, to the Secretary of the Navy, August, 1830, quoted by J.H.T. McPherson, *History of Liberia*, (Michigan: Michigan University Press, 1891), 41.

"not to connect . . . with the views or plans of the Colonization Society, with which, under the law, the Government of the United States has no concern."[11]

Paul Cuffe had jumpstarted the "experiment" and made two voyages to Sierra Leone to arrange for a black settlement on his own. He received national and international praise for his colonization initiative, even among blacks. However, the founding of the American Colonization Society instantly changed everything. Blacks and other abolitionists cast doubtful suspension on the back-to-Africa scheme, although it was similar to Cuffe's plan. The ACS came under immediate attacks from black leaders, including former supporters of Paul Cuffe.

## Criticism of the ACS

The composition of the ACS made it an easy target for criticism and speculations, whether real or imagined. According to its opponents, the ACS had a clandestine plan to preserve slavery in America. The scheme, according to critics, was intended to remove freedmen from the United States, while leaving the slaves behind to fend for themselves. With no freed agitators, slavery was said to be guaranteed longevity, with the help of the ACS.

Incidentally, before the American Colonization Society emerged, some states had begun restricting blacks from entering their towns and cities. Others demanded that African Americans carry passes, away from home. During this state of turmoil, the American Colonization Society emerged and offered free passage to those who wanted to leave for the Colony of Liberia. Immediately, critics contended that what the states were doing at a local level was now going to be enforced on a large scale at the federal level by the ACS. All free blacks were going to be forcibly deported to Africa.

Two prominent black leaders, businessman James Forten and Rev. Richard Allen, were supporters of Paul Cuffe's colonization scheme. Their support continued until the death of Cuffe, but they denigrated the American Colonization Society. On January 15, 1817, 3000 opponents gathered at Rev. Richard Allen AME Bethel Church in Philadelphia to deliberate on the question of colonization.[12] The prevailing view was unanimous. The ACS, just a few days old, was said to be under

---

[11]     Ibid, 12.

[12]     James Sidbury, *Becoming African in America: The African-American* (NY: Oxford University Press, 2007), 169.

the influence of Southern slaveholders. The objective was to get rid of influential freedmen and leave the slaves in their misery. Rumors spread fast that repatriation might not only be limited to volunteers, as the Society claimed, but all black people could eventually be deported.

Some prominent people in the audience were apprehensive and did not want to denounce the ACS outright. However, the assembly was aggressive, accusing some leaders of betrayal. The will of the majority prevailed.

Forten once wrote to his friend, Paul Cuffe, about the opposition among blacks against colonization: "They think that the slaveholders want to get rid of them so as to make their property (slaves) more secure."[13]

The Bethel Church assembly set up twelve committees to oppose the American Colonization Society in every conceivable way possible, and Forten served as general chairperson.[14] In retrospect, he also admitted to Paul Cuffe: "My opinion is that they will never become a people until they come out from amongst the white people."

The following resolution was adopted by the assembly: "Resolved, that we never will separate ourselves voluntarily from the slave population in this country; they are our brethren by the ties of consanguinity, of suffering, and of wrongs."[15]

Reverend Finley and other abolitionists, especially influential leaders like Daniel Coker, Richard Allen, and James Forten, were stunned by the negative and hostile response of the African community. They argued that the American Colonization Society initiative was misunderstood or misrepresented. But most Africans saw the removal of free blacks by the ACS as an attempt by slaveholders to purge the United States. Getting rid of vocal blacks would minimize opposition to slavery, according to opponents. On the other hand, as supporters of the ACS argued, because slaves were legal property of their owners, it was important for any repatriation plan to focus on freedmen and not slaves. The captives were regarded as personal property in the same sense as horses or other farm animals. Only with the consent of their masters could they be repatriated out of the United States.

Author of the Liberian Declaration of Independence, Senator Hilary Teage, defended the colonization scheme that created Liberia. He also expressed support for those who chose not to immigrate. He argued

---

[13]   Wilson Jeremiah Moses, *Classic Black Nationalism: From American Revolution to Marcus Garvey* (NY: New York University Press, 1996).

[14]   http://www.pbs.org/wgbh/aia/part3/3h484.html (access July 2, 2011).

[15]   The First Annual Report of The Board of Managers of The New England Antislavery Society (Boston: Garrison & Knapp, 1833), 36.

that blacks did not have to immigrate, if they were granted the same opportunities whites had. In a speech called "Calumny Refuted by Facts From Liberia" the Senator declared:

> No one can object to the Colonization of Africa, so long as it is perfectly voluntary on the part of those who go out as Colonists; in which case, connected with legitimate commerce and plans of civil and Christian improvement, great benefit may accrue; and which, for the sake of Africa, is worthy of encouragement. But, to hold up such a scheme, merely as a mode of expatriating the whole of the African race from America, merits the strongest disapprobation.

> If "the aristocracy of the skin" were laid aside, and the Coloured population of America were invested with the full rights of citizenship, and every civil prize, every useful employment, and every honourable station were thrown open to their exertions, there can be little doubt, as J. J. Gurney observes, in his Remarks on a Speech of Henry Clay's, "that the mixture of colours, in the same population, would soon be found perfectly harmless, Every man, white or black, would rest on his own responsibility ; character, like other things, would find its natural level; light and truth would spread Amliout obstruction; and the North American Union would afford, to an admiring world, a splendid and unsullied evidence of the truth of that mighty principle on which her constitution is founded; viz., that, 'all men are created EQUAL, and are endowed by the Creator with certain NALIENABLE rights, LIFE, LIBERTY, AND THE PURSUIT OF HAPPINESS'. (Sic)[16]

## Why the Outcry?

The following circumstances of black people in the United States have been mentioned before in other chapters. However, the incidents are presented here again to give a wholesome picture of the brutality against Africans, especially in the south.

---

[16]   *Calumny Refuted by Facts From Liberia.* http://www.archive.org/stream/ calumnyrefuted00armi/ calumnyrefuted00armi _djvu.txt accessed April 10, 2014).

Slaves had no civil rights, and it was against the law for them to resist enslavement, sue, witness against whites, or run away. In most states, assembly of slaves, without the presence of whites, was forbidden by law. Wandering away from home without permission was prohibited. A violation of any of the restrictions was punishable by any means the masters deemed necessary, including the cutting off body parts such as ears or hands, flogging, hanging, or lynching.[17] It was not unusual to see the heads of decapitated bodies or charred corpses of blacks dangling from trees as a reminder to all slaves that resistance had deadly consequence.

In many Southern states, slaves were not allowed to get married, but if they did, the families had no legal protection. In states like Texas, for example, contubernium[18] was allowed, as long the cohabitation was not construed as marriage. Enslaved blacks did not own their children and each family member could be sold separately, never to be seen again. An instance of this was the sale of Richard Allen (founder of the AME Church) and his family by their master to Stokley Sturgis, a wealthy plantation owner near Dover, Delaware. Later, Sturgis sold Mrs. Allen and three of the children, leaving behind young Allen, his older brother, and sister, to work as field hands.

Sexual abuses were common, although amalgamation was illegal. It was rare for white men to accept responsibility for fathering mulatto children. Notwithstanding, it was not uncommon, for some slave masters to treat their black children or relatives exceptionally well, in comparison to other slaves.

The alleged black son of George Washington, West Ford, and Thomas Jefferson's alleged black children worked around their masters' homes. They escaped the harshness of slave life in the plantation or cotton fields. On the other hand, all mulatto children were not so fortunate. Alfred F. Russell, who became the ninth president of Liberia, was bought as a child with his mother in 1825. His father was John Russell, Mary Owen Todd Russell's son.[19] While on vacation from Princeton, John impregnated

---

17  Henry S. Cooley, *A Study of Slavery in New Jersey* (MD: Johns Hopkins University Press, 1896), 40.

18  Contubernium: "Among the Romans, slaves had no civil state, their marriages, although valid according to natural law, when contracted with the consent of their masters, and when there was no legal bar to them, yet were without civil effects; they having none except what arose from natural law; a marriage of this kind was called contubernium. It was so called whether both or only one of the parties was a slave. Poth. Contr. de Mariage, part 1, c. 2, Sec. 4. Vicat, ad verb." http://legal-dictionary. thefree dictionary.com/Contubernium (accessed May 20, 2012).

19  http://www.bluegrass.kctcs.edu/LCC/HIS/scraps/liberia2.html (access June 1, 2011).

Milly. The issue was never discussed again in the Russell's family. Instead, the black family was sent to Liberia when Alfred was ten years old.

In some cases, slaves were forced to procreate with whomever their masters chose, especially to big and strong black workers. The historian Randolph B. Campbell provides the following graphic slave narrative: "Women were put with men . . . like "the cows and the bull" and bred for "bigger niggers."[20]

Abolitionism was an act of desperation and a daring venture to dismantle the hideous institution of slavery and restore dignity to its victims. Humanitarians in the 1800s demanded immediate emancipation of slaves, followed by granting of civil rights. However, this apparent zealotry led to a split in the abolition movement. One camp came to be called "abolitionists" or "immediatists" and the other called "gradualists" or "colonizationists."

Abolitionists demanded immediate emancipation and granting of civil rights to all blacks. The gradualists preferred a piecemeal approach, to be followed by colonization. Abolitionists opposed gradual approaches and maligned the concept of colonization. After more than two centuries in the United States, immediatists contended that blacks were to be awarded citizenship and not colonized in a foreign land like Africa.

The gradual emancipation movement turned out to be a dichotomy of individuals with diverse motives. It was a coin with different images on both sides. First, there was the philanthropic group, made of religious and other altruists. Its goal was to repatriate freedmen to a region outside of the United States, with their consent, and induce the emancipation of slaves for the purpose of emigration. Another group in this category was slaveholders who welcomed the idea of getting rid of freedmen, but not slaves. The evil hybrid became the focus of critics, branding the goal of the slaveholders as the cooperate aim of the ACS. It was obvious that slaveholders welcomed the repatriation of freedmen but not slaves. The field hands were needed to work the plantations.[21]

Christian groups urged the removal of blacks from America as a moral imperative. They concluded that, given the increased violence and dejected status of freedmen, people of African descent could not gain freedom and live happily and respectfully among white people. To enjoy basic human rights, African Americans needed to have their own country outside of the United States.

The idea of relocating freed blacks was attractive to slaveholders. Many were men of means and political influence. They became

---

[20]    Campbell, 154-154.

[21]    http://personal.denison.edu/~waite/liberia/history/acs.htm (accessed June 6, 2011).

members of what was first known as "The Society for the Colonization of Free People of Color of America." The organization was renamed The American Colonization Society. Plantation owners had other motives, and altruism was not one of them. They wanted to enforce the removal of freemen out of America. Commenting on the strange relation, Bronwen Everill of Kings College noted:

> That early antislavery movements such as colonization found themselves allied with slaveholders not out of a compromise in their belief in antislavery or a cynical calculation of political-economic realities, but as a reflection of slow imperial communications, complex relationships between formerly enslaved people and the institution of slavery.[22]

In 1787, when the U.S. Constitution was completed, Madison wrote that he would return to Virginia without one of his slaves, Billey. According to Madison, "On the view of all the circumstances I have judged it most prudent not to force Billey back to Virginia even if it could be done. Billey's mind was too thoroughly tainted to be a fit companion for fellow slaves in Virginia."[23]

Madison could see that Billey was profoundly affected by the spirit of freedom in Philadelphia to the extent that he could not be a good fit for a normal slave life back in Virginia. Madison was concerned about the possibility of Billey being a bad influence on the other slaves. Instead of setting him free, he was sold to a Quaker as an indentured servant for seven years. Billey became free and served as an associate correspondent for Madison's finances, handling most of the families business.

As slave masters became more entrenched and created laws to safeguard slavery, it became inconceivable that the evil empire could be demolished without the full cooperation of abolitionists and slaveholders. Slaves were considered legal property, and it was against the law to take away personal property without just compensation. Hence, the ACS became an alliance of necessity with racist elements. It was a problematic alliance, even for slave masters.

Slaveholders who were members of the ACS found out quickly that the Society's plan was not limited to the removal of liberated blacks only,

---

22    Bronwen Everill, *Those That are Well Off do Have the Natives as Slaves: Humanitarian 'Compromises' with Slavery in Sierra Leone and Liberia* JOUHS, 7 (Special Issue—Colloquium 2009).

23    John P. Kaminski, *James Madison: Champion of Liberty and Justice* (Parallel Press, 2006), 36.

as stipulated in its constitution. The organization was actively seeking to secure the freedom of slaves by appeal or purchase for emigration. This was more than slave owners had bargained or hoped for.

ACS member John Randolph Johnson had campaigned for slaveholders to support the Society, with the understanding that it would not interfere with slavery. Now, members were being urged to manumit their slaves and send them to Liberia, or wherever they could go and enjoy freedom.

## William Lloyd Garrison: "All on Fire"

Voices of abolitionists that demanded immediate emancipation grew louder. One of the most vocal was William Lloyd Garrison. He became the total embodiment of all fanatical antislavery sentiments could express within a generation, and Garrison was a white man. From the beginning of his campaign, he wrote in his propaganda newspaper, the *Liberator*: "I do not wish to think, or speak, or write, with moderation . . . . I am in earnest—I will not equivocate—I will not excuse—I will not retreat a single inch—AND I WILL BE HEARD."

*William Lloyd Garrison*
*(December 12, 1805 – May 24, 1879)*

Certainly, Garrison was heard. From 1831, no abolitionist did more to shame slaveholders or denounce supporters of colonization than he did. His most ferocious disparagement was transfixed on the American Colonization Society like a guided laser beam to track and vilify its actual, speculative, or imaginary schemes.

Garrison commenced his antislavery discourse as a gradualist. He called for gradual emancipation and education of slaves to fit in civil society.[24] Perhaps, one other lesser known fact about Garrison is that at one time, he also shared the same prevailing prejudices other whites held against black people,[25] but three events transformed him completely to become the firebrand antislavery ambassador he became.

While Garrison shared what he called "ordinary prejudices" of the commonwealth toward free blacks, his mother helped to redirect his path by narrating the story of a black woman named Henny. According to Mrs. Garrison, "Although a slave to man, (she is) yet a free-born soul by the grace of God." She admonished Garrison to remember Henny "for your poor mother's sake."

Garrison got hold of a pamphlet entitled *The Book and Slavery Irreconcilable*, which was written in 1816 by a Presbyterian minister named George Bourne. Reverend Bourne was outspoken against slavery and held every slaveholder's feet over a blazing and never quenching hell fire. He was eventually booted out of Virginia. However, from the pamphlet, Garrison raised the slavery question to a higher moral platform of sin. He adapted Bourne's maxim, "Moderation against sin is an absurdity."

Moreover, an English Quaker, Elizabeth Heyrick, had an impact Garrison's worldview. She outright denounced gradualism as a "masterpiece of satanic policy," and urged abolitionists to become "Christian combatants." Garrison relinquished his formal ideology of gradualism to embrace immediatism. He considered himself cleansed from past sins and prejudices and was ready to confront the evil empire of slavery.

Garrison's transformation was notable in his forceful attacks against the American Colonization Society. He supported the organization up to 1830, before delivering an incinerating rebuke against slaveholders and promoters of gradual emancipation at an ACS event on July 4, 1828.[26] He called for the expulsion of all slaveholding members from the Society.

---

[24]  Henry Mayer, *All On Fire* (NY: W.W. Norton & Company, 1998).

[25]  Ibid, 68.

[26]  Martin Robison Delany, *The Condition, Elevation, Emigration, and Destiny of the Colored People of the United States* (NY: Arno Press, 1968).

That meant everyone but a few, including himself. Apparently, that was not to be. Slaveholders who sought a graceful exit from the evil trade and those bent on securing slaves as property were prime supporters of the organization. To expel them meant the end of the venture, which would have aborted plans to establish what turned out to be the viable African nation of Liberia.

Rev. Ralph Gurley, Secretary General of the ACS, was put between the hammer and anvil when Garrison delivered his address. Some members called for condemnation of his comments. Gurley took a stand to deflate the tension. In a carefully worded statement, he wrote: "The Society had no interest of promoting general emancipation or interfere with the right of private poverty."[27] This was the breaking point for Garrison. He concluded that the ACS was a scheme to preserve slavery because it avowed not to push for immediate emancipation or confront slaveholders for their sins. Thus, "The ACS was constantly forced to renegotiate its moderate position, seeking affirmation from their British counterparts that they were not patrons, directly or indirectly, of slavery."[28]

In the 1840s, a rift developed in the Garrison camp. The moderates broke away and formed their own group, with the hope of working with others to find solution to the slave problem. One of his supporters, Frederick Douglass, condemned Garrison for burning the American Constitution and calling it a "proslavery document." Douglass disassociated himself when Garrison called for disunion of the federal government.

Another brutal critic of the ACS was John Brown Russwurm, editor of the anticolonizationist newspaper, "Freedom's Journal." As an opponent of the ACS, he once proclaimed, "Never shall we consent to emigrate from America until the prior removal from this land of their degradation and suffering. Even then, we would not ask the aid of the American Colonization Society to carry us to their land "flowing with milk and honey."[29]

After fourteen years in the United States, Russwurm had enough. He could see no discernible change in the conditions of black people or attitude of whites toward racial integration. In 1829, Russwurm reconsidered his prospect in America. "Can the justice of God tolerate

---

[27]  Nichols Guyatt, *Providence and the Invention of the United States* (NY: Cambridge University Press, 2007; *Error Corrected,* African Deposity 5, no. 7 (Sept. 1829) 215-6).

[28]  *African Colonization-Slave Trade-Commerce, Report of Mr. Kennedy, of Maryland, from the Committee on Commerce of the House of Representatives of the United States* (Washington, 1843), 1007.

[29]  Winston James, *The Struggles of John Brown Russwurm: The Life and Writing of A Pan-Africanist Pioneer: 1799-1851* (NY: New York University Press, 2010), 31.

so much iniquity and injustice?" he asked, "and when will the monster prejudice be done away, even from among the Christians?"[30] He came to the same conclusion as the ACS: "There was no better option than to immigrate to Africa." He argued that it was a waste of time to talk of ever enjoying citizenship in this country. "It is utterly impossible in the nature of things: all therefore who pant for this must cast their eyes elsewhere."[31]

Russwurm filed an application with the ACS in January of 1829. He was approved in July of the same year. The Board had its doubts about the wisdom of enlisting him, after his barrage of attacks on the Society from the editorial of the paper he edited, "Freedom's Journal."

On February 14, 1829, Russwurm wrote that he had a change of heart about colonization and called his former anticolonizationist position an "error." The ACS published the recantation in the *African Repository Journal,* with the title, *Candid Acknowledgment of Error.* The ACS announced elatedly, "The Editor of Freedom's Journal, Mr. Russwurm, (a very respectable, and well educated coloured man in New York) who has for several years, been decidedly and actively opposed to the Colonization Society, in his paper of 14th February, candidly and honourably confesses that his opinions in regard to our Institution, have become entirely changed."[32]

Russwurm immigrated to Liberia in 1829 and served as editor of the *Liberian Herald*, school superintendent, and governor of what is now Maryland County in Liberia.

---

[30] James, 60.

[31] Ibid.

[32] Winston James, *The Struggles of John Brown Russwurm: The Life and Writings of a Pan-Africanist Pioneer, 1799-1851* (NY: New York University Press, 2010), 54.

# CHAPTER X

# BACK-TO-AFRICA CONSPIRACY THEORY

As early as 1773, Samuel Hopkins and Ezra Stiles discussed the possibility of sending two freedmen as missionaries to Africa.[1] Two young men were trained at Princeton College for the mission. However, the American Revolutionary War affected the plan for what could have been the first American mission station or colony in Africa. The endeavor was abandoned.

Some doubts still linger whether Hopkins intended to establish a colony or just an evangelical mission station in Africa. In a letter to Granville Sharp, dated January 15, 1783, Hopkins wrote, "This plan I have had in view for some years, and had wished and attempted to promote."[2] The lack of funds delayed its implementation.

Hopkins and Stiles were associates of Rev. Samuel J. Mills, editor of the *Evangelical Magazine*. His son, by the same name, was born in 1783 and consecrated to be a foreign missionary.[3] It can be recalled that Mills, Jr. and Ebenezer Burgess went on the first expedition to West Africa in 1818, which paved the way for the Colony of Liberia in 1822.

The British took the lead in the resettle scheme. Its naval ship arrived in West Africa with 411 free slaves on May 10, 1787, as a humanitarian act, "because blacks stood a better chance of independence in a free community based on Christian principles in Sierra Leone."[4] Two other waves of black immigrants followed. In 1792, another group of blacks

---

[1]   Grace G. Niles, *The Hoosac Valley—Its Legends and Its History* (MD: Heritage Books, 1997), 409.

[2]   Ibid, 410.

[3]   Ibid.

[4]   Kenneth Morgan, *Slavery and the British Empire* (Oxford: Oxford University Press, 2007), 158.

who fought for the British emigrated from Nova Scotia. The second wave included exiled Maroons from Jamaica after the Maroon War of 1795.[5]

The deportation of blacks was a standing policy in the South, although it was not aggressively pursued in some states. Deportation laws existed before the ACS was organized. The slave codes took effect in the early 1700s and allowed for the deportation of blacks who committed certain types of crimes such as rape and theft.[6] The owners were to pay the deportation fees, but if the culprit was not a slave, the individual was flogged and branded.[7]

As President of the ACS, James Clark defended the Society initiatives in 1829, when he argued that emigration was a humane paradigm. Clark made reference to a Virginian law that called for emancipated blacks to leave the State in twelve months or forfeit their freedom. According to him, the law provided no asylum or destination for deportees, therefore the Liberian colony was a necessary alternative for stateless black victims.[8] In defense of the Liberian Experiment, the ACS leader said the country was open to both freeborn and emancipated slaves. It was an opportunity for slaveholders who chose to manumit their slaves, for whatever reasons. Slave owners who agreed to manumit also paid the cost for transportation or the ACS did, when it could.[9]

The decision to accept freedom for emigration was a quandary. Most slaves wanted freedom and wished to live in the United States. However, slavery was not the opposite of freedom, as some were led to believe. Emancipated blacks were neither slave nor free. They were not eligible for citizenship.[10] Many states barred them from residency and the U.S. Constitution made African Americans a stateless race in antebellum America. As such, they had no hope, beyond what their masters were willing to offer, and that was servitude, with perpetual degradation.

When a slave was offered freedom in exchange for emigration, they had to make a decision and accept the consequences. Those who refused freedom for emigration risked remaining in bondage, risked being sold to cruel masters; women risked gang rape and forced procreation to breed bastards, or brutalized in other ways with impunity. On the other hand, those who chose freedom for emigration were also taking risks of dying in transit, infected with tropical diseases, and drawn into tribal conflicts.

---

5    Morgan, 159.

6    http://www.jstor.org/pss/1886908 (accessed November 2, 2011).

7    Ibid.

8    *The American Repository*, Vol. 5, No. 2, American Colonization Society. (1830)

9    The American Repository, 21.

10    Allen C. Guelzo, *Lincoln's Emancipation Proclamation: The end of Slavery in America* (NY: Simmon & Schuster, 2004).

However, if the emigrants survived and were willing to work hard, they had a real opportunity to rise socially, economically, politically, and command respect for their achievements. Blacks in America could not hope for such opportunity. It was a difficult position for those who had to make the precarious decision to stay or to go. It was still their decision, and that is how the evil empire of slavery worked, unfortunately.

Opponents of colonization point out the inhumane and forceful removal of blacks from the United States. However, there is no significant data to demonstrate an ACS forced removal initiative. No doubt, there were blacks who preferred America to Liberia, but they had to migrate to Liberia as a condition for liberty, which was imposed by the terms of freedom. However, once in Liberia, some immigrants returned to America, while others retreated to Sierra Leone. Most decided to stay and endure the hardships on the West Coast of Africa.

There had been cases of slave masters making a will and including emancipation of their slaves or reselling them, as Thomas Jefferson did. As it relates to Liberia, the decision was made by the "property" owner, not the ACS. If the decision was for them to be repatriated, they could accept the plan or challenge it in court as others did.[11]

There were instances when emancipated individuals appealed to the ACS for help to emigrate, but the organization turned them down due to the lack of funds. Churches and other sources had to help and this is especially true of immigrants from Arkansas. There were individuals who sold their possessions just to get a ticket or make partial payment to hold a seat on a boat for Liberia as in this case, as is evidenced in the following narrative: "They expected emigrants to make some payment for their transportation which cost around $100 per adult passenger . . . The Conway applicants expected a spring departure and had sent in a total of $197 to the ACS office in Washington for their passage."[12]

It would have been incomprehensible for a financially stripped organization to go after people who did not want to be repatriated, when there were others who wanted the opportunity to immigrate. In some cases, the organization did not have the funds to help those who were willing to go, and it avoided acts that would drag it into litigation.

The ACS was often aware of its precarious political position with critics of colonization. It did what it could to avoid litigations over slavery. While there are unsubstantiated claims that the American Colonization

---

[11] How voluntary was the return to Africa? http://www.liberiapastandpresent.org/ ColonizationSociety.htm (accessed October 1, 2011).

[12] Kenneth C. Barnes, *The Back-to-Africa Movement in Faulkner County*http://www. faulknerhistory.com/ articles/backtoafrica.htm (accessed February 5, 2012).

Society forcefully removed some freedmen from the United States against their will, no documented evidence has surfaced to suggest that such was the case. All litigations about slave freedom and whether or not they immigrate were the prerogative of the slave owners and not the ACS.

The concept of colonization was highly controversial in the black community, and most African Americans opposed the idea. They strongly believed that, by removing freed blacks, slaveholders would have less opposition or pressure to liberate their slaves. However, most emigrants to Liberia were emancipated slaves (individuals who gained freedom with or without the help of the ACS or bought their own freedom to go to Liberia).

Including those who purchased their own freedom to go to Liberia as indicated, 4885 emigrants were freeborn. Nearly 5957 of the settlers were former slaves who gained their freedom with help from the American Colonization Society.[13] That is more than the combined number of freeborn and those who purchased their own freedom. With such a disparity, it is obvious that the ACS clearly demonstrated that it was more concerned about the emancipation of slaves as an organization than some of its individual members had intended. Therefore, the argument that the organization only intended to remove freedmen and leave slaves in bondage to perpetuate slavery is erroneous. The evidence demonstrates otherwise.

Among the emancipators were slaveholders and supporters, like ACS Board member William H. Fitzugh. He manumitted 300 slaves and offered to pay their passage to Liberia.[14] The organization also sought to secure the freedom of slaves by appeal or purchase if they chose emigration. This was a challenge to slaveholders. Henry Clay and Randolph had warned in 1816 that nothing be done to challenge slavocracy,[15] but in practice, the ACS did not yield to the grand bargain, whenever it was politically and legally feasible.

In 1819, ACS member Randolph manumitted all his slaves in his will, and noted, "I give and bequeath to all my slaves their freedom, heartily regretting that I have ever been the owner of one."

During one of his early tours in the South, ACS founder, Rev. Robert Finley once said, "The constant and increasing tendency of the plan of Colonization is to lead to the emancipation of slaves, and that this had already taken place, and is still, in a very encouraging manner."[16]

---

[13] J. Gus Liebenow, *The Evolution of Privilege* (NY: Cornell University Press, 1969).

[14] *The African Repository and Colonial Journal*, Vol. 2, June 1826, no. IV.

[15] Nikki Taylor, *Reconsidering the 'Forced' Exodus of 1829: Free Black Emigration from Cincinnati, Ohio to Wilberforce, Canada* (The Journal of African American History No. 87 ((2002), 288.

[16] The African repository, Volume 9, No. 1, *American Colonization Society* (Washington DC: James C, Dunn, 1834), 124.

# CHAPTER XI

# THE ANATHEMA:
# COLONIZATION OR EMIGRATION

No subject ever proved to be more divisive in antebellum America than the concept of colonization. Many blacks had ancestors who left Africa more than two centuries earlier. They considered America as their homeland. The thought of going back to a land once considered the "dark continent" hardly seemed fair and practical. In retrospect, racism plagued the nation with hatred for blacks, and even freedmen were not welcome in America, especially in the South. In view of this reality, some freedmen decided to form their own colonization societies, and the goals were similar to the plan of the American Colonization Society. The essential differences were the substitution of the word "colonization" with "emigration" or "civilization," headed by black colonizers.

A difference emerged between colonization and emigration mainly as a resentment against whites. According to General Martin Delany, colonization "was the racist removal of blacks from the United States, and emigration was an independent initiatives by blacks to leave the United States."[1] It was not a question of removing blacks from the United States, but who was removing them, whether black or white.

In 1818, the *Haytian* "Emigration" Society of colored People was formed, with Rev. Peter Williams as chairman. It avoided the use of the despised racist term, "colonization" so not to be identified with the ACS. Its goal was to repatriate freedmen to Haiti, not Africa.[2] Rev. Williams made this point clear in 1834 when he objected to the belief that blacks were best suited to be colonized in Africa: "We are NATIVES of this country and ask only to be treated as well as FOREIGNERS . . . we ask

---

[1]    Michele Mitchel, *Righteous propagation: African Americans and the politics of racial destiny* (NC: University of North Carolina Press, 2004), 23.

[2]    Leslie Alexander, *African or American? Black Identity and Political Activism* (NC: University of North Carolina Press, 2004).

only to share equal privileges with those who come from distant lands, to enjoy the fruits of our labor. Let these modest requests be granted, and we need not to go to Africa or anywhere else to be improved and happy."[3]

Five years after the Forten 3000 freed slaves forum passed a united resolution echoing defiantly, "Never will (we) separate voluntarily from the slave population in this country . . . ," James Forten and Bishop Richard Allen formed the *Haytian Emigration Society* in 1824 in the same Bethel African Methodist Church where a resolution was passed in 1817 to denounce colonization and emigration. They planned to recruit free blacks and encourage slaveholders to emancipate their slaves and prepare them for Haiti, with one critical difference: no compensation to slaveholders for emancipation, as the ACS was inclined to do.[4] The Haytian Society planned to ship thousands of freed blacks to Haiti and Santo Domingo, if they consented to go; similar to the ACS platform. The venture envisioned the possibility of settling about two million blacks. Moreover, the Haitian government was willing to pay blacks to settle on the island.[5]

The Haytian Emigration effort did not succeed, after the initial attempts. The organization stalled in the midst of white opposition. The venture was too close to the empire of slavery in the South and some slaveholders argued it could encourage rebellion among the slaves. Also, the Haitian government terminated subsidy for black settlements. Language barrier, religious differences, and high death rate in the immigrant community caused surviving blacks to return to the United States.[6]

Notwithstanding, from 1824-1827, 13,000 emigrants settled in Haiti initially, about the same number that settled in Liberia over half a century from the United States.[7] Slaveholders also supported the Haiti Emigration Society for the same reason others joined the ACS: "to promote their own agenda and expedite the expulsion of all black people from the United States."

---

[3]  *Debate Over Emigration and Colonization*, http://www.inmotionaame.org/ migrations/topic.cfm ;jsessionid= f830197974136 4920007408?migration=4&topic= 7&bhcp=1

[4]  Léon Dénius Pamphile, *Haitians and African Americans: a Heritage of Tragedy and Hope* (Gainesville: University Press of Florida, 2001).

[5]  Donald Yacovone, *Freedom's Journal: African American Voices of the Civil War,* (Chicago: Lawrence Hill, 2004), 31.

[6]  Yacovone, 31.

[7]  *Colonization*, http://www.loc.gov/exhibits/african/afam002.html (accessed June 1, 2013).

Rev. Henry Highland Garnett formed the *African "Civilization" Society* in 1858. Though he was indifferent to earlier emigration endeavors, the preacher became convinced that "African Americans had little chance of attaining true independence in their country," but they could benefit the continent by promoting "civilization" and "Christianity," while achieving independence for themselves. He made a authoritative argument against opponents of emigration and cautioned his critics thus: "No man should deprive me of my love for Africa, the land of my ancestors."

In response to Frederick Douglass' criticism against immigration to Africa, Garnet addressed him in February 1859 thus:

> But I entreated you to tell your readers what your objections are to the civilization and christianization of Africa. What objection have you to colored men in this country engaging in agriculture, lawful trade, and commerce in the land of my forefathers? What objection have you to an organization that shall endeavor to check and destroy the African slave trade, and that desires to co-operate with anti-slavery men and women of every grade in our own land, and to toil with them for the overthrow of American slavery?—Tell us, I pray you, tell us in your clear and manly style. 'Gird up thy loins, and answer thou me, if thou canst.'"[8]

—Letter from Henry Highland Garnet

After doing missionary work in Jamaica, he was appointed by President James A. Garfield as minister to Liberia in 1881, where he died in 1882.[9]

Opponents of the African Civilization Society were adamant in their claim that the goals of the organization were essentially the same as the goals of the ACS. The only difference was that the ACS promised not to interfere with slavery in the United States, while removing emancipated blacks who volunteered to leave for Africa. The Civilization Society also promised to repatriate blacks voluntarily with their consent.

General Martin R. Delany, a prominent abolitionist, was a former associate of the ACS. Later, he defected and denounced the Society for

---

[8]    African Civilization Society http://teachingamericanhistory.org/library/document/african-civilization-society/

[9]    Kenneth Barnes, *Journey of Hope: The Back-to-Africa Movement in Arkansas in the Late 1800s*. (NC: UNC Press, 2004), 154.

cooperating with slaveholders. Notwithstanding, he did concede that racial integration in America was an elusive dream. After terminating his membership with the ACS, he displayed contempt and outright hostility toward Liberia.

From his youth, Delany learned quickly that being a black person in the United States was difficult. He was born into freedom to Pati and Samuel Delany in 1812 in Charles Town, West Virginia (a part of Virginia at the time). Pati's parents originated from Angola and her husband's father was a native of the Gola Tribe from present day Liberia[10] They were brought to America as slaves. The family later purchased freedom.

Pati was literate and decided to teach her children at home, despite the anti-black education law of Virginia. The government issued her a citation for violating the prohibition.[11] She acted quickly and took her family to Chambersburg, Pennsylvania, out of the reach of the Virginian authorities. Young Delany took note of the provocation. Three other incidents occurred to radicalize him, as he grew older. First, he barely escaped death in Ohio when a white mob attempted to chase him out of town. He and a companion hastily retreated to a hotel, while the mob built a bonfire outside the building. The manager stopped the crowd from entering the building. Delany later escaped town but addressed the experience as follows: "Then came the most horrible howling and yelling, cursing and blasphemy, every disparaging, reproachful, degrading, vile and vulgar epithet that could be conceived by the most vitiated imaginations, which bedlam of shocking disregard was kept up from nine until one o'clock at night . . ."[12]

In 1850, Delany matriculated to Harvard Medical School to study, along with three other African Americans. The faculty seemed enthusiastic about their enrollment. However, before they settled in, a large number of Anglo students rose in opposition and objected to the presence of blacks in the school. They passed a motion that read: "Resolved: That we have no objection to the education and evaluation of blacks but do decidedly remonstrate against their presence in college with us." The Dean of the College, Oliver Wendell Holmes, caved in and ejected Delany and the other black students out of the college.

Also in 1850, the government passed the Fugitive Slave Act, mandating the capture and return of runaway slaves. Blacks were affected

---

10    Frank A. Rollins, *Life and Public Services of Martin R. Delany,* 1883, reprint 1969, Arno Press, pp. 14-17, accessed 21 February 2011

11    http://www.post-gazette.com/pg/11037/1123210-51.stm#ixzz1 G3KoZeas (accessed June 4, 2011).

12    Martin Robison Delany and Robert Steven Levine, *Martin R. Delany: A Documentary Reader* (NC: UNC Press, 2003), 107.

by the Act, resulting to the re-enslavement of some freedmen. This legislation outraged Delany, leading to his self-exile in Canada in 1856 until after the Civil War. Thereafter, he became an advocate for emigration outside of the United States.

In his book, *The Condition, Elevation, Emigration and Destiny of the Colored People of the United States*, Delany declared, "Let no visionary nonsense about habeas corpus, or a fair trial, deceive us; there are no such rights granted in this bill . . . There is no earthly chance, no hope under heaven for the colored person.[13]

## Delany's Emigration Initiatives

Delany became a strong supporter for emigration and was willing to find a place outside of the United States—anywhere but Liberia. Most blacks opposed going to Liberia because it was associated with the American Colonization Society. Discussions about Liberia generated angry responses from some blacks. Delany himself referred to the First African Republic as a mockery and "burlesque on government. He considered the ACS to be . . . one of the most arrant enemies of the colored man."[14]

Yet, African Americans had to face the same facts as members of the ACS did, that whites were in opposition to the presence of freemen in America. Blacks could only realize their full capability and command respect outside of the United States, but that was a hard reality, especially coming from whites and slaveholders.

Instead of Liberia Delany favored the Caribbean islands, Canada, and Central America, or elsewhere in Africa, as a last result. He listed a few reasons for his dislike of the First African Republic. Among other things, the country's location was poorly chosen (6th of latitude and North of the equator) and was unhealthy. Secondly, the country was founded by slaveholders who had evil motives to get rid of blacks, and the origin being sufficient to justify us in impugning the motives. Besides, "it is not an independent republic . . . but a poor miserable mockery—a burlesque on a government."[15]

---

[13]   Delany, 107.

[14]   Alphonso Pinkney Red Black and Green: Black Nationalism in the United States (London: Syndics Cambridge University Press, 1976), 24.

[15]   Ibid, 24.

On second thought, Delany said there was a possibility of Liberia succeeding, however, that was not going to change his mind. He did not care about the end result but the process, the "motives of the slaveholders."

General Martin decided to visit the Slave Coast (Nigeria) to negotiate for settlements. Rev. Ralph Gurley invited him to Liberia, and the ACS would defray the cost. Delany objected to a free passage on an ACS boat. However, he was unable to raise enough funds. He refused to accept donations from whites. The unfavorable condition humbled him to take a small financial support from the ACS "and its close cousin, the African Civilization Society."[16] He had to ride in a boat flying the Liberian flag and owned by three Liberian businessmen, Messrs. Hon. John D. Johnson, Joseph Turpin, and Dr. Dunbar.[17]

Delany made it to Liberia, the country he had vilified for more than two decades, before he ever laid eye on the former ACS Colony on July 10, 1859, he arrived in Monrovia, a town named in honor of former U.S. President and slaveholder, James Monroe.[18] It was enthralling when Liberia's critic-in-chief arrived in the city. The news of the advent to these shores of this far-famed champion for the elevation of colored men in the United States, and this great antagonist to the American Colonization Society, spread throughout the country of Montserrado with astonishing rapidity, and persons from all parts of the county came to Monrovia to see this great man.[19]

Once in Liberia, Delany met President Stephen A. Benson and other government officials. He was mesmerized and emotionally overwhelmed by the progress the country had made. Delany stayed until September 5, before leaving for Yoruba land (Nigeria).

Delany's plan for settling freed blacks in Nigeria did not materialize. Notwithstanding, in 1877, he helped to transport 206 emigrants from the United States to Liberia.[20]

After the Civil War, General Delany joined the Freemen Bureau to help other blacks. While in service for the United States government, he encouraged many blacks to immigrate to Liberia.

In a speech to celebrate 20 years of perseverance for civil liberty for blacks, Fredrick Douglass said:

---

[16]   Delany, 332.
[17]   Ibid, 332.
[18]   Ibid.
[19]   Delany, 333.
[20]   Wilson Jeremiah Moses, *Classical Black Nationalism: From the American Revolution to Marcus Garvey* (NY: New York University Press, 1996), 161.

> Nothing has occurred in these 20 years which has dimmed my
> hopes or caused me to doubt that the emancipated people of
> this country will avail themselves of their opportunities and by
> enterprise, industry, invention, discovery and manly character,
> vindicate the confidence of their friends and put to shame the
> gloomy predictions of all their enemies.[21]

Other abolitionists in the gathering rose to toast to the future of
blacks in America. Martin Delany stood up, raised his glass, and asked for
a toast to the future success of the Republic of Liberia.[22]

These few examples show that blacks' opposition was largely based on
a conspiracy theory that the ACS planned to remove "only freedmen" and
abandoned the slaves to fend for themselves. In practice, the organization
offered free passage to freedmen who wanted to immigrate. In addition,
it induced slaveholders to set their slaves free for repatriation. This did
not mean that slaveholders could not manumit their slaves for settlement
elsewhere. Congressman John Randolph or Roanoke, who was an original
founder of the ACS, set all his slaves free and relocated them in the free
state of Illinois. Edward Coles freed his slaves also in 1819 and settled
them in Illinois. Moreover, the ACS paid slave owners for emancipation, if
the free slaves chose to relocate to Liberia.[23]

There are some instances when individuals sued their masters for
attempting to send them to Liberia in exchange for freedom. It is not
certain if any of these cases ever involved the ACS directly. It is also
important to note that some emigrants chose to return to America
because they were not happy in Liberia.

It must be said emphatically that slaves were entitled to unconditional
freedom, including the means to integrate in a freed society, whether in
the United States or elsewhere. Under normal circumstances, offering
freedom in exchange for repatriation to Liberia was uncivil. On the
other hand, the era of slavery was not a normal time for blacks. In view
of that reality, it was not uncommon for slaves to be offered freedom in
exchange for something they might not have volunteered to do, under
normal circumstances. For instance, slaves were offered freedom if they
chose the Christian faith and were baptized, irrespective of their religious
backgrounds. They were also promised freedom if they agreed to fight in

---

[21]   Delany, 459.

[22]   Mark Roth, *Martin Delany, Father of Black Nationalism,* February 06, 2011 (accessed
       March 4, 2012) http://old.post-gazette.com/pg/11037/1123210-51.stm.

[23]   http://www.newworldencyclopedia.org/ entry/American_ Colonization (accessed
       February 18, 2012).

American battles. Certainly, going to Liberia could not have been worse than dying on a battlefield in the South where blacks lost their humanity and were considered a mere thing.

Nearly 10% of the Union Army was black and 40,000 died, excluding 30,000 incapacitated or wounded men. A great number of the black warriors were freedmen. Slaves who signed up to fight in exchange for freedom died—their dreams were never realized.

William Garrison and most abolitionists approved the enlistment of blacks in the civil war, with slaveholding officers. Garrison did not denounce blacks for cooperating with the racist white officers. Rather, he vilified the ACS for granting membership to slaveholders, while disparaging the founding Liberia.

Arguably, life for blacks after the Civil War was "worse than slavery."[24] For a few years, though, the world of free forced labor seemed to be a thing of the past. For the first time, the U.S. government extended citizenship to blacks born in the United States, according to the Fourteenth Amendment. However, at best, former slaves became second class citizens, with a tantalizing hope that faded away quickly.

Southern whites erected legal obstacles that kept blacks from voting. Although blacks were denied educational opportunities in slavery, they were required to be able to read and write to vote. After 1863, there was a renewed interest to migrate from America. About 1000 African Americans chose Liberia over the United States, and the ACS, which declared bankruptcy in 1848, improved its standing among blacks. They denounced America for their enlistment to fight in a war that left them impoverished and without civil rights or citizenship.

There were laws against enlisting blacks in the army, and some of those dated as far back as 1790. Later, when enlistment became necessary, blacks were not allowed to carry guns, but they were promised freedom after the war. 40,000 did not live to enjoy the freedom they fought to achieve.

> In addition to the perils of war faced by all Civil War soldiers, black soldiers faced additional problems stemming from racial prejudice. Racial discrimination was prevalent even in the North, and discriminatory practices permeated the U.S. military. Segregated units were formed with black enlisted men and typically commanded by white officers and black noncommissioned officers. The 54th Massachusetts was

---

[24]   Leon F. Litwack, *Been in the Storm So Long: The Aftermath of Slavery* (NY: Random House, 1980), 290.

commanded by Robert Shaw and the 1st South Carolina by Thomas Wentworth Higginson—both white. Black soldiers were initially paid $10 per month from which $3 was automatically deducted for clothing, resulting in a net pay of $7. In contrast, white soldiers received $13 per month from which no clothing allowance was drawn.[25]

This was not the freedom black soldiers risked their lives for. Therefore, irrespective of the motives, racist or benevolent, repatriating blacks to the continent from which their ancestors were violently removed was a noble endeavor.

[25] Black Civil War, http://thomaslegioncherokee.tripod.com /black_civil_war_ soldiers_black_civil_war _soldier_civil_war_blacks_in_the_civil_war.html

# CHAPTER XII

# THE GRAIN COAST BEFORE 1800

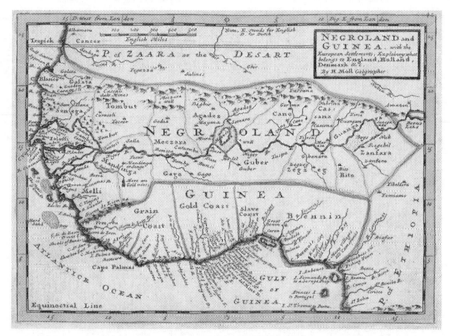

*Negroland and Guinea with the European Settlements*

Hanno of Carthage (modern day Tunisia) provided some of the earliest written accounts about the coast of West Africa. In 520 B.C., he recorded his travel down the coast of West Africa. The convoy included 30,000 men and women in sixty ships.[1] Hanno wrote that he met men who were as fast on their feet as horses, and the interpreters said the hairy people were called gorillae. The voyagers attempted to capture some of the so

---

[1]    http://ancienthistory.about.com/od/africangeographers/a/Hanno.htm (accessed February 18, 2012).

called stone-throwing men, but they escaped. Three of the hairy women were captured but attempt to take them to Carthage as evidence of the exploration failed. They fought fiercely, biting and tearing the flesh off their captors. The crew killed and flayed their captives and took the stripped skins with them for display in Carthage.[2]

Hanno related the drama as follows:

> In the recess of this bay there was an island, like the former one, having a lake, in which there was another island, full of savage men. There were women, too, in even greater number. They had hairy bodies, and the interpreters called them Gorillae. When we pursued them we were unable to take any of the men; for they had all escaped, by climbing the steep places and defending themselves with stones; but we took three of the women, who bit and scratched their leaders, and would not follow us. So we killed them and flayed them, and brought their skins to Carthage. For we did not voyage further, provisions failing us.[3]

Debates about the hairy creatures' real identity have not resolved the mystery. Some historians argue that what Honno saw were real gorillas, while others say the swift moving hairy humans may have been pygmies.

## European Explorers in Africa

In 1364, the Europeans set out for West Africa. The coastal area was called the *Grain Coast*, but other explorers called the region *Malagueta Pepper Coast*.[4] The Normans arrived and built trading centers in Sinoe and Bassa, in present day Liberia. Nearly 100 years later, Pedro de Cintra arrived from Portugal. He named a few physical features and drainages, including Cape Mount, Cape Mesurado, Cape Palmas, St. Paul, St. John, Cavalla, Cestos, and Junct Rivers. He also named Bulombel "Sierra Leone," which means mountain of lion. While on the West African coast,

---

2    Douglas Brooke Wheelton Sladen, Ethel M. Stevens, Joseph I. Spadafora Whitaker, *Hanno and Tunis: the Old and New Gates of The Orient.* (London: Hutchinson and Company, 1906).

3    *The Voyage of Hanno,* http://www.metrum.org/mapping/hanno.htm(accessed January 15, 2014).

4    The coastline from Sierra Leone and Ivory Coast was called Malagueta Coast or Pepper Coast. The Malaueta Pepper was used for spices. "Grains of Paradise" became a preferred name for the English and Dutch explorers for the same product.

Pedro captured a man, as evidence of his visit to the region. He carried the native back with him to Portugal.

King Alphonso sponsored the trip and was elated when Pedro returned with a specimen of a man from the last country visited "by force or by love." The captive met a black slave woman in Lisbon and they seemed to have been able to communicate with each other. However, the Portuguese did not learn much from the African man, except that there were unicorns in Liberia.

In 1626, Belgian geographer Levinus Hulsius compiled the work of other navigators to the Grain Coast. He published the first map of the West African coast. It included names of places visited on the coast such as Sinoe, Cape Palmas, and Grand Bassa. Another Dutchman, Olfert Dapper, published a book in 1668 that described the social life of the people in the region. He noted that they lived in kingdoms between the Mano River and Cape Mesurado, and identified two of those kingdoms as Quoja and Falgia, occupied by the Vai and Kru. The third kingdom was in the north, called the Mandingo Kingdom, which was ruled by King Mandi Manou.

The Chevalier des Marchais of France visited the Grain Coast in 1724-1725. King Peter offered him Bushrod Island to grow sugar cane and possibly establish a colony.[5] Instead of taking the offer, the overture was referred to the Senegal Company. It also declined to establish any settlements at the site where the capital of Liberia is currently located.

According to the French traveler, the natives of the area practiced human sacrifices. To some extent, the slave trade diminished the tradition, when headmen found out their captives could be sold in exchange for needed commodities. The Chevalier estimated that about 2000 slaves were being sold off the Grain Coast annually.

Chattel slavery on the West Coast of Africa was largely induced by European explorers, and eventually it became a common business practice among African chiefs. European bought slaves or kidnapped them from the coast. The following narrative reveals the craftiness of the traders, according to one account:

> I am known to sail up a river with some large craft. Arriving in a town, I give some speech to get their attention. I would open a puncheon or two of rum and I would invite the people to sit around and drink. At night when I have got them all

---

5    Johnson & Stanfield, 30.

thoroughly drunk, I would give the signal to my people who are waiting in the craft to secure all the party ready to be sold.[6]

In 1562, Captain John Hawkins became the first Englishman to engage in commercial slave trading in West Africa. After his successful voyage, Queen Elizabeth "sent for him when she expressed her concern lest any of the African Negroes should be carried off without their free consent which she declared would be detestable and would call down the vengeance of heaven upon the undertakers."[7] Hawkins expressed regrets and assured the Queen he would comply, but he never kept his promise. "Here began the horrid practice of forcing the Africans into slavery; an injustice and barbarity which, so sure as there is vengeance in heaven for the worst of crimes, will sometime be the destruction of all who act or who encourage it."

Hawkins' father, William Hawkins, visited the Guinea Coast in 1530 and purchased slaves. Nearly thirty two years later, his son went to Africa with three ships and 100 crewmen. They took about 300 slaves and sold them for profit to Santo Domingo. Hawkins and his men returned again in1562, 1564, and 1567 to trade for slaves in the Gallinas territory, along the coast of West Africa.[8] On his second voyage, he had four armed ships, the largest named *Jesus*, a vessel of seven hundred tons, and a force of one hundred and seventy men. The Captain took nearly 800 slaves on the three voyages, mostly in violent conflicts with the natives. The chiefs were forced to provide slaves. Those who refused had their villages burned, along with the people. Every conceivable form of inducement was used to turn tribes against each other. Eventually, manufactured goods from Europe were traded for slaves, instead of ivory, rice, spices, and other African goods, as before. Slaves became another medium of exchange.

Captain Hawkins was a Christian. Yet, he did not believe his cruelty to Africans was wrong, because they were not Christians. Most Europeans felt it was a religious duty to enslave non-Christians whom they called *infidel or pagan*. As a result, after raiding villages, Hawkins would host religious services, admonishing his men to "serve God daily, love one another, preserve their virtues, beware of fire, and keep good company."[9]

---

[6]    Samuel R. Watkins, *Liberia Communication* (Indiana: Authorhouse, 2007), 4.

[7]    The English's first trade to the coast of Guinea: *Violently carry off some of the Negro,* http://www.gutenberg.org /files/11489/11489-h/11489-h.htm *(accessed January 2, 2014).*

[8]    Sir Harry Hamilton Johnston, *The Negro in the New World* (New York: Macmillan Company, 1910).

[9]    Sir Admiral John Hawkins, http://www.findagrave.com/cgi-bin/fg.cgi?page=gr&GRid=80478739 (accessed February 12, 2014).

The Cubans built a slave trading station in western Liberia. Pedro Blanco had a contract to supply 5000 slaves for seven years, from 1822 to 1839. The destination was Cuba, South Carolina, Georgia, the Bahamas, and Brazil.[10] His chief lieutenant was a French seaman called Theodore Canot. He joined the Spanish, Portuguese, American, and Russian vessels to transport slaves, although British and French cruisers intercepted a large number of the ships.

To protect his illegal trade, Blanco hired Africans as watchmen, spies, and policemen. "From a hundred look-outs on the Gallinas beach and the islands of the lagoon these men, trained to use telescopes, watched the horizon for the arrival of British cruisers."[11]

The center of Blanco's slave activities was western Liberia, especially in the Gallinas territory. Those affected were largely the Mende, Gola, Lorma, Vai, and Kissi tribes. The Kru resisted slavery more sternly than all other tribes in Liberia. Only few of them were captured or sold, but they also served as middlemen for slave traders.

The American Colonization Society shutdown the Gallinas slave stations by 1847, with help from the British, eight years after Pedro Blanco retired. He returned home but lost a large sum of money in political battles with the Cuban government. As a wealthy man, he left for Genoa and spent the rest of his life quietly on the Italian Riviera.

---

[10]    Johnston, 41.
[11]    Ibid.

# CHAPTER XIII

# PEOPLING OF THE GRAIN COAST

Pedro de Cintra first named what is now Liberia the Grain Coast during his historic visit in 1461. The first immigrants to settle in the region were indigenous Africans who migrated from other parts of Africa to escape ethnic, political, or religious violence.

Migration was common after the disintegration of the Ancient Sudanic Empires of Ghana, Mali, and Songhai. Some of the tribes pushed toward the coast to gain access to the sea for trade and commerce with Europeans.

When the Kingdom of Ghana fell in 1076 to the Almoravids (Muslim invaders), an Islamic government replaced the Negro leadership. Before the conquest, King Bassi ruled over the capital of Ghana, Kumbi-Salem, which was divided into two quarters. The Muslims lived in one section and non-Muslim Negroes lived in another. Thus, the two groups were kept apart and Kumbi-Salem flourished. This changed gradually when the Almoravids took over control. A poll tax and Islamic religious rituals were imposed on all inhabitants, including non-Muslims. The tedious rituals required unquestionable regimented conformity, which the Negroes detested. They battled constantly to gain control or extricate themselves, while others left to start a new life elsewhere in Africa.

The desiccation of the Sahara Desert also created a hostile environment for agriculture and agrarian life that caused a wave of movement of people toward the north or south of the Sahara. Other migrants ended up on the Grain Coast, currently Liberia. Those who arrived on the coast met an indigenous group of people whose identity is still unknown to historians. The eminent Liberian historian, Abayomi Karnga, called them Pygmies.[1] The mysterious little people are known

---

[1]    Ellen Johnson Sirleaf, *The Child Will Be Great: Memoir of a Remarkable Life by Africa's First Woman President* (NY: HarperCollins Publishers, 2009).

locally as *jinna*.[2] They were described as food gatherers who lived in caves and hollow of trees. The Gola arrived in the region between 1000-1400 and engaged in various wars for settlements. The newcomers settled primarily in the Kongba Kingdom. Others sparsely relocated elsewhere.

The Almoravids sacked the Empire of Ghana in 1076, putting the kingdom in Muslim control. Many ethnic groups migrated over time to avoid the intertribal conflicts and rigid Islamic rituals that were imposed on all the inhabitants. Moreover, the Sahara Desert continued to desiccate, thus making the region increasingly uninhabitable, when farmlands became scarce.

The Gola engaged the Islamic rulers in three of the Kumbi wars.[3] After losing the third battle, the ethnic group headed for the West African Coast, through the region now called Sierra Leone. Battles with the Mende in Sierra Leone forced the Gola to settle in Liberia. A series of battles with the Gbandi and Lorma in the hinterland pushed them further towards the coast, which resulted into constant conflicts with the Dei Tribe, until the Liberian government intervened, after 1822.

No one knows what happened to the legendary pygmies the Gola first met in the region. They died or migrated to other parts of Africa. Although there is no evidence that pygmies ever inhabited the country, stories of the little people are numerous in Liberian folklores and are loved by both children and adults.

Modern day Liberia is ethnically diverse, with sixteen major ethnic groups, divided in three linguistic classifications as follows: Mel (tribes of the Gola and Kissi), Kru (including Bassa, Bella, Dei, Grebo, Krahn, Kru) and Mande (Bandi, Gio, Kpelle, Loma, Mandingo, Mano, Mende, and Vai).[4]

The Kpelle, Gio, Mano, and Vai groups migrated from the Empire of Mali at different intervals. They escaped political upheavals and chose to migrate to West Africa for better living conditions.

The Vai arrived in 1500, through Sierra Leone, a nation outside the northwestern boarder of Liberia. On arrival, they engaged the Gola in series of battles and conquered the western end of the country, now Cape Mount. They settled on the coast to gain access to the sea for salt and trading opportunities with the Europeans.

---

[2]   Tarnue Carver Johnson, *Education and Social Change in Liberia: New Perspectives for the 21st Century* (Indianna: Authorhouse, 2004).

[3]   http://www.liberianonline.com/modules.php?name=Content&pa=showpage&pid=74 (accessed July 20, 2011).

[4]   http://www.liberiapastandpresent.org/index.html (accessed January6, 2014).

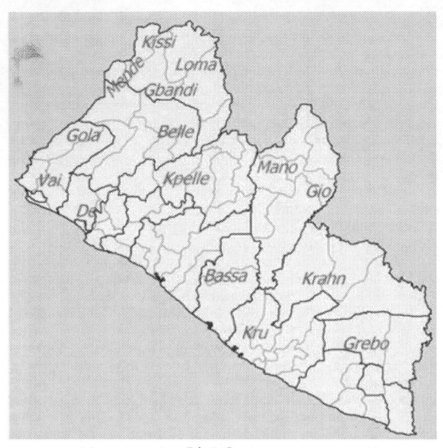

*Ethnic Groups*

The Vai language was the first tribal language in Liberia to have its own script. Momolu Duwalu Bukele invented the script in 1833, after being inspired in a dream to create a writing system for his people. The scripts, written from right to left, are unique and not based on Latin characters. While elderly Vai men mostly use the writing, it is not widely used in the country. It was never adapted in the general school curriculum, as a required course. However, during World War I, German intelligent officers used the Vai script to transmit secret information codes in their command units.[5]

The Kru (including Bassa, Dei, and Belle) arrived in the 1550s from the Ivory Coast. The Krahn emerged from intermarriage between the

---

5    Patricia Levy and Michael Spilling, *Cultures of the world*: Liberia (Cavendish, Marshall Corporation, 2008).

Bassa and Dei or Belle. The Gbandi, Lorma, and Mende arrived about 1530. They descended from the military-like Mane. They conquered the Sape and Sherbro Islanders from 1515-1530. Shortly before 1600, the Kpelle arrived and settled in Jorquelli in present day Bong County. Also about the same time, the Kissi arrived from Upper Niger and eventually settled south of the Madonah River in the early 1700s. The Grebo arrived from the Ivory Coast in two waves and settled near the Cavalla River in 1700. Other arrivals at the same time were the Gio and Mano.

About the 17th century, the Mandingos began to arrive in Liberia. They were Muslims and descendants of the Mende of West Africa. They too originated from the Western Sudanic Empire of Mali, under King Sundiata Keita. Askia Mohammed conquered the Empire in the sixteenth century, sparking a migration of many ethnic groups to other parts of Africa.

Almost all the tribes that settled on the Grain Coast originated from other parts of Africa. They migrated to escape political violence, draught, or to engage in trade and commerce with the Europeans on the West African coast.

All tribes had to fight their way to take possession of the lands they occupied. It was a hostile experience for both the invading and invaded tribes. The slaughter was brutal for the indigenous because new-comers were more equipped with better weapons. They conquered and imposed coexistence. In this light, everyone travelled to the region in search of freedom. The Grain Coast provided relief, and the love of liberty became the rallying cry for all ethnic groups.

The last major group to migrate to the Grain Coast in search of liberty was black immigrants from the United States. They became known as the Americo-Liberians. They were not a homogeneous group. Generally, they can be divided into three groups: freed slaves from the U.S.A, freed slaves from the Caribbean Islands (West Indies), and recaptured slaves from slave vessels.

The recaptives became known in Liberia as Congo or Congo people because many of them originated from Central Africa, near the Congo River. These immigrants were culturally uprooted. They were torn away from their homelands and set adrift without a country or common language. Eventually, the recaptives were rescued and taken to Liberia and Sierra Leone to live.

# CHAPTER XIV

# THE LIBERIAN COLONY

By the early 19<sup>th</sup> century, most black immigrants had rejected Africa as a possible destination for colonization. The attraction was Haiti, the first black republic in the world. The nation did all it could to entice freedmen and runaway slaves from America.

The Haitian government provided subsidies and farmlands to new arrivals. However, many of the immigrants resented agrarian life and the drudgery of farming, to the disappointment of the citizens and Haitian government.

The concept of a black empire in Haiti faded rather quickly, and most of the settlers returned to the United States. They complained about voodoo, language barriers, and cultural conflicts.[1]

Similar immigration took place in the Caribbean nation of Trinidad, after the 1812 British-American War. The outcome was different. Each person received at least five acres of land initially, and the natives of the country were more hospitable. As a result, the American immigrants integrated and became a part of the Afro-Trinidadian society, which remained predominately as a community of African descent.

Despite the setbacks, the founders of the Liberian Colony had high hopes for the return of Africa's lost sons and daughters to the cradle of their ancestors. On arrival, they were not to engage in polygamy, sorceries, and witchcraft, as some did in Haiti. Rather, the settlers were to serve as civilizing agents, educators, and Christian missionaries to evangelize Africa.[2]

The Society engaged Rev. Samuel Mills to explore the west coast of Africa for a suitable location to settle free slaves from America. Mills contacted his friend, Professor Ebenezer Burgess, to accompany him with a compelling appeal: "My brother, can we engage in a nobler effort? We

---

[1]   Yacovone, 35; http://www.inmotionaame.org/migrations/ topic.cfm;jsessionid= f830190383132630685 6494? migration=4&topic=5&bhcp=1 (accessed June 9, 2011).

[2]   *African Repository*, Vol. XLIII, 1872.

go to make freemen of slaves. We go to lay the foundation of a free and independent empire on the coast of poor degraded Africa."[3]

The two men left the United States on November 16, 1817, and went by way of England to get more information and endorsement for settlements on the coast of Africa.[4] On arrival in Sierra Leone on March 22, 1818, they contacted John Kizell on the March 27. John was a repatriated African Baptist minister from the United States. He took Mills and party to the disputed Island of Sherbro to negotiate for land. The party was well received by the natives, with an initial assurance that black Americans would be welcome to return to the land of their ancestry. The Americans were ecstatic and hoped to take the good report to the American Colonization Society. Unfortunately, Rev. Mills died and was buried at sea. Burgess made it home safely to present the report to the ACS.

*Old Map of Liberia*

---

3    Ibid, 117.
4    Benjamin Griffith Brawley, *A social history of the American Negro* (NY: McMillian Company, 1921).

John Kizell was an indigenous African. He had been kidnapped and taken to South Carolina three years before the American War of Independence. At twelve years old, the lad was snatched from his uncle's village in Sherbro, while visiting some relatives. Warriors overran the village, slaughtered some villagers, and took the rest as captives, including Kizell.

Three years after his arrival to America, the Revolutionary War began. The boy was about fifteen years old at the time, but his desire for freedom turned him against the Americans. He joined the British who promised freedom to slaves who defected. After the war, he was taken to Nova Scotia. He later joined other blacks to be transported to Sierra Leone, in 1787.

Kizell became a successful businessman and preacher in Sierra Leone. He founded a small colony for freedmen. Based on the horrible experiences of American blacks in the United States, John was hopeful that they would return to Africa in huge numbers. "Africa is the land of the black men," he said, "and to Africa they must, and will come." However, he was mindful of those who would not: "Some would not be governed by white men, and some would not be governed by black men, and some would not be governed by mulattoes; but the truth was they did not want to be governed by anybody."[5]

The Americans had high admiration for the African preacher. Governor Edward Columbine of Sierra Leone said John was not only dependable and trustworthy, but had extensive knowledge about the natives and traders of the region. The Governor appointed him as envoy in the hinterland to dissuade the African chiefs from cooperating with slave traders.[6]

Once in Sierra Leone, Mills and Burgess befriended John Kizell and found his advice to be immensely useful. Before his death, Mills recorded in his private journal, "No man in Africa could probably be useful to the colonization society as John Kizell."[7]

In response to a letter from Bushrod Washington, President of the ACS, Kizell replied: "I thank you for the first and will take care of the last. Africa is wide and long—Africa is fertile and healthy—Africa is afflicted— "Rachel mourneth for her children," and "will not be comforted till they come home."[8] [Sic]

---

[5]   Ibid, 175.

[6]   James Sidbury, *Becoming African In America: The African American* (New York: Oxford University Press, 2007), 171,

[7]   Sidbury, 172.

[8]   *Address of the Board of Managers of the American Colonization Society to Auxiliary Society and the People of the United States* (Pennsylvania: Davis and Force, 1820).

Notwithstanding, the Americans found out that, though the Sierra Leonean government was hospitable, the governor did not want an American colony near Sierra Leone. The intent was to avoid trade and commerce competition between the two colonies.[9] On the other hand, the African eminent historian, Dr. Amos Beyan, has contended in his book, *African American Settlements in West Africa* that John Kizell was deceptive and worked to undermine the mission of the settlers. He writes, "Kizell's misleading statement that the chiefs around Sherbro Island area had approved the establishment of the proposed American colony on the island was accepted at the face value by Mills and Burgess."[10] The reason for Kizell's apprehension, according to Dr. Beyan, was fear of competition. He added, "Kizell decided to turn wholeheartedly against earlier reluctant commitment to the establishment of an American colony on Sherbro Island. He successfully persuaded the Sherbro chiefs, for example, to reject the request by the American to establish a settlement in the area."[11]

However, the Americans blamed the government of Sierra Leone and local slave traders for the troubles: "We expect that all who are engaged in the slave trade at the Galenars, both white and natives, will try to do us all the harm they can, by setting the chiefs against us. They well know, if we get foot hold, that it will be against the slave trade."[12]

Rev. Coker had this to say about Kizell: "He is considered by the natives a head-man, and his influence is great. He has built a small meeting house in his town . . . He is no friend to division among us. He wishes Mr. Bacon, himself, and me, to be closely united, and to keep our respective societies, as much like one as possible."

Nevertheless, the chiefs expressed a genuine concern about selling land to the Americans for fear that the whites would declare war and take additional land by force. The natives used Sierra Leone for an example, which had a white governor. Tribal people were forced out of their land at gunpoint. Moreover, the natives told Mills, in the presence of John Kizell, that they had another problem with the return of the former slaves, and that was revenge. They dreaded the thought of the possibility for retribution from the immigrants for being sold into slavery by their ancestors. Already, before Mills-Burgess' arrival, a former slave from Europe returned and was angry for being sold initially. He threatened to kill anyone who would ever dare to lay hands on any of his relatives again.

9    http://www.westporthistory.com/Lowther_Kevin.pdf. Accessed January 13, 2012.

10   Amos Beyan, *African American Settlements in West Africa* (New York: Palgrave Macmillan, 2005), 43.

11   Ibid, 43.

12   Julius H. Bailey, *Race Patriotism: Protest and Print Culture in the A.M.E. Church* (Knoxville: University of Tennessee Press, 2012), 12.

After that incident, the chiefs wondered what it would be like to build a settlement, with many free slaves from America who might turn on the natives in revenge.

John Kizell encouraged the chiefs to sell some land to the Americans, because "they had good intention." He informed them of the benefits of having schools, agricultural programs, and trading partners. After a visit to another village, he wrote to the Sierra Leonean governor and said:

> I went to take a walk with one of my boys and was surprised to see so many coffee trees some places being entirely covered with them. I was concerned to think that there was no man to be found who had the welfare of this country and people at heart to observe what is in it and what it will produce instead of taking the natives and carrying them to European islands to raise coffee which is the natural plant of Africa.[13]

According to the Mills-Burgess Report, the visit to Africa was promising. Besides being cautiously but warmly received in Sierra Leone, the natives were willing to provide lands for black settlements, if the payment was proper.[14] However, it was noted that the Sierra Leonean government was uneasy about having an American colony next to its colony.[15]

In the United States, however, most blacks objected to the back-to-Africa scheme. They claimed a de facto citizenship to America and hoped for integration. However, others lost hope of ever gaining racial equality with white people. Some of those who lost hope repatriated with Paul Cuffe in 1811 and 1816 and settled in Sierra Leone, before the colony of Liberia was established.

The ACS sent out its first eighty eight black settlers in 1820 on the *Elizabeth,* escorted by the *USS Cyane*, a 32-gun warship. This was nearly two years after the natives in Sherbro declared their desire to welcome the former slaves for resettlement, if the price was right. However, by the time the settlers arrived, the chiefs changed their initial plan to sell land to the immigrants.

The Americans believed slave traders influenced the natives. On arrival, Coker recorded that there were about 300 slave ships along the

---

[13]  Wilson Armistead, *A Tribute for the Negro: Being a Vindication of the Moral, Intellectual, and Religious Capabilities* (Manchester: William Irwin, 1848), 349.

[14]  http://www.fullbooks.com/History-of-Liberia.html (accessed March1, 2012).

[15]  Ibid.

coast.[16] Many of the ships were American but disguised as Spanish vessels. The traffickers had the interest and the resources to discourage antislavery activities or construction of abolitionist settlements along the Grain Coast.

After the death of Rev. Mills on June 16, 1818, John Kizell did not hear from the Americans again until the arrival of the *Elizabeth*, in 1820. The ship finally anchored at Kizell's trading haven, after six weeks of travelling. The Americans had not purchased any land before they arrived. Their host, Rev. Kizell, bought a piece of land and built a small settlement, with huts at Sherbro as temporary shelters for the Americans.[17]

In a few months, torrential rainfall proved deadly. Forty-nine of the immigrants and all the agents died of yellow fever. Those that survived retreated to Sierra Leone and remained there until the *Nautilus* arrived. It carried 28 more immigrants. On board the ship were two government agents, Jonathan B. Winn and Ephraim Bacon; Joseph R. Andrus and Christian Wiltberger represented the ACS. This time, the Nautilus went past Sherbro Island to Cape Mesurado (Montserrado), but again, the natives refused to sell land to the Americans. Disappointed with the turn of events, Winn opted and returned to the United States.

When the immigrants arrived in 1822, the natives refused to accommodate them. This must have been a great surprise, because the Mills-Burgess Report had alleged otherwise. Apparently, something happened to disengage the natives from earlier commitment to welcome the Americans. The settlers were prohibited from even landing on the island that later became the country of Liberia. The chiefs demanded the pioneers to return to Sierra Leone.[18]

The chiefs refused to trade or offer free lands for settlements. Though it was not customary to sell community properties, it was usual for ethnic peoples to accommodate strangers by providing lands for farming or community building. The unfortunate encounter may have been the work of slave traders. Their influence extended over a great portion of the West African coast. It was unlikely that they could welcome antislavery settlements in the region.

The settlers did not return to Sierra Leone immediately, as the chiefs had demanded. A mulatto slave dealer, John S. Mills, came to their rescue. Cape Mesurado comprised two small islands, and the chiefs had already sold one portion to the slave trader for commercial trading. When the

---

16      Coker, 6.

17      Yarema, 35.

18      Jehudi Ashmun, *History of the American Colony in Liberia: From December 821 to 1823* (Washington City: Way and Gideon, 1826).

chiefs refused to sell the other piece of land or allow the immigrants to disembark, he offered a temporary accommodation to the settlers on his island.[19] He had several houses, mostly used as slave depots. Many of the captives were strangers far from other parts of the region and felt like strangers on the coast, while they waited to be sold to plantation owners in the Americas.

Finally, when the immigrants succeeded in purchasing the land, Mills sold his piece of land to the settlers.[20] For a while, he even worked briefly as secretary for the Colony and helped the agents negotiate land deals with the natives. However, in few weeks as colonial secretary, Mills left and returned to slave trading.

President James Monroe decided to step up the pressure on the African chiefs. He sent a new agent, Dr. Eli Ayres, to secure a place for the recaptives and free slaves from the United States. A naval armed schooner, the *Alligator*, under the command of Lieutenant Robert F. Stockton of the U. S. Navy, accompanied the expedition.[21]

Once in Sierra Leone, Dr. Ayres and Stockton were warned by Governor George McCarthy about the difficulties in dealing with the coastal tribes. They were wholly engaged in trading with the Europeans and serving as intermediaries. The Governor cautioned that it was practically impossible to obtain the land peacefully because:

> They (natives) are the most ferocious, warlike, and depraved
> of all the tribes on the coast . . . They were constantly engaged
> in wars of rapine and invasion with the feeble nations of the
> interior, from whom the captives were obtained with which
> they supplied the slave-ships. Many efforts had been made
> during the previous century, both by the British, French, and
> Portuguese, to purchase this country from the chiefs and head-
> men; but they had uniformly refused to negotiate for a sale of
> any part of it, or listen to any propositions for such a purpose
> from any quarter.[22]

With the cautionary advice, the agents headed toward Cape Montserrado. They resolved to take precaution to gain the trust of the chiefs by not using their own gunboat on the coast. They rented an

---

[19]   Ibid, 9.
[20]   Harvey Newcomb, *Cyclopedia of Missions: Containing Comprehensive New of Missionary Operations Throughout the World* (NY: Charles Scribner, 1856), 517.
[21]   Ashmun, 9.
[22]   Samuel John Bayard, *A sketch of the life of Com. Robert F. Stockton: with an appendix* (New York: Derby and Jackson, 1856), 41.

ordinary commercial boat to create a friendly atmosphere. Stockton talked through interpreters about the possibility of trade and commerce, education, agriculture, and most of all, the benefit of having civilized Africans from America who had many skills to help develop the region. Everything to allure the natives was said, without mentioning the suppression of slavery, not to provoke opposition from the natives and their allies.

The Ayres-Stockton party, beaming with optimism, was pleased with the treatment accorded them by the natives. After the first encounter, Ayres and Stockton felt they had a deal with the African elders finally to secure a place for settlement. During the meeting, a reference to the slave trade or its suppression was intentional omitted to avoid opposition from the benefactors of the illegal trade in the area, especially the Afro-European merchants. A date was set to finalize the discussion or *palaver*, but the chiefs never show up at the appointed meeting site.[23]The Americans, with their Kru interpreter, were surprised. They were told that King Peter and all his men had gone to a village in the interior and left instruction for General Stockton to follow, if he dared to venture.[24]

Stockton and company took the bait. To some extent, King Peter had gained the trust of the Americans as being a candid and honest broker. The General was not convinced that the chiefs deliberately planned to be deceptive, after their first encounter and amicable reception. He blamed the change of events on a mulatto slave trader in the area.[25]

The twenty miles journey was prolonged due to heavy rainfall. The men of the village were indeed surprised to see the white men in a town where Europeans did not generally venture to go. Nevertheless, when the meeting convened, there were about 500 Africans, some dressed as warriors. The mulatto whom Stockton suspected of spreading the rumors appeared in the assembly also. Stockton proceeded to declare his carefully crafted statement of goodwill to the people, without mentioning slavery. While speaking, however, the suspected mulatto slave trader stood up defiantly and told the assembly that the Americans were enemies of slave traders. According to him, they had already captured many slave ships and removed the captives. He urged the chiefs not to listen or cooperate with the abolitionists.

Stockton's next move clearly demonstrated the level of frustration he felt:

---

23    Ibid, 43.
24    Bayard, 43.
25    Ibid, 43.

Stockton instantly, with his clear, ringing tone of voice, commanded silence. The multitude was hushed as if a thunderbolt had fallen among them, and every eye was turned upon the speaker. Deliberately drawing a pistol from his breast and cocking it, he gave it to Dr. Ayres, saying, while he pointed to the mulatto—"Shoot that villain if he opens his lips again!" Then, with the same deliberation, drawing another pistol and leveling it at the head of King Peter, and directing him to be silent until he heard what was to be said, he proceeded to explain the true object of his refusal to execute it, threatening the worst punishment of an angry God if he should fail to perform his agreement.[26]

The sagacious King Peter sat quietly and listened to Stockton make his case for black settlements in the region. In the final analysis, the chiefs committed to comply reluctantly, with the sense of being under duress. A new date was set to meet at the original agreement site to sign the treaty. The pressure paid off for the Americans, at least for a while. A date was set for December 15, 1821. The sale secured a 130 by 40 miles strip of land for about $300.00 along the coast.[27] The actual items included: six muskets, one small barrel of gun powder, six iron bars, ten iron pots, one barrel of beads, two casks of tobacco, twelve knives, twelve forks, twelve spoons, one small barrel of nails, one box of tobacco pipes, three looking glass, four umbrellas, three walking sticks, one box soap, one barrel of rum, four hats, three pairs of shoes, and three pieces of white calico.[28] The following additional payment was required, when the Americans could afford to do so: six iron bars, twelve guns, three barrels of powder, twelve plates, twelve knives, twelve forks, twelve hats, barrels of salt beef, five barrels of salt pork, twelve barrels of ships' biscuits, twelve glass decanters, twelve wine glasses, and five, pairs, of boots . . . in a miscellaneous assortment of trading goods, gunpowder, rum, tobacco, umbrellas, hats, soap, tools, and other things.[29] The treaty was signed by Ayres, Stockton, King Peter, King George, King Zoda, King Long Peter, King Governor, and King Jimmy.[30]

[26]   Ibid, 46.
[27]   Ibid.
[28]   Sir Harry Johnston. *Liberia*. Vol. 1 (London: Hutchinson & Company, 1906), 129.
[29]   Johnston, 129.
[30]   Sarah J. Hale, *Liberia of Mr. Peyton's Experiments* (New York: Harper & Brothers, 1853), 155-156.

After the deal was done, angry natives blamed King Peter for the sale of the land and had him impeached.[31] George, Governor, and most of the native leaders contended that, "The Americans were strangers who had forgot their attachment to the land of their fathers; for if not, why had they not renounced their connexion with white men altogether and placed themselves under the protection of the kings of the country?"[32][Sic]

The two leaders, Peter and Bristol objected to the alienation of the African Americans and argued that they were not strangers. They contended that the "The increased numbers of the Colonists gave them a superiority which would insure their success that they were not a settlement of foreigners and enemies but of their countrymen and friends as was proved by the identity of their colour and therefore had a right to reside in their country." However, King George took a commanding lead in the alliance for war and attempted to coerce other chiefs to comply to the invasion plan. Some followed his lead wholeheartedly; others objected. A few cooperated reluctantly.

> King Peter presuming still to dissent from the general voice of his chiefs was principally thro the influence of George obliged to shut his mouth during all the following deliberations of the assembly. King Bristol returned home. Messengers were then dispatched in every direction to solicit the aid of the neighbour tribes. The king of Junk refused to take any active part in person and sent to assure the Colony of his neutrality but did not prohibit his people from following individually their own inclinations . . . . The war King Tom of little Bassa entirely declined. King Ben of Half C(ape) Mount and his people came into the conspiracy . . . . Ba Caia whose island is overlooked by the settlement was too much agitated by his fears to resolve on any decided course. He tarried at home . . . but many of his people gave themselves to the war. Bromley, Todo, Governor, Konko, Jimmy, Gray, Long Peter, George, and Willy, with their entire force and all king Peter's warriors and the auxiliaries already named were in the last week of October perfectly combined and assembled under arms on Bushrod Island about four miles from the settlement and on the St Paul.[33]

31    Jehudi Ashmun, *History of the American Colony in Liberia from December 1821 to 1823* (W Washington City: Way and Gidean, 1826), 9.
32    Ashmun, 24.
33    Ashmun, 25.

The chiefs disputed the sale of their land and opposed having the settlers as neighbors. In a few days, the Dey, Gola, and Vai, former political rivals, formed an alliance to depose the colony. They were supported by slave traders who opposed the antislavery sentiments of the Americans.[34]

Dr. Eli Ayres appealed to King Sabsu, (aka King Boatswain) from Bopolu. He was the foremost eminent chief in the region. During the 1822 crisis, the King arrived on the coast with a large force to warn the Dey, Gola, and Vai that he would behead anyone who interfered with the Americans. "Having sold your country and accepted payment, you must take the consequences . . . . Let the Americans have their lands immediately. Whoever is not satisfied with my decision, let him tell me so."[35]Turning to the Agents, he said, "I promise you protection. If these people give you further disturbance send for me. And I swear, if they oblige me to come again to quiet them, I will do it by taking their heads from their shoulders, as I did old king George on my last visit to the coast to settle disputes."[36]

Chief Gehtumben who claimed to have been at the treaty signing event blamed a drunken native woman for depriving the chiefs from reclaiming their land.[37] According to the narrative, among the articles of exchanged for the land sale was a barrel of rum. Chief Baguerah's wife, Gbi Bono, was happy about the transaction. She quickly pulled some liquor from the barrel and drank it all. Gehtumben contended, "One drunken woman sold the land to the Americans."

According to tradition, a purchase made with money or other articles could not be reversed, unless the exact medium of exchange was returned to the seller, if the buyer was not satisfied with the exchange. In the case of the initial purchase of Cape Montserrado, the chief's wife had already drunk some of the rum. Although all other items were returned to reclaim the land, the consumed liquor was irretrievable. Chief Boatswain concluded that the deal was irreversible because the chiefs had already accepted payment. The Americans were entitled to their land.

Boatswain learned to read and write, while working on a British ship on the West African coast. That is how he got the *Boatswain* name, which means unlicensed dock worker or trainer. After some years, he returned

---

34    Johnston, 136.
35    Andrew Hull Foote, *African and the American flag* (New York: D. Appleton & Company, 1854), 121.
36    Ashmun, 14.
37    M. Teah Wulah, *Back to Africa: A Liberian Tragedy* (In: Authorhouse, 2009), 201.

home and set up a large slave trading post in the Bopolu area. He was ruthless and sold his victims to slave traders.

Working with the British helped Boatswain to develop appreciation for western culture. Until his death in 1836, he was one of the friendly chiefs the colony could count on.[38]

Unhealthy conditions delayed the arrival of the settlers from Sierra Leone until April 25, 1822, when the immigrants returned. The surviving emigrants of the previous expedition arrived from Sierra Leone and the Liberian colony was officially planted.

## The Colonial Period: 1822-1839

The first seventeen years of the colony marked the early beginning of the Liberian settlements, under the supervision of colonial agents. The period lasted from 1822 to 1839, with eleven agents, including eight white and three black.

Dr. Ali Ayres was the first principal agent of the colony. He and Robert Stockton purchased the first parcel of land from the natives by putting their chiefs under duress. Shortly after the settlement began, Ayres became sick and threatened to leave the settlement.

Although subtle, tension was brewing between the white leaders and settlers over governance and control of the settlement. Ayres decided to retreat to Sierra Leone with the colonists, thus abandoning the colonization scheme, at least temporarily. Elijah Johnson objected and declared, "Two years long have I sought a home; here I have found one; here I remain."[39] This crucial declaration made a difference and determined the survival of the young colony. Johnson remained with the colony. (His son, Hilary Johnson, became President of Liberia from 1884 to1891).[40]

Christian Wiltherger, agent of the ACS, decided to leave the unhealthy lowland area for the highland, but he also contracted fever and returned to the United States with Dr. Ayres. Elijah Johnson took charge of the colony, with eighty inhabitants.

---

[38]   S. E. Holsoe, *The Condo Confederation in Western Liberia* (Liberia Historical Review), III, 1 (1966).

[39]   Johnston, 130.

[40]   http://books.google.com/books?id=P7fA6zZyHc0C&pg=PA26&dq=Hilary+Johnson%2Bliberia&hl= en&sa=X&ei=vua4Uc_NG8fJqgGzx4HABA&ved=0CDwQ6AEwAw#v=onepage&q=Hilary%20Johnson%2Bliberia&f=false (accessed June 12, 2013).

A conflict with the natives was about to break out over construction on the promontory. With only twenty fighting men, the survival of the colony was uncertain. It seemed like an angel appeared in the whirlwind, when a British gunboat appeared on Cape Montserrado, heading to the Gold Coast. The captain heard gunfire in the settlement vicinity and he stopped to inquire. Unwilling to engage in a battle with a British gunboat, the natives decided to retreat. The captain offered support to punish the tribal invaders, if Johnson would give him a piece of land to hoist the British flag. Johnson declined on the grounds that it might be easier to deal with the natives than to put down a British flag. The gunboat, with its crew, sailed away without an incident.

In August of 1822, more supplies arrived from Baltimore on the *Strong*, with 53 immigrants. Liberia's most notable agent, Jehudi Ashmun, was on board. Perhaps, more than any other, he was largely responsible for establishing and expanding the colony. The chiefs called him "The White Devil of Cape Mesurado,"[41] due to his relentless pursuit for land and unpromising stance against slave traders among the natives and colonists. He named the Liberian capital *Christopolis* at first (City of Christ),[42] before it was renamed "Monrovia," by the ACS.

Rev. Lott Carey travelled on the *Nautilus* to Liberia in 1821. He had purchased his family's freedom for $850 eight years earlier.[43]Carey worked closely with Ashmun to expand and provide security for the settlement, which had only forty muskets and one cannon. Ashmun added five guns to the arsenal, which he carried with him from the United States.

Ashmun established a command structure from the thirty five men of fighting age and put the settlement under military law to deal with the security need of the colony. He proceeded to assign military officers at various command posts as follows:[44]

1.  Elijah Johnson became the commissary of stores
2.  R. Simpson . . . . . . . . . . . . . . Commissary of Ordinance
3.  Lott Carey . . . . . . . . . . . . . . Health Officer and Government Inspector
4.  Federick James . . . . . . . . . . . . . . Captain of the Brass Mounted Field piece, assisted by Ralph Newport, M.S. Draper, Williams Meade, and J. Adam

---

41  Foote, 141.

42  D. Elwood Dunn and Svend E. Holsoe, *Historical Dictionary* (NJ: The Scarecrow Press, 1985).

43  Miles Mark Fisher, Lott Cary, *The Colonizing Missionary*, March 15, 2012 (March 21, 2012) (http://docsouth.unc.edu/church/fisher/fisher.html

44  Johnston, 136.

5. A. James .............. Captain of the Long 18, assisted by J. Benson, E. Smith, William Hollings, D. Hawkins, John and Thomas Spencer
6. J. Shaw .............. Captain of the Southern Picket Station, mounting two iron guns; assisted by S. Campbell, E. Jackson, J Lawrence, L. Crook and George Washington
7. D. George .............. Captain of Eastern Picket Station, mounting two iron guns; assisted by A. Edmondson, Joseph Gardiner, Josiah Webster, and J. Carey
8. C. Brander .............. Captain of carriage mounting two swivels to act in concert with brass piece, and moving from station to station, as the occasion may require; assisted by T. Tines and L. Butler.
9. Every man to have his musket and ammunition with him, even when at the large gun
10. Every officer is responsible for the conduct of the men placed under him, who are to obey him even to their peril
11. The guns are all to be got ready for action immediately, and every effective man is to be employed at the pickets
12. Five stations are to be occupied by guards at night till other orders shall be given
13. No useless firing permitted
14. In case of alarm, every man is to repair instantly to his post and do his duty.

## Battles with the Chiefs

On November 11, about 800 warriors overwhelmed the settlers in an attempt to settle a disputed land sale. The warriors captured some women and children. Slave traders in the area provided ammunition to demolish the colony. The natives were successful in ousting the settlers, but instead of continuing their advancement, they stopped to plunder the settlers' homes. The break gave enough time to Ashmun and his soldiers to regroup and pushed the natives back with firepower, which resulted to the death of many invaders.

The number of people who died among the Africans had never been affirmed, but according to Ashmun, several boatloads of dead bodies or fatally wounded warriors hurried across the river. Meanwhile, the natives took children and women as prisoners of war. They did not harm them. Some elderly women who took charge of the kidnapped babies visited the settlers to get information about how to care for the children. As Ashmun recorded, when the day came to return the prisoners, some of the children did not want to return to their mothers in the settlement, because they were attached to their African surrogate mothers.

Ashmun proposed November 11 as Thanksgiving Day. The survival was attributed to divine intervention, and the date was set aside to reflect on that providential intervention. However, because many natives died during the brief war, critics believe the holiday promotes disunity in Liberia and should be abolished.

The conflicts with the natives continued. On November 29, a British ship from Liverpool stopped by on its way to the Gold Coast. Captain H. Brassey replenished the Liberian depleted supply stores and arsenals. Again, on December 1, nearly 1000 natives, mainly of the De Tribe, attacked the Colony.[45] Four settlers died, three wounded, and Ashmun had three bullet holes in his clothes. At sunset, the invaders abruptly withdrew, when they spotted a British ship approaching. It was the *Prince Regent* from Sierra Leone on its way to Cape Coast Castle. Its crew, mainly Major Laing and Gordon, helped to broker a peace accord between the warring parties.

A timeline of the early major native-settler conflicts began with the Battle of Crown Hill on November 11, 1822. Native warriors, mainly Dey, Vai, and Mamba people, attacked the first settlement, with Elijah Johnson leading the Liberian forces. The colony won, and a peace agreement was interceded by King Sao and Captain Laing of the Royal Navy. King Peter of the Dey Tribe eventually allied with the colony. The Vai and Mamba people, on the other hand, conceded to sign treaties for land and peace.

The Battle of Trade Town erupted April 10, 1824. The Liberian militia, with Jehudi Ashmun and Elijah Johnson leading the band of men, stormed three Spanish and French slave strongholds at Trade Town on the Cestos River. With help from the U.S. Navy and native allies, nearly 350 warriors were defeated. 80 slaves were liberated.

In 1832, the government sought to stop a conflict between the Gola and Dey tribesmen. The Gola fighters remained defiant, until General Elijah Johnson forced them to surrender.

The second Battle of Trade Town occurred in1838, after the slave merchants resumed trading in the vicinity. Governor Thomas Buchanan

---

45    According to the available accounts, Matilda Newport was not a part of Ashmun command structure, but the two men she had relationship with were included. At the time of the December 1 assault by the De, her husband, Thomas Spencer, was killed. Later, she married Ralph Newport, who was also a part of the military command structure. Erroneously, December 1 was once celebrated as Matilda Newport Day for firing cannon that drove the native warriors away. If a Newport fired cannon, it had to be Ralph Newport, her new husband.

sought volunteers to demolish slave trading centers completely in the second battle. Again, the slave traders were defeated.

In September of 1838, the Fish Town War claimed the life of Governor I. C. Finley of Mississippi in Africa (Sinoe settlements), son of the founder of the American Colonization Society. He was mugged and executed by Krus at Bassa Cove. The Fish Town War lasted about a year, before it ended in favor of the Liberians.

The second Gola War took place in 1840, under Chief Gatumba. The Dey fled and took refuge in Arthington and Millsburg to escape annihilation, as they were being decimated by Gatumba. When the Gola Chief pursued the Dey remnant into the Liberian territory, the militia counter attacked, with help from native allies. The Gola settled for peace.

The Grebo War of 1856 broke out over land dispute in Cape Palmas. President Joseph Jenkins Roberts sent in the militia to help. As a result of that war, Maryland dropped resistance to be annexed to Liberia. It became a Liberian county in 1857.

One tall tale about the December 1, 1822 war is still controversial. After the conflict, various accounts credit Matilda Newport, over the years, for firing a canon, allegedly, that drove the native warriors away and kept them from overrunning the colony. According to one account, she was smoking a pipe, while the war was raging, and she dropped a coal of fire into a cannon. The gun exploded and the bellow frightened the warriors.

Historians who have studied Newport's life in Liberia concluded that she never performed the legendary role that raised her to stardom. In his report, *Putting to Rest the Matilda Newport Myth*, (Part 2), Siahyonkron Nyanseor wrotes:

> Based on available sources, Matilda Newport was a real person who resided in Liberia during this period. She came to Africa on the "Elizabeth," March 9, 1820 at the age of 25 as Matilda Spencer, the spouse of the 32 years old, Thomas Spencer. According to records, she could not read nor write (illiterate). During the Battles of Fort Hill, Matilda Spencer was 27 years old. Had she performed the deed she is credited with, she would have been known as Matilda Spencer, and not Matilda Newport. Probably, her husband, Thomas Spencer was killed in one of the conflicts. According to the Emigrant List, he died as a casualty in 1822. Matilda Spencer married to Ralph Newport sometime after 1822. Her story borne of the need to pass on the so-called victory of the Settlers over the natives, and it was nurtured through myth of larger-than-life proportions, passed

on as a 'Griot' would to his family. In passing on this tradition, the 'Griot' acted as if truth is woven within every treasured word of myth, fable, etc., that's how this story was passed on from generation to generation.

In order to secure a lasting peace with the natives, Ashmun invited them to trade with the settlers, and he built a market place where they could transact business.[46] Some chiefs were beginning to develop tolerance for the man they dubbed, "The White American Devil of Cape Mesurado."

In the first five years of landing, some colonists endeavored to travel inland to learn more about the natives. They hoped to sign treaties for land and improve opportunities for trade, amidst sporadic scrimmages. The explorers found out that some of the natives were more advanced intellectually than previously assumed, but due to their mutual distrust, trips to the interior were infrequent.[47]

## Unrest in the Colony

The wars and struggles to survive with little supplies had their negative effect. Some settlers, including Rev. Lott Carey, became dissatisfied with Ashmun hard handiness in dealing with administrative issues. According to the ACS Secretary Ralph Gurley, Ashmun took charge of the colony, when Dr. Ayres returned to the States, but tension was already brewing against the authorities for mismanagement and impropriety.[48] Allegedly, some leaders used the supplies from the public store to trade with the natives and converted the proceeds to their own use, while others complained about unfair rationings and lands distribution.[49]

Rebellion broke out, when Ashmun attempted to redistribute the town lots that were already allocated for the first settlers. The colonists protested and refused to cede any land or accept relocation. Moreover, some of the earliest pioneers felt they were the true defenders of the colony and therefore deserved special privileges by getting more lands or granted preferential treatment over the newcomers.

---

[46]    Johnston, 140.

[47]    James Fairhead, Time Geysbeek, Svend E. Holsoe, Melissa Leach, *African American Exploration in West Africa: Four-Century Diaries* (Indiana: Indiana University Press, 2003).

[48]    Ibid, 398.

[49]    Ibid.

A complaint was filed against Ashmun. Some Board members already had doubts about Ashmun's role in the colony. Newspapers in the United States maligned him. Ashmun himself claimed that the accusations prevented him from advancing in the colony or gaining ACS acceptance.[50]

A committee was set up to investigate the allegations. From the report and deliberation of the Board, a guilty verdict was brought against Ashmun, to the great surprise of Gurley, the Secretary General of the ACS. "The Committee to whom these proceedings were referred, arranged them in their Report, under six heads; upon each, they pronounced an unfavourable judgment; and this Report, adopted by the Board, was transmitted to Mr. Ashmun."[51]However, the decision was reversed after another committee examined the finding. Obviously, some members were not pleased and had doubt about Ashmun's administrative role in the colony.[52] Nevertheless, in considering his effort in his de facto governing capacity, the Board voted January 11, 1825, to appoint him as agent.[53]

Ashmun had a difficult life, and it had little to do with his divisive encounters in Liberia. He was born in New York on April 21, 1794. Eighteen years later, Ashmun enrolled at Middlebury College. When the funds for school ran out, he transferred to the University of Vermont in 1814. After leaving his parents at age 22, he never returned home. His mother finally saw him on his deathbed in 1828.

Ashmun served as a Presbyterian minister, while at Vermont. He completed his studies with literary honors in 1816 and started dating another lady, while having a committed relationship with a female teacher; she later became his wife. Two years later, Ashmun became principal of a theological academy in Maine. He travelled from there to New York and married his first fiancé. His controversial marriage to Miss Catherine D. Gray in 1818 ended his seminary career. Apparently, he married to Gray, while involved with another lover he met in 1816.[54] Ashmun admitted bringing shame on himself and he had wished to disappear from the face of the earth. He became a hate object and scandals turned other Christians against him. "I almost sometimes wish that I might sink out of existence and vanish from the memory of all my friends and the world forever."[55]

---

50    Gurley, 226.
51    Ibid, 228.
52    Martin, 247.
53    Ibid.
54    Gurley, 35.
55    Ibid.

Ashmun left for New York where he became editor of the "Theological Repertory," an Episcopalian Church magazine.[56] While in the State, he learned about the American Colonization Society's mission to establish a homeland for freedmen in Africa. By then, controversies were mounting from opponents of colonization, but Ashmun remained undeterred.

Noticeably, the ACS had many white supporters, like Ashmun, who devoted themselves religiously to the cause of black people, though they considered blacks inferior to white. As for Ashmun, that superiority complex, camouflaged with messianic calling, plunged him into conflict with the settlers, especially Rev. Lott Carey, and some members of the ACS Board.

Perhaps Ashmun's greatest fault was his paternalistic tendency and lack of confidence in the settlers to govern themselves. That changed greatly after the Gurley Constitution was set up, which provided more authority to the colonists. Thereafter, Ashmun was less visible in the public square, as he acknowledged that the Liberians capability for self-governance was superb.

Before leaving for Africa, Ashmun started the *African Intelligence* newspaper in 1820 to promote the ACS. Like his other ventures, the publication also failed. However, the failure did not dissuade him from following his calling enthusiastically to help establish the Colony of Liberia. He sailed June 19, 1822, with his wife, but she died shortly after their arrival from malaria. It was the beginning of Ashmun's struggle for personal redemption, and in some measures, he did just that in Liberia.

When Ashmun landed in Monrovia in 1822, the colony had about 120 discouraged people, without provisions or designated leadership, and under military threat from the natives. He took charge of governance, without authorization from the ACS and managed to establish a fortified fortress in Monrovia, and successfully defended the settlement. Some call him the Father of the Nation and the George Washington of Liberia.

The ACS Board sent Secretary Ralph Gurley to investigate allegations against Ashmun. The Secretary reported that the public storehouse was short of rice and other supplies. The Liberian authorities disparately attempted to buy more rice, but there were numerous slave ships on the coast buying slaves and rice at the time. Though tobacco was in high demand for exchange, the colonial storehouse did not have any to trade for rice. As a result, the ration was adjusted for each family, but some settlers objected to the cutting of their allotments.

---

[56]  Radhika Madana Mohan, *Jehudi Ashmun, the Father of Liberia One man's devotion: One man's dream* http://www.apnmag.com/spring_2008/madanamohan_ashmun. php (accessed March 3, 2012).

The report further stated that the colonists had the responsibility to cultivate their own acreages and build their own homes. The government provided seeds and tools, but each family had to work their own land. The labor was tedious and not everyone succeeded. Some pioneers relied on the government for supplies. Those who received assistance, however, were required to work two days a week on public projects. Meanwhile, an ultimatum was given to healthy families whose ration period had ended to expect termination from the supply list. Individuals who were affected protested, along with their sympathizers. Some settlers challenged the mandate, which called for:

> Every adult male emigrant should, while receiving rations from the public store, contribute the labour of two days in a week, to some work of public utility. Before . . . On the 5th of June 1834 all rations would cease except in case of special necessity and that unless those who had appealed to the Board on the subject of their lands should while their case was pending cultivate some portion of land designated by the Agent they should be expelled from the Colony. There are in the Colony more than a dozen healthy persons who will receive no more provisions out of the public store till they earn them. This notice proved inefficient except as it gave occasion for the expression of more seditious sentiments and a bolder violation of the laws. On the 19th the Agent directed the rations of the offending individuals to be stopped.[57]

Twelve of the men refused to do public work, while demanding rations. Rev. Lott Carey, according to the Gurley investigation, encouraged others to oppose the government policy, because he viewed it as being unjust. To this charge, Gurley reported:

> He (Lott Carey) acknowledged frankly, that his influence had seduced others, and seemed to view the evil in all its extent. He told the Agent it was his wish hereafter to receive no more supplies from the Colonization Society, and live less enthralled with secular connexions; but professed his willingness to be useful in the way the Agent thought fit to propose. The latter then suggested to him the care of the liberated Africans. To

---

[57]  Ralph R. Gurley, *Life of Jehudi Ashmun, Late Colonial Agent of Liberia* (Washington: James C. Dunn, 1835), 186.

this proposition he very promptly acceded, and it is believed, he will discharge the trust with fidelity and ability.[58]

The protesters went to Ashmun's home and demanded a change of policy. When they could not get him to comply, the group proceeded to raid the public store and removed what supplies they could.

Ashmun assembled the colonists and spoke to them lengthily about their responsibility to themselves, the colony, God, and posterity. He warned that insubordination was making governance impossible and making the lives of the recalcitrant difficult.

Before the uprising, Lott Carey had been supportive of the administration and allied with Ashmun in most of the decisions, until it came to the town lots redistribution scheme. Gurley wrote:

> It is well known, that great difficulties were encountered in founding a settlement at Cape Montserrado. So appalling were the circumstances of the first settlers, that soon after they had taken possession of the Cape, it was proposed that they should remove to Sierra Leone. The resolution of Mr. Cary was not to be shaken: he determined to stay, and his decision had great effect in persuading others to imitate his example.[59]

The Colony complained to the ACS Board that:

- The Agents demanded that the government should be obeyed or all recalcitrant would be expelled from the Colony
- Those that disobeyed were being punished, while the obedient enjoyed special privileges.
- The complaint charged "Mr. Ashmun with oppression, the neglect of obvious duties, the desertion of his post, and the seizure and abduction of the public property."[60]

When no information came from the ACS to suggest what action to take, Ashmun became convinced that the allegations had turned the Society leadership against him also. Meanwhile, the unfortunate circumstances had altered his view of Carey. From being a trusted friend, Ashmun described Lott Carey as "wretched," "obstinate," "narrow,"

---

[58]   Martin, 150.
[59]   Gurley, 149.
[60]   Fisher, 207.

"disobliging," and "corroding temper . . ."[61] But, when order was restored and a new constitution was proposed for the colony, the two men became amicable again. Ashmun later described Carey as "more obliging, affectionate husband, display of tenderness, moral innovation, habit of holiness . . ." Surprisingly, Lott Carey did not leave any written records of the account and the role he played in the conflict.

The colonists did not push Ashmun out of the settlement, as has been alleged, nor is there evidence that his life was endangered by the settlers or native people. Nevertheless, as tension was building up, he felt increasingly unsafe.

Ashmun's health deteriorated after breaking an artery, while attempting to extract an infected tooth from his mouth. He took his personal possessions and boarded a ship for the Cape Verde Islands. During the voyage, a physician assisted him to stop the forty eight hours of sporadic bleeding.

Some of the settlers were also angry for Ashmun's aggression against the slave traders. Obviously a few, including officials in the Liberian government, got entangled with the nefarious trade and other practices that were contrary to the principles of the ACS. There were allegations of quasi polygamous lifestyle also, implicating some settlers and white leaders like Ashmun himself and Mechlin.[62]

In a separate incident, the white agent, Dr. Joseph Mechlin, Jr., seduced settler Joseph Blake's wife and she conceived a mulatto child. Blake complained that he was left to support "a mulatto child" produced by their "criminal intercourse."[63]

Blake thought of killing Mechlin but became concerned about the impact his action would have on the colony and "repercussions for the colony's reputation." When his complaint was ignored by the ACS, Blake left and resettled in Sierra Leone.

Drunkenness became a social pastime for some Liberians, as the natives and visiting European slave merchants did so often. The anticolonizationists attempted to use the accusations against the Colonization Society to demonstrate that the Society was never interested in abolishing slavery but to promote it in American and Africa.

The ACS Board argued that its colony was an unfairly target for criticism in the United States press. The managers defended their effort,

---

[61]  Miles M Fisher, *Lott Cary, the Colonizing Missionary*, The Journal of Negro History, Vol. 7 No. 4 (October 1992), 394.

[62]  Beyan, 61.

[63]  Joseph Blake to R. R. Gurley, A.C.S., March 9, and May 13, 1835, *American Colonization Society Papers*, Library of Congress, Reel 153. Blake never received the redress he petitioned for, and left Liberia for Sierra Leone in 1837.

contrasting what was happening in Liberia and the United States at the time: "They (Board) have not the sole authority in the civil government of the colony. In this city of Boston public opinion has not risen to that elevation which enables the police to prevent the sale of ardent spirits . . . There is not a grog shop in Liberia."[64]

While other administrative steps were taken to discourage the use of alcohol, such as raising the license fee to $300.00, the Board did not believe enacting laws was the best way to end the practice, especially when alcohol was used as a medium of exchange with the natives in some instances.[65] The authorities depended on the power of the gospel to transform the colonists and their neighbors, without legalism.

Both the British and Americans attempted to rely on diplomacy in combating slavery in the hinterlands. Sometimes they were able to get some chiefs to cooperate by disassociating with the European slave traders. The strategy did not always work, and it ended up in hostilities. Often, the British or Americans looked away, as their own nationals engaged in the nefarious trade in plain sight, as the case was in Sierra and Liberia.

The ACS Board was also aware of slavery in the colony and the tendency for some settlers to indulge in polygamous or concubinary practices. "A treaty concluding a war with the Dey includes an article declaring that 'No woman shall be given or sold as a wife to any of the recaptured Africans or other persons under the protection' of the colony."[66]

Many former slaves who rose to permanence in the United States also became slaveholders. Some of them ended up in Liberia. In 1837, Louis Sheridan, for instance, a former wealthy black merchant in the South, arrived from North Carolina.[67] As a rich farmer, he owned 16 slaves,

---

[64] *The Seventh Annual Report of The American Society For Colonizing the Free People of Colour Of The United States With An Appendix* (Washington, DC: Davis and Force Franklin's Head, 1824).

[65] *The Seventh Annual Report.*

[66] Archives of the Ministry of Foreign Affairs, Monrovia. *Treaty of Peace and Amity between the Colony of Liberia and the Kings and Chiefs of the Dey Country* (n.d.), quoted in Bronwen Everill, "Those That Aare Well off Do Have The Natives as Slaves: Humanitarian 'Compromises' With Slavery in Sierra Leone and Liberia." JOUHS, 7 (Special Issue—Colloquium 2009).

[67] John Hope Franklin, *The Free Negro in The Economic Life of Antebellum North Carolina* (North Carolina Historical Review, Vol. XIX, No. 3, July 1942; Allise Portney, *Their Right to Speak: Women's Activism in The Indian and Slave Debates* (MA: Harvard University Press, 2005).

but they were emancipated to settle in Liberia with him.[68] On arrival, he accused the authorities for condoning slavery, poor treatment of the colonists, and denounced the colonization scheme. Sheridan refused to become a Liberian citizen. However, he leased 600 acres of land from the Liberian authorities for 20 years.[69] Another renegade, Augustus Curtus, who arrived in Liberia in the early 1820s, was accused by Joseph J Roberts as a slave trader in the Colony.[70] Other leading Liberians, such as John Lewis, Hilary Teage and James S. Payne, had also been implicated in trading Africans to Europeans.[71]

There is no evidence that the ACS aggressively addressed the slave issue in its colony, due to the complexity of the scheme and inadequate resources. Some slave traders were friends of the settlers like John Mills, Bob Gray, and Boatswain. Although Chief Gray helped to save the colony and consented to trade with the Americans, he remained an aggressive warrior for slaves, though the settlers attempted to induce him to stop.

The colony was not large, and its few lightly armed inhabitants generally only acted in self-defense. As a result, some events were ignored. Others were underreported for fear of confirming the anticolonizationist self-fulfilling prophecy or "mischaracterization of free African Americans as immoral or unintelligent."[72]

Ashmun left the colony and went to the Cape Verde Islands alone to avoid the upheaval in the settlement. His wife, Catharine D. Gray, died September 15, 1822 from fever, after three months in the country.

Dr. Eli Ayres returned to Liberia the second time, while Ashmun's departure was being probed by the ACS. After returning, he attempted to appease the settlers by allocating more lands for their use, but the contention continued. Eli returned to the United States finally. He, too, like Ashmun, lacked people management skills. Both men were tactless and paternalistic.

---

[68]   Franklin, *The Free Negro in North Carolina*, (NC: University of North Carolina Press, 1943).

[69]   *The African Repository and Colonial Journal*, Vol. XV (Washington: American Colonization Society, 1839); Louis Sheridan's reason for not becoming citizen of Liberia: "My having refused to become a citizen of this realm by swearing to be a white man's slave threw me out of the pale of regal favor and I had to take a lease of 600 acres to enable me to carry out my verbal promise made to the Society who sent me here," 36.

[70]   Joseph J. Roberts to President, *American Colonization Society*, Jan. 24, 1845 in Maryland Colonization Journal 2/21 (March 1845) "Slave Trading," 334-335.

[71]   Beyan, 62.

[72]   Bronwen, 14.

The greatest fallout in the conflict was Rev. Lott Carey, who apologized later to the Board of Directors for his role in the brawl. Gurley writes:

> In December, 1823, Mr. Cary was unfortunately engaged in a transaction which inflicted a deep wound upon his conscience, and which but for his speedy and sincere repentance, might have left a lasting stain upon his reputation. He was one of those who appeared at that time to have lost confidence in the Society, and who ventured to throw off those restraints of authority, which though severe, were deemed absolutely necessary for the general safety of the settlers. In the ninth chapter of the Memoir of Mr. Ashmun, we have given some account of the origin and progress of that spirit of insubordination, which finally resulted in abduction by a few individuals, of a portion of the public stores, in open violation of the laws. Mr. Cary had no small influence and share in this seditious proceeding. But there is reason to believe, that in this conduct, prejudice and passion were permitted to usurp the place of reason, rather than, that he deliberately sacrificed his integrity.[73]

Regardless of Lott Carey's role in the uprising and subsequent denouncement by Ashmun, the Agent later told the Board:

> The services rendered by Lott Cary in the Colony, who has with very few, (and those recent exceptions,) done honor to the selection of the Baptist Mission Society, under whose auspices he was sent out to Africa, entitle his agency in this affair, to the most indulgent construction which it will bear. The hand which records the lawless transaction, would long since have been cold in the grave, had it not been for the unwearied and painful attentions of this individual—rendered at all hours—of every description—and continued for several months.[74]

Gurley went to the Cape Verde on the U.S. warship, *porpoise*, and encouraged Ashmun to return with him to the colony. An investigation launched by Gurley reported:

---

[73]   Gurley, 150.

[74]   Ibid.

The causes, to which most of the moral disorders of the Colony were to be attributed, as specified in the report made on my return to the Board, were:

1.  First and principally: the dissatisfaction of the earliest settlers, with the decision of the principal Agent about the distribution of the town-lots.
2.  An imbecility traceable to the former habits and condition of life, of many of the settlers.
3.  The turbulent and malicious temper of two or three individuals.
4.  Jealousy kindled by the proceedings of a commercial company established at Baltimore, for the prosecution of the African trade.
5.  The trials and hardships incidental to the founding of a Colony on a remote and uncivilized shore; and
6.  The deficiency of power in the Government to meet exigencies, to restrain the first tendencies towards insubordination, and enforce the authority of the law.

At the end of the investigation, Ashmun was vindicated of the changes.[75] However, important changes were implemented. A new constitution made provision for the sharing of power with the colonists. Ashmun was not happy with the provision because he did not think the settlers had the ability for self-governance. He changed his mind when he saw how the colonists carried out their duties with absolute diligence, which resulted to his admission:

> The official decisions communicated to them, along with the new modification of the Government, were received with unanimity of acquiescence, which I confess, was painful to me. I feared either that they could not understand them, or thought opposition, at that moment, unseasonable. But the event has proved my fears unfounded; and I now consider myself authorized to state, that there is an enlightened and growing attachment rooted in the bosoms of the great body of the people to their laws, their officers, and the authority of the Society.[76]

---

75   Gurley, 248.
76   Alexander, 217.

## First Constitution

While in the settlement, Gurley unfurled the first constitution he drafted, with the help of Ashmun, giving the name *Liberia* to the country and *Monrovia* to its capital. General Robert Goodle Harper recommended the name of the country to replace another name that was under consideration at the time, *Freedonia*.[77] Both names were suggested to the ACS and U.S. government by Harper, after whom the city of Maryland was named. Congress granted its approval and so did the American Colonization Society on March 14, 1825. According to the *Gurley Constitution*, the agents were to be appointed by the parent organization in the United States and the settlers appointed the assistants, with the approval of the agents. Gurley returned to America August 22, 1824.

Ashmun insisted on having a security force to protect him, but Gurley told him it was not necessary.[78] However, he was given the option to do what he felt was necessary, but Gurley "thought the guard inexpedient, and that it would not be sustained." Ashmun later abandoned the plan because he saw that it was not necessary. After the new government was instituted, the Ashmun became less visible and trusted the colonists to carry on their duties according to the law, and they did. Relationship between the settlers and government improved remarkably before Ashmun ended his service in Liberia, due to poor health.

Critics of Ashmun denounced him as being dictatorial and paternalistic. He and other white agents believed that the blacks were not intelligent enough to share in governance, without the guidance of the agents. This attitude was the foundation to most of the conflicts between white and black in the colony, because the Africans did not like being treated as children.

Ashmun's behavior during the upheaval in the colony also demonstrated that he did not have extensive skills in managing people. Delisting settlers from receiving supplies and showing no willingness to negotiate favorable terms with the angry colonists was probably imprudent. It was also noted that, although Ashmun was dutiful, he spent a lot of time on personal affairs, including his own business venture. Attempts to redistribute lands or reallocate people who had already invested on their lots were a risky preposition. This policy got Lott Carey involved in the rebellion.

---

[77]    Eric R. Papenfuse, *The Evils Of Necessary: Robert Goodloe Harper and the Moral Dilemma of Slavery* (Philadelphia: American Philosophical Society, 1997), 53.

[78]    Gurley, 215.

After the palaver was over, Ashmun reengaged in his land purchase scheme. He bought more land around the St. Paul River by signing treaties with the neighboring chiefs, Peter, Long Peter, Gouverneur, Yola, and Jimmy, as relationship with the tribes became less hostile. They began doing business and working for the Liberians. Some natives sent their children to live with the settlers for education.

When the indigenous children began moving into the settlements to live and work for the Liberians, a new system of relationship developed. It was the BIG HOUSE concept, which the former slaves from the United States were accustomed to on the plantations. While many children benefitted from this tradition and went on to hold important positions in the Liberian government, others were abused and held in a condition that was indistinguishable from slavery. That continued into the late 20th century. It appeared to be a replication of the plantation experience with the slave masters over the Big House. Historian Everill pointed out that, "Those African Americans who were sent by former slave masters to colonize Liberia often created new identities based in part on their plantation experiences, replicating the Big House, employing slaves of their own, and emulating the only form of freedom they had seen in America.[79]

July 4, 1825, was a celebratory moment. The immigrants celebrated the Independence Day of the United States in grand style, with special American and British guests.[80] They raised their glasses and toasted to:

- The President of the United States: the champion of the people's rights. He deserved the people's honor.
- The Day we commemorate.
- The colony of Liberia. May the history of the nation which has founded it become its own.
- Africa: may it outstrip its oppressors in the race for liberty, intelligence, and piety.
- The heroes and statesmen of American Independence. They fought and legislated for the human race; even the people of England are freer and happier for their labors.
- The Monrovian Independence Volunteers, armed for the defense of rights, which it is the trade of war to destroy. May they never forget their characters.
- General Lafayette of America. We honor him not because we are Americans, but because we are men.

[79] Everill, 5.
[80] Johnston, 146.

- His Britannic Majesty, the Constitutional King of England.
- Success to agriculture.
- Health to the President of the United States and prosperity to the Colony of Liberia.

From 1825, the settlers focused on ending slavery in the area under their jurisdiction. This was accomplished primarily by expanding their territories, especially in areas where the slave trade was still active. As late as 1825, about 200 slaves were still being shipped to America from around the St. Paul River. The building of settlements, such as Millsburg, disbanded many of the trading centers near the coast. As many chiefs conceded lands to the colony, King Boatswain's envoys visited the Liberian leaders and signed a treaty with the pioneers on May 14, 1828. More land concession was made from other chiefs without much hostility as in time past. Cape Mount was purchased on April 12, 1826, from the chiefs with one stipulation that the settlers could not resell the land to foreigners.

With the help of U.S. marines and two warships, Ashmun destroyed the slave station at Trade Town. Attempts were made to revitalize it, but the British finally helped to burn it down in 1842.

The first printing press was set up February 7, 1826. In the same year, the first public library was set up with about 1,200 books.

When Liberia seemed to start improving its relations with the natives, Ashmun's health seriously deteriorated from malaria and had to return to the States. The scene of his departure from Monrovia was emotional. Historian Benson Lossing recalls:

> His departure was a great grief to the colonists who now numbered twelve hundred souls. He felt that the hand of decay was upon him and he expressed a belief that he should never return. Like the friends of Paul they kissed him. Sorrowing most of all for the words which he spake that they should see his face no more. And they accompanied him to the ship. Men, women, and children parted with him at the shore with tears. His anticipations were realized for on the 25th of August 1828 only a fortnight after his arrival at New Haven he departed for the happy land at the age of thirty four years.[81]

---

[81] Benson J Lossing, *Emminent Americans Comprising Brief Biographies of Leading Statesmen, Patriots, Orators, and Other Men and Women Who Have Made the American History* Vol. II. (NY: American Publishers Corporation, 1890), 325.

Ashmun established a legacy in Liberia. Besides building a fortress to defend Monrovia, he enlarged the territory by annexing native lands under some controversial treaties. As a farmer, Ashmun saw trade with the Africans as lucrative, and he attempted to improve trade with the natives. He published a *The Liberian Farmer* (1826), to boost agriculture among the settlers. Ashmun's accounts to the American Colonization Society provide insightful resources about the founding of Liberia. He also published *History of the American Colony in Liberia*, 1821-1823 (1826). After six years in Liberia, mostly in poor health, he returned to the States in 1828 and died August 25, in New Haven. He was 34 years old. Unmistakably, "The survival of Liberia is his only principal monument."

In 1827, Maryland State organized its own colonization society, after breaking away from the American Colonization Society. There were charges of funds mismanagement in the parent organization, and some of the philanthropic members in Maryland charged leaders of the ACS of allowing drunkenness in the colony. Eventually, they established their own colony in Cape Palmas, known as the Colony of Maryland.

The State of Maryland actively promoted resettlement of free Negroes. The philanthropists who attached themselves to the scheme did so with the special aim of upholding the principles of temperance or total abstinence from alcoholism in the colony. The anti-alcoholic sentiments were based on reports that Europeans and educated natives of West Africa were avid drinkers. The Liberians were being accused of indulging in the same practice.

The temperance principles became divisive in Liberia. The Liberian officials and Hall separated, and he took his colonists to Cape Palmas over the liquor issue. Dr. Hall departed for the States and returned to Monrovia in 1833, "with twenty eight fresh colonists and several Methodist and Presbyterian missionaries. He was instructed to pick up at Monrovia the thirty one colonists whom he had deposited there two years previously and to take all his party beyond Liberian limits, there to found another state to be called Maryland."[82]

Hall and party went to the eastern limit of the Liberian Colony to settle at Cape Palmas. The chiefs refused to concede any territories due to the temperance controversy. "Here he found the Grebo chiefs very ill disposed to receive the colonists or to give them any rights over the land chiefly because of the temperance or total abstinence principles which were inculcated. The chiefs were furious at the idea of giving up brandy, which had become quite a vice along the Grain Coast."

---

[82]  *Liberia*, Vol 1, 154.

The issue was resolved temporarily by presenting lavish presents to the Grebo chiefs, but not everyone was happy. Some natives decided to starve the colonists by refusing to sell food to them, unless the Americans were willing to barter with brandy or rum. When the settlers threatened to burn the Grebo villages, the natives dropped their resistance.

Another philanthropic group from Edinburgh in the United States formed its own colonization society and sent a large number of blacks to settle on a land purchased from Chief Bob Gray on the bank of the St. John River. It became known as the settlement of Edina in Grand Bassa. Moreover, the Pennsylvanian Young Men Society (PYMC), largely Quakers, sent out 126 immigrants in 1835, with instructions against drunkenness. The Liberian authorities were careful not to alienate the Quakers group as it did the Marylanders. Indifference had already caused the establishment of a colony in Cape Palmas, which both colonies later regretted. The PYMC acquired lands from two Bassa chiefs, Chief Harris and Bob Gray. However, Harris was induced by Spanish slave traders in the vicinity to burn the settlement. Eighteen pioneers died in the process.

According to the University of Chicago anthropology professor Frederick Starr (1858-1933):

> In 1835 this little colony (Edina) was wiped out of existence by a brutal attack on the part of natives instigated by a slave trader who feared that the presence of the colonists would interrupt his trade. Joe Harris and Bang Peter, brothers, were the active agents of destruction; for several days their people spied upon the settlers, informing themselves whether any arms were in the place ; there was one gun only there ; the assault took place at night, and about 20 persons, mostly women and children, were killed ; the agent Hankinson and his wife were rescued by a Kruman who concealed them; those who escaped were taken to Monrovia and cared for; the authorities at Monrovia took immediate action, marched an armed force against the aggressors, put them to flight, and destroyed their towns; King Peter and Joe Harris agreed to forever abandon the slave trade, to give free passage from the interior through their country, to rebuild the settlement, and return the property; a better spot was selected and a new settlement made.[83]

Bob Gray was a friendly chief and remained loyal to the Americans. He joined the Liberian government to attack Harris. Later, Chief Harris

---

[83]    Starr, 74.

sued for peace, and he rebuilt the settlement near the St. John River and named it Bassa Cove.[84] He promised to refrain from attacking the colonists.

In 1838, the Mississippi Colonization established a colony in Greenville, Sinoe. Its governor was IFC Finley, son of Rev Robert Finley who founded the American Colonization Society. In September of 1838, he left his colony to go to Monrovia on a business trip.[85] A French slave trader, Theodore Canot, lured him to his slave trading territory, robbed and killed Finley. Canot accused the governor of cooperating with the Liberian government to subdue Joe Harris and destroy slave-trading centers. The incident led to the Fish War between the natives and the settlers. They fought for nearly a year around Fishpoint, until they settled for peace.[86]

## Commonwealth Period: 1839-1847

According to the censor of 1839, there were 2,281 settlers and 30,000 recaptives and natives in all the settlements, excluding Maryland County, which was not a part of the Liberian Colony at the time.[87] Tropical diseases caused the death of many, forcing others to resettle in Sierra Leone permanently.

The Commonwealth formally comprised eight settlements. They included Bexley, Buchanan, Caldwell, Edina, Marshall, Mesurado (Montserrado), Millsburg, New Georgia.

There were more churches than schools in the settlements. In 1839, Thomas Buchanan arrived as an envoy from the colonization societies of New York and Pennsylvania. He and Joseph J. Roberts were appointed the first governor and vice governor respectively. Buchanan built the first lighthouse in Monrovia and the capital of Grand Bassa, Buchanan, was named in his honor.

The slave trade posed a major obstacle in Liberia. It was still flourishing on the coast, with European and American traders. Native chiefs and headmen served as middlemen. The illicit business was primarily responsible for a great part of the intertribal-settler conflicts, perhaps even more so than controversial land treaties. European slave

---

84    Sir Harry Johnston, *Liberia*, Vol. 1, (NY: Dodd, Mead & Company), 156.
85    Frederick Starr, *Liberia: Description, History, Problems* (Chicago, 1913), 77.
86    *The Commonwealth of Liberia*. July 11, 2013. http://www.freefictionbooks.org/books/s/17773-a-social-history-of-the-american-negro-by-brawley?start=113.
87    Johnston, 183.

traders provided firearms and urged the natives to destroy the settlements to ensure the perpetuation of the slave trade. When attacked, the settlers fought back, with a deadly force, which resulted to the loss of lives largely on the side of the tribal people. In most of the wars or scrimmages between the two groups, the natives initiated the fight to push the settlers away. Sometimes the aggression was intended to reclaim land allegedly gained illegally from the natives. Mostly, however, the fight was to secure slave trading in the regions where it existed.

By the end of the colonial period, the colony was taking on a form of a nation, with four printing presses, newsmagazines, a system of paper money created to trade with the natives. Some of the bills had images to help the natives who could not read to understand the transactions. Schools and churches were emerging, and a large number of natives began to move into the Liberian colony to live or do business. Those of legal age of 21 years, who were born or moved to live in the colony, were required to pledge allegiance to the Constitution to become citizens of Liberia. Those that lived within the colonies but refused to confirm, especially Muslims, were not considered citizens, but they were not driven out. Moreover, foreigners were not allowed to own land within the territorial limits of the Colony, without special permits from the ACS Board or its agents.

# CHAPTER XV

# NATIVE-SETTLER CONFLICTS

The American settlers on the Grain Coast of Africa were descendants of African ancestry. Their ancestors had been violently captured and sold as common laborers in Europe and the Americas over a period of 300 years. A few of those who gained freedom repatriated to the land of their forefathers in the 1800s and founded the First African Republic in West Africa.

When addressing conflicts with the indigenous, historians have often failed to address whether former slaves in the Diaspora had rights to reclaim or establish a homeland in Africa. Without any doubts, their ancestors had been violently captured and sold into bondage on other continents. After several centuries of enslavement, a great part of their African heritage disappeared. People from different tribal groups could not communicate with each other due to language barriers. The loss of language led to the extinction or diminished cultural practices. They developed a pidginized form of communication for survival.

Adaptation to different kinds of foods and tastes, dressing styles, sociopolitical orientation, and religious practices became a sine qua non for Africans in slavery. For most of the hyphenated or Americanized blacks, the only thing they had in common with Africa was the color of their skin. Also, as demonstrated during the call for black repatriation, some freedmen harbored intense hatred for Africa and chose not to identify with the continent due to the degradation and anguish of slavery, which included the active participation of African chiefs.

The slaves experience and acculturation in America created a perfect condition for tempestuous conflicts with indigenous people in West African. The native religions and political system were dissimilar to the ethos of Christianity and western democracy. Irrespective of these cultural differences, the prevailing sentiment among African historians tends to lay blame on repatriated Africans for adapting western culture, instead of embracing African traditionalism. This is what tribal leaders expected.

Traditional leaders expressed opposition to the black Americans westernized culture. Apart from skin color and hair texture, everything else seemed different. The settlers generally spoke English, with no knowledge of any local language, although there were several to pick from. The dressing was western, and the houses styled after southern architectural designs, generally lifted from the ground on bricks, with attics in the rooftops. Some foodstuff like flour, corn meal, and sugar were imported from abroad. Truly, Africa may have been their ancestry homeland, but they had more cultural ties with the United States, which was more probable, after being in captivity for more than three hundred years. They chose to become hyphenated Africans, with the designation of *Americo-Liberians*. In conclusion, they were also monotheistic, and all other forms of worship were viewed as pagan practices.

As early as 1822, some chiefs contended that, in order for black Americans to be established on the land, they had to sever ties with America in exchange for tribal customs and protection. On the other hand, other chiefs contemplated at the daunting task of de-Americanizing the settlers in order to Africanize the newcomers as pointless, because the number of colonists was increasing, and with that, the power to protect the settlements from invasions was inevitable.

How tribal control over the colony would have affected the code mission of the immigrants is uncertain. Undoubtedly, efforts to end the flourishing and coveted slave trade between natives and Europeans may have been prolonged and more brutal. The spreading of the gospel through education may have suffered a greater setback, without American philanthropic support. Slave traders in West Africa did not create institutions of learning or health centers. They did not build worshipping houses such as churches or mosques for the indigenous people. Slave traders impoverished the African continent to build western civilizations in Europe and the Americas.

Slavery was the greatest menace and irritant and the primary basis of bloody conflicts between the natives and settlers. In *Bitter Canaan*, Johnson writes: "These natives, longer used to the Europeans, were sophisticated, spoke a maxed jargon of Portuguese and English, had adopted European names, and indulged in a lively slave trade with the coast as a consequent of incessant intertribal wars."[1]

Most tribal chiefs and European traders opposed the building of settlements for fear that the colonists would obstruct the lucrative but hideous slave trade. The practice was deeply rooted in West Africa, as the basic form of commerce and trade, by the time the repatriates arrived.

---

[1]    Johnson, 29.

As a consequent, slave traders encouraged constant resistance against settlers' partnership in trade and peace initiatives with the chiefs. Some European merchants provided arms to the natives to overrun and burn settlements. As historian Yekutiel Gershoni argues, "Their allies, slave traders, provided no middle grounds for acculturation and integration."[2]

After the death of Chief Boatswain, Chief Gatumba of the Gola tribe sought to exterminate the settlers for interfering with slavery. He designed a policy of sustained resistance and provocations by refusing to stop wagging war against neighboring tribes. After nearly decimating the Dey people, the tribe remnant turned to the colonial government for protection. Gatumba invaded Millsburg, a settlement on the St. Paul River, where the fleeing Dey villagers sought rescue.[3] Governor Buchanan attacked the invaders and killed a large number of tribesmen, out of a fighting force of nearly 700. Joseph Jenkins Roberts led the counterattack against the Gola warriors. Their capitulation gave Buchanan the advantage he needed to purchase more lands from beleaguered tribes.

A dispute of a different kind emerged between Governor Buchanan and the Reverend John Seys of the Methodist Church. The Methodist Minister was involved in missionary work, which included evangelism and education of the native inhabitants. At the same time, he also had business interest in Liberia. As a missionary, he protested against taxation of goods imported by the Church, even if some of the cargoes were intended for personal business. Governor Buchanan objected and argued that goods brought into the country primary for business were subject to taxation, except for goods designated for missionary work or education. As a result of the dispute, John Seys returned to America.

Notwithstanding, intertribal wars to capture slaves, secure safe trading routes, or fan off invaders for dominance, remained frequent, bloody, and alarming. Historian Fred van der Kraaij noted that:

> In the region which is now called Liberia the (slave) trade thus contributed to the impoverishment of and the hostilities between tribes. Up till the present day the inter-tribal relations are affected by the events of this period. The Golas, Krus, Kpelles and Kissis were notorious slave traders conniving with unscrupulous Europeans who looted the coastal areas. Besides this, the northern tribes of the Mano and the Gio were feared

---

[2]     Yekutiel Gershoni, *Black Colonization: The Americo-Liberian Scrambles for the Hinterland* (London: Westview Press, 1985), 7.

[3]     Randall Miller, *Dear Master: Letters From a Slave Family* (GA: University of Georgia Press, 1990), 76.

because of their cannibalism, a practice which was also not uncommon among the Greboes and the Krus.[4]

## Poro-Sande Governance

The Poro and Sande traditions posed a challenge to coexistence and governance in colonial Liberia. The two tribal societies had been in existence for hundreds of years in West Africa. Both have served as educational, political, and spiritual guide for boys and girls.

When it comes to governance, there is a great difference between Poro-Sande jurisprudence and western democracy. This difference made the formation of an integrated and a unified government problematic in Liberia.

The settlers had a mission to evangelize and educate the indigenous inhabitants. Obviously, "The Founding Fathers of Liberia were determined to form a democratic government supportive institutions. To do so, they had to overcome impediment of other sociopolitical ideology (Poro and Sande) of the numerically superior indigenous Africans among whom they settled."[5]

The settlements were created and supported by Christian organizations in the United States. The founders prohibited any indulgence or tolerance of antichristian values or practices, such as animism, drunkenness, polygamy, fetishism, and voodoo. These were considered acts of paganism. The spread of Islam was to be contained, if not stopped, and slavery on the coast abolished. These, of course, were tall orders. With that realization, the ACS cautioned that the power of the gospel could make the difference, without using force to ensure compliance. In *Crisis of State*, authors Kapferer and Bertelsen write:

> The founding of Liberia was intended to displace the natives but eventually win them over through evangelism and education, but these mediums did not always prevent intertribal conflicts or natives against settlers. But where the control of government was not firm, slave traders took charge and encouraged more intertribal conflicts.[6]

---

[4]   http://www.liberiapastandpresent.org/Peppercoastbefore1822.htm (accessed April 12, 2012).

[5]   Bruce Kapferer, Biorm E. Bertelsen, *Crisis of State: War and Social Upheavals* (NY: Berghalm Books, 2009), 110.

[6]   Kapferer, 276.

It is important to take into account the vast ideological differences between the natives and settlers. Traditional authority rested with a council of Poro elders who relied on ancestry worship for influence, control, and power. Fetishism was the basis for the spiritual authority to mediate in cases of life and death, punishment of criminals or war declaration. Dr. Olukoju makes the following insightful statement in his book, *Culture and Customs of Liberia*:

> Beliefs in spirits has always been fundamental to Liberian life, worldview and religious beliefs. Traditional religionists . . . believe in the existence of a variety of spirits: ancestral spirits, various water and bush spirits, genies, spirits of the associations, and specific Poro spirits. Ancestral spirits are believed to protect and play mediatory roles in the affairs of their offspring and in their offspring's dealings with the spirit world, and generally maintain an interest in their well-being. Bush and water spirits and genies are believed to possess humans and to be capable of transferring specialized knowledge or power to them . . . These spirits are also believed to govern the mysterious world that exists outside of human control. Spirits (or totems) of the associations govern the affairs of the snake and leopard societies, which often act as the agents of the Poro . . . The spirit world of benign and malevolent spirits and ancestors is usually represented by masquerades in which participants wear wooden masks. Though the man behind the mask is a mere mortal, the wooden mask shields his identity from the human gaze, and the ancestral spirit or any spiritual force that comes upon him is believed to take him beyond the level of non-initiates.[7]

After nearly 200 years in bondage, both slaves and freedmen were acculturated to adopt western political and religious institutions, as would be expected. Obviously, they chose western democracy, based on Christian values over tribal beliefs. Christian values became the basis for divine inspiration, instead of ancestry worship. Therefore, the cultures were at odd from the start, and it took many decades to negotiate peaceful coexistence. However, due to the vast dissimilarities, it was not abnormal for both groups to take as long as they did to create a hybrid society, which was neither wholly African nor American. Somewhere in between is the amalgam, the new Liberian identity. Nevertheless, the Church remained

---

[7]     yodeji Olukoju, *Culture and Customs of Liberia* (CT: Greenwood Press, 2006), 24.

the most powerful symbol in the nation's sociopolitical system, although some traditional practices were allowed to exist.

When the returnees settled on Cape Montserrado in 1822, the Poro and Sande Societies were the dominant tribal institutions in the territory. They were highly secretive and initiation ceremonies took place in seclusion, about a mile away in the bush for girls and much farther for boys. The time spent in the bush camps varied from three years for girls and four years for boys.[8] During those years, neither the boys nor girls associated intimately with the opposite sex outside of the groves.

In general, women are not allowed to see the Poro boys in or outside of their camps, but this practice varies, depending on tribal regions. To avoid any encounter, the women sing special songs or announce their presence, while travelling on public roads or trails. On the other hand, when the Sande girls are in camp or when travelling, they sing and clap their hands intermittently to alert males in the vicinity. This keeps men off the trails to avoid encounter with the young women, as they go by. Failure to comply generally result to some forms of punishment for both men and women. A serious violation of some Sande or Poro customs may result to immediate fine or death of the guilty individuals.

## Origin of the Sande and Poro

Most anthropologists report that the Sande Society was initiated by the Gola people of Liberia. The custom spread and was adopted by other tribes and adjacent regions.[9] Eventually, most of the sixteen tribes embraced the initiation practices, including some Bassa people, Belle, Dei, Gbandi, Gola, Kissi, Kpelle, Kru, Loma, Mano, Mende, and Vai, among others.

An important aspect of the Poro and Sande initiation in Liberia is circumcision. The removal of the foreskin for boys is not much of a secret, because nearly all young men go through the process in the Poro or at home. When done at home, the circumcision rituals takes place early in the morning behind a hut or away from public view, and the children are returned to their parents shortly after. Sometimes celebratory ceremonies may follow. Uncircumcised boys who join the Poro are cut before graduation.

---

[8]    Joseph Jeffrey Walters, Gareth Griffiths, John Victor, *Singler Guanya Pau: A Story of an African Princess* (Broadview Press, 2004), 32.

[9]    Filomina Chioma Steady, *Women And Collective Action in Africa* (NY: Palgrave & Macmillan, 2006), 97.

Most girls are also circumcised, but the practice is done secretly in the groves or camps. The act is known as female genital mutilation or cutting (FGM/C), and is generally associated with the Sande Society.

Although the Sande may have originated from the region now called Liberia, the source of the cutting tradition is unknown. Evidently, females were being circumcised long before the Sande Society came to existence. A Greek source, dating as early as 163 B.C., indicates that Egyptian girls were undergoing circumcision at the time, but there is no consensus on the origin of the practice.[10]However, according to most anthropologists, the Gola ethnic group founded the Sande that is largely responsible for promoting FGM in West Africa. In 1688, the Dutch physician and geographer, Olfert Dapper first reported the existence of what he called the Sandy (Sande) among some tribes on the Grain Coast.[11]

In all Poro and Sande tribes, secrecy enforces the spiritual component underpinning the privacy of each society, and members are prohibited from disclosing the rites to nonmembers.[12] There is a penalty for violation, including death. In *The Meaning of Secrecy in a Secret Society*, author Bellman affirms, "Poro and Sande initiation rituals are primarily concerned with teaching initiates how to keep a secret. Knowing when, how, and even whether to speak about various topics is a prized virtue . . . of all mature members of their society."[13]

There is a religious and civil aspect of the Poro and Sande. They make all major laws governing the community under their jurisdiction. Only Poro members and, generally, elderly women with high ranks in the Sande are allowed in the selective governing council. Many of the important meetings take place outside of the towns or villages, even in contemporary society.

The initiation process is conducted in bush camps. Older women perform clitoridectomy (female circumcision) and scarification (small shallow cuts in the skin as evidence of initiation) on the girls when they enter the camp to allow for healing.[14] The process could involve laminectomy or cutting of the labia. These procedures presumably make a woman whole or complete by removing that part of her, the clitoris, which

---

[10]    Sabine R. Huebner (2009), *Female Circumcision as a Rite de Passage in Egypt—Continuity Through the Millennia?* Journal of Egyptian History, Volume 2, Numbers 1-2, 2009, pp. 149-171(23). http://www.ingentaconnect.com/ content/brill/ jeh/2009/00000002/F0020001/art00004 (accessed January 12, 2013).

[11]    Fima Lifshitz, *An African Journey Through Its Art* (IN: AuthorHouse, 2009).

[12]    Stephen D. Glazier, *Encyclopedia of African and African-American Religions* (NY: Routlege, 2001), 297.

[13]    Bery Bellman, *The Language of Secrecy* (NJ: Rutgers University Press, 1984), 51.

[14]    *Sande Society*, http://afrikadawn.com/africa/sande.html (accessed. April 2, 20120.

is analogous to the male penis.[15] The intent varies in the countries where it is practiced. Generally, the cutting is intended to make women less erotic or sensual for their own safety.[16]

Dr. Idowu of Obafemi Awolowo University in Nigeria, points out:

> In Africa, the preponderance of evidence establishing culture as one of the factors for Female Genital Mutilation in different ethnic groups is that people have a resolute belief that women's unmutilated genitals are ugly and bulky. That a woman's genitals can grow and become unwieldy, hanging down between her legs unless the clitoris is excised. It is also believed that a woman's clitoris is dangerous and that if it touches a man's penis he will die. Similarly, if the baby's head touches the clitoris during childbirth, the baby will either die but if it manages to survive, he or she may not succeed in life.[17]

The centuries old practice is now facing a global challenged to stop mutilating women sexual organs. The World Health Organization (WHO) has continued to popularize the negative effect of FGM, including "severe pain and bleeding, shock, difficulty in passing urine, infections, injury to nearby genital tissue and sometimes death; death through severe bleeding leading to haemorrhagic shock, neurogenic shock as a result of pain and trauma, and overwhelming infection and septicaemia." WHO also warns that, "When giving birth, the scar tissue might tear, or the opening needs to be cut to allow the baby to come out." In addition:

> Risks for complications from infibulations include urinary and menstrual problems, infertility, surgery (defibulation and reinfibulation) and painful sexual intercourse. Sexual intercourse can only take place after opening the infibulation, through surgery or penetrative sexual intercourse. Consequently, sexual intercourse is frequently painful during

---

[15]   Ibid.

[16]   "The 2007 Liberia Demographic and Health Survey, the most recent statistics, showed the prevalence of circumcision among Liberian women ages 15 to 49 is about 58 percent. The procedure is usually practiced by 10 of Liberia's 16 tribes, and is reportedly intended to reduce sexual pleasure and, consequently, the unlikelihood of promiscuous," http://www.theworld.org/2012/03/ female-genital-circumcision-temporarily-stopped-in-liberia/ (accessed April 10, 2012).

[17]   Amos Adeoye Idowu, *Effects of Female Genital-Mutilation on Human Rights of Women and Female Children: The Nigerian Situation*, Research Journal of International Studies, Issue 8 (November, 2008), 13.

the first weeks after sexual initiation and the male partner can also experience pain and complications.[18]

The masculinity of males is as important as the femininity of women. With circumcision, the male removes "the remaining femaleness (foreskin) of a Poro man." Unlike the female,[19] circumcision was intended to have an opposite effect for the Poro male, by enhancing his sexual gratification.[20]

After the initiation, the females learn skills about family life, cooking, nutrition, health, sexuality, marriage, motherhood, and other traditional industries for women. The males develop other social skills relevant to the males' roles in society, such as farming, fatherhood, building, and acquiring and keeping secrets about traditional leadership.

In both societies, some adoptees rise to higher ranks in degrees, involving more fetish practices or spiritualism. However, most members never advance past the preliminary initiation.

The Poro and Sande were not merely puberty rites of passage or a process of metamorphosis, and transition from child to adulthood. They were the source of spiritual power and a mystical religious experience deeply rooted in deep secrecy. Arguably:

> Once rebirth in the bush occurred, each individual was bound to the society and vowed to uphold secrecy of the initiation and to abide by Poro-Sande authority. Allegiance was no longer to parents and kin but to the society as foremost arbiter. Thus, Poro-Sande instituted a regulatory process with sociopolitical duties implemented to fulfill collective and societal goals. The Poro council was supreme. It stopped village quarrels, tried and condemned social criminals, intensified holiday spirit, and gave permission to declared war. Although the chief was a nominal ruler, real power rested with the council, which was

---

18    *Effects of FGM*, http://www.endfgm.eu/en/female-genital-mutilation/what-is-fgm/effects-of-fgm/ (accessed April 16, 20120.

19    According to a 2002 study in Nigeria, "Circumcised women experience sexual arousal and orgasm as frequently as uncircumcised women . . . Proponents of female circumcision claim it makes virginity at marriage and marital fidelity more likely. Opponents condemn it as dangerous and painful," http://www.circumstitions.com/FGM-sex.html (accessed April 3, 2012).

20    Position Paper on Neonatal Circumcision: *No Valid Evidence To Date, However, Supports The Notion That Being Circumcised Affects Sexual Sensation or Satisfaction, Circumcision*: http://www.aafp.org/ online/en/home/clinical/clinicalrecs/children/circumcision.html (accessed April 10, 2012).

composed of senior members of both Poro and Sande societies and could even depose a chief.[21]

## Religious Differences

Islam was also a major force in Liberia. Muslims arrived in the region from 1500-1600 and settled in the rural area and the coast over time. They carried on commerce and trade, without involving themselves deeply into native affairs in meaningful ways. In part, as a result of their isolation, the natives considered Muslims to be strangers or foreigners. Nearly 400 years since they settled on the West African coast, many Liberians still consider Muslims as foreigners.

Muslims were anti-Sande or Poro practices. On the other hand, only Poro and Sande members could be a part of the hierarchy of decision-makers. Muslims remained in their own communities by adopting a de facto isolationist policy. They had their own burial sites, worship houses, and forbade intermarriage with nonbelievers.

Islam is a monotheistic religion and its concept of one Supreme Being meant that he only was to be worshipped. Muslims called nonbelievers *karfi* or infidel, who would go to hell after death.[22] Notwithstanding, from the offset, some native people resisted, especially the Via, Kpelle, Gbandi, Lorma, Mane people. Overtime, some of these indigenous people were converted.

The African Americans arrived in 1822, with an evangelistic endeavor. Like the Muslims, they were monotheistic, with strong opposition to animism. The Christians believed that both the natives and Muslim needed salvation through Jesus Christ.

The xenophobic spirit among the three groups complicated attempts for political or social integration. The natives considered both Muslims and Christians as strangers, but that perception gradually changed, as more natives enrolled in church schools and became Christians. However, as the resistance weakened, Muslims remained undeterred. Most of them left the coastal areas and went farther inland away from the Christian government control. On the other hand, most natives remained in their villages in Liberia although a few continued sporadic resistance against the government into the 20th century.

---

[21]    Joseph E. Holloway, *Africanism in American Culture* (IN: Indiana University Press, 2005), 162.

[22]    http://www.islamicinformation.net/2008/05/hell-in-islam-jahannam.html (accessed, April 15, 2012).

## Racism in the Colony

The settlers had their own racial issues between dark and light skin immigrants. The rift developed to a de facto class system. The mulatto emerged as the ruling class, and the darker settlers followed. The recaptives or rescued Africans from slave ships were next in line, followed by the civilized (educated) Africans. The natives served at the bottom of the sociopolitical hierarchy.

The epitome of the racial divide was embodied in the pan-Africanist Edward Wilmot Blyden. Born in the Danish West Indian Island of St. Thomas on August 3, 1832, Blyden arrived in Liberia in 1857, ten years after the nation's independence. Racial identity was vital. He joined the racial struggle, and it was the fight that defined his legacy in Liberia.

Blyden viewed the presence of mulattoes in the country as an insult to the Negro race. He argued against the Anglo American view that a Negro was anyone with any amount of Negro blood. Blyden responded, "Mulattoes were not part of the Negro race any more than the Negro is a part of the Caucasoid and Mongoloid races . . . If the difference between the mulatto and the Negro is understood hereafter, it will much simplify the Negro problem and the (Negro) race will be called upon to bear its own sin only, and not the sin also of a mixed multitude."[23]

*Edward Wilmot Blyden*
*(3 August 1832 – 7 February 1912)*

---

[23] Hollis Lynch, *Edward Blyden: Pan-Negro Patriot: 1832-1912* (Oxford: Oxford University Press, 1967), 58-59.

Critics view Blyden as a racist for denouncing mulattoes. However, the pan-Africanist defended his position by pointing to the mulattoes' tendency to identify with white and not black. They saw themselves as white. It was that predisposition that animated the rivalry. Blyden said mulattoes reminded him of the raped womanhood of Africa, as a system which brought humiliation to the Negro race. He concluded, "When I am dead write nothing on my tombstone but . . . he hated mulattoes."

The 1840s was the beginning of reality check for the Commonwealth and its relation with the ACS or the United States. Communication with America became infrequent and some Liberians began to question the role of ACS in the colony. Meanwhile, the United States stepped up its criticism against the 18 years old colony for not being self-sufficient, especially in food production.

The British became Liberia's major ally. They teamed up to eradicate the active slave trade on the Grain Coast. The United States played a marginal role. From 1840, the French also increased its antislavery patrol on the region. Of all the European commercial traders, the French were less brutal and most acceptable to the natives. The English were most aggressive and highly detested on the West African Coast.

As the slave trade diminished, palm oil and palm kernels production replaced it, ultimately. Europeans supported palm production in Liberia and slavery eventually lost its commercial attraction.

On September 4, 1841, Governor Thomas Buchanan died of fever in Bassa Cove. General Joseph Jenkins Roberts, an octoroon, became the first and only black governor of Liberia.[24]

Roberts was the second of seven children from Norfolk, Virginia. His biological father was a planter of European descent. Joseph's mother was Amelia Roberts, a mulatto. She became the planter's slave concubine. The family was manumitted later, but to identify who the father of her children was, she made the mystery father's name the middle name of six of her children, "Jenkins."[25] She married a black boatman named James Roberts. He became a successful businessman and raised the children as his own.

---

[24]   Joseph J. Roberts registered in Virginia as a mulatto in 1825, but technically, he was an octoroon, with one-eighth black ancestry. His father was a white planter and his mother a mulatto.

[25]   Many slave masters who had children by black women remained anonymous. It was against the law for whites to have sexual affairs with blacks in most states, therefore interracial relations remained a family secret, especially for men with political status.

The Roberts sailed from Norfolk, Virginia, for Liberia on the *Harriet* in March, 1829. Amelia went with five of her children, while J. J. Roberts travelled with his wife Sarah and infant.[26]

Four years after arriving, Roberts was appointed High Sheriff of the colony and assigned to collect taxes and lead excursions to put down uprisings in the tribal regions near Monrovia.[27] In the process, he befriended many chiefs in the hinterland. Roberts also became a successful businessman and a Methodist preacher in Liberia.

## Border Disputes

### The Gallinas Territory

The Gallinas is a river that flows between northwestern Liberia and Sierra Leone. It empties into the Atlantic Ocean, about 100 miles from Monrovia. The river got its name from a cluster of slave factories or warehouses built on several small islands in the region. The adjacent territory became known as the Gallinas Territory.

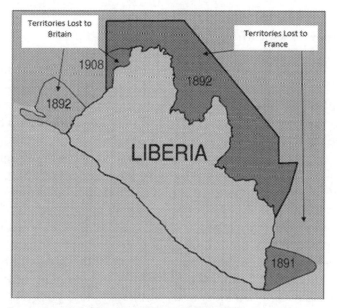

*Location of Lost Territory Map*

---

[26]  Sarah and infant died within a year in Liberia.

[27]  http://www.educationalsynthesis.org/famamer/NinthPresident.html(accessed May 30, 2012).

The Gallinas was once known as a depot for slaves from rural West Africa. It had no other known value at the time but was a delight for slave traders. The islands in the region had several slave factories. Some of the warehouses could hold from 100 to 500 persons, and sometimes more. As many slaves or more were shipped to American and European plantations or sugar farms daily.

The famous Amistad story originated from the Gallinas Territory. In 1839, fifty three Africans were seized from this notorious region and taken to Havana, Cuba, in the ship *Tacora*. Against international law, the forty nine adults and four children of the Mende ethnic group were bought by two plantation owners and headed for Puerto Principe, Cuba. However, after three days at sea, the trip was aborted, when a twenty five years old Sengbe Pieh led a revolt and seized the ship, La Amistad (Friendship). The captain and his cook were killed. Amistad was detained off Long Island, New York, by the U.S. brig *Washington*. The captives were jailed in New Haven, Connecticut. After the Supreme Court finally heard the case in January 1841, with former President John Quincy Adams arguing for the defendants, the accused were released. Thirty five of them were sent back to Africa. The others perished at sea or in U.S. custody.

## Antislavery Campaigns

Roberts had a good relationship with the natives. He developed friendly ties during his years of military expeditions in the hinterland for settling disputes. He concluded a treaty with King Yoda on February 22, 1842. According to the treaty, the Gola chiefs vowed to give up the slave trade and trial by poison ordeal.

Roberts visited the United States in 1844, when European merchants were challenging the colony's right to impose custom duties on foreign traders. The British government sent a letter to Roberts stating that it was not willing to recognize the rights of "private persons" to levy custom duties. The Governor called on the U.S. government to declare the commonwealth its protectorate. He hoped that the public declaration would keep powerful European nations from encroaching on the colony, but the American government remained indifferent. The U.S. Foreign Ministry had never given an official reason for ignoring Liberia's request, but the Monroe Doctrine could have played a role.

President James Monroe addressed the United States Congress on December 2, 1823. He declared that "further efforts by European nations to colonize land or interfere with states in North or South America would be viewed as acts of aggression requiring U.S. intervention." The speech stated that the United States would neither interfere with existing European colonies nor meddle in the internal concerns of European countries. Historians generally interpret the speech to mean that the government was banned from owning colonies in foreign lands. But since that declaration, there were occasions when the United States got involved in foreign disputes in countries like Mexico, Cuba, and the Philippines, to name a few. Therefore, since the United States and the ACS created the colony of Liberia, it was expected naturally to protect the territory from foreign encroachment, but it never did.

As the boundaries disputes dragged on, the U.S. reluctantly sent a note to the British government to request cooperation with the Liberian custom laws. The request was ignored.

Liberia seized the Captain Davidson's *Little Ben* in 1845 for refusing to pay custom duty. Another Englishman, Captain Jones, appeared in Grand Bassa with a gunboat from Sierra Leone and impounded the *John Seyes*, a Liberian ship. The vessel ended up in a Sierra Leonean court in Freetown. The judge ruled against Jones and the Liberian ship was returned to Monrovia. Similar provocations became increasingly frequent and menacing for the impoverished Commonwealth.

Liberia purchased the Gallinas in 1850 from the chiefs of the area.[28] Roberts was determined to shut down the slave activities in the Gallinas by expanding the power of the government in the region. He made an unsuccessful appeal for funds from the United States to sustain the antislavery campaign. The ACS was deeply in debt and could not help finance the project.

Slave traders in the area fermented hate against Liberia. They convinced some of the chiefs to reclaim the territory and push away "the American dogs," as they called the settlers. As a reward for getting rid of unwelcome Americans, the natives would be able to purchase merchandise, without duties or taxes.[29] Moreover, the slave trade would be unrestricted. As a result, some of the chiefs who signed treaties with Liberia became reluctant or hostile toward the government.

Meanwhile, the provocations increased, when an English slave trader, John Harris, settled on a portion of the land and established ownership. He had several wives from various tribes of the area. Harris became a kinsman and was able to assert great influence over leaders of the tribes.

The Secretary of Interior, Edward Wilmot Blyden, appealed to the British government to intervene. The British urged Liberia to forego claim

---

[28]   The African Repository and Colonial Journal, Volume 45, 1869.

[29]   Ibid, 370.

over the territory because the tribal people in the area did not want to be a part of Liberia.

The natives in the Gallinas were dissatisfied with the Liberian government for another reason, besides being urged by the slave traders to resist Liberia's authority. The government was unable to extend protection over the territory. The tribal people charged that Liberia signed a conditional treaty with them to build schools, provide education, protect the territory from foreign interference, and ensure peaceful coexistence.[30]

The Liberian government acknowledged its obligation to the Gallinas. However, it blamed the lack of funds to build schools or assign personnel to provide instruction. Fewer immigrants were arriving from the United States at the time and not in sufficient numbers to locate personnel in the disputed region.

Disputes over the Gallinas began when English slave traders accused the Liberian military of destroying their property. Along with other incidents of scrimmages, the claim for damages was set at $80,000.00.[31] The amount varied from time to time, during the fifteen years of conflict. But, Liberia blamed the action of the military on aggravations by the natives who failed to yield to warnings against uprising and disrespecting the Liberian authorities.[32] Slave traders were urging their tribal allied to attack tribes that were friendly with the settlers. Here is how the ACS defended the action of the Liberian military in the Gallinas:

> An armed force was sent up to the Manna country for the purpose of compelling Prince Manna to return to his own country, the Gallinas and of seizing the goods, and breaking up the trading factories of the Sierra Leone people dealing unlawfully in our territory. Prince Manna retreated, but the factories in the Manna country were broken up, and the schooner Elizabeth, lying in the Manna River, and a portion of their goods, were seized and were condemned in the Admiralty court the goods being sold upon decree. In breaking up these factories a number of letters were found, written by residents of Sierra Leone, in which they encouraged each other to resist our officers; and in several of them, written by one George M Macauley, he urges his friends to get swords and guns and defend themselves and call on the natives to assist. He tells

---

[30]  Ibid.

[31]  *The Liberian Repository and Colonial Journal*, Vols. LVII, LVIII, LIX (Washington D.C.: American Colonization Society, 1883).

[32]  Ibid.

them that should they see any "American dogs!"—as they call us—coming toward them, they must "stop them far off:" and he expressly hopes the natives "will kill all the American dogs."[33]

The British government was drawn in the dispute on the side of the English merchants, while relatively friendly to Liberia. The government recommended that the quarreling parties settle by arbitration, with the American government as mediator. An attempt was made but the mediation failed. The United States abdicated and recommended that the African nations settle their own differences.

Surprisingly, the Governor of Sierra Leone, Author E. Havelock, arrived in Monrovia on March 20, 1882, under the escort of British four gunboats and proposed that Liberia forgo the entire Gallinas Territory.[34] The Liberian Legislature objected and informed President A. W. Gardiner not to sign any agreement with Havelock. The Governor revised his demand and extended the Liberian boundary to the Mano River. Still, the government refused to endorse the loss of nearly forty miles of coastal line to Sierra Leone.

The United States remained indifferent in the border crises. Liberia eventually lost large parcels of land to the British and French. Included in the loss was the land across the Cavalla River that was a part of Cape Palmas in eastern Liberia. The French seized the land and became a part of its colony, the Ivory Coast. The French also annexed a part of Liberia's northern territory to its colony, French Guinea. These seizures became legal between Liberia and France in 1891 and 1892.

In 1883, the British seized land north of the Mano River based on what became known as the Havelock-Blyden Treaty. Blyden was Secretary of Interior and President of Liberia College at the time. Liberian leaders accused him of being bribed by the British to cede the land to the English Colony of Sierra Leone. Opposition to the Havelock-Blyden Treaty was so fierce that Blyden fled for his life to Cape Palmas.

President Anthony W. Gardiner found himself in a sea of fire, when his Vice President, Alfred F. Russell, accused him of cowardly capitulating to the British. The criticism from local people and the gunboat diplomacy employed by the British to annex the territory culminated to the resignation of the President. He became the first Liberian president to resign from office and was succeeded by Vice President Alfred Russell.

---

[33]   The African Repository and Colonial Journal, Volume 45, 1869, 370.
[34]   Lynch, 158.

Finally, Liberia legally ceded two parcels of land at its northwestern border to the British in 1891 and 1908.

The French-Liberian dispute dragged on, and the British contended that they would not relinquish claims to land between Liberia and Sierra Leone until the French abandoned their encroachment in eastern Liberia.

Since the French were adamant, Liberia made the following appeal to the world:

> We appeal to all the civilized nations of the world Consider we pray you the situation. Having been carried away into slavery, and, by the blessing of God, returned from exile to our fatherland, are we now to be robbed of our rightful inheritance?

> We do not consent to France's taking that portion of our territory lying between the Cavalla and San Pedro Rivers; nor do we recognize its claims to points on our Grain Coast, which as shown above, our government has been in possession of for so long. We protest too against that government's marking off narrow limits of interior land for us. We claim the right to extend as far interior ward as our necessities require. We are not foreigners, we are Africans and this is Africa. Such being the case, we have certain natural rights—God given rights to this territory—which no foreigners can have. [35]

---

[35]    Frederick Starr, *Liberia: Description, History, and Problems* (Chicago: n.a., 1913), 114.

# CHAPTER XVI

# DECLARATION OF INDEPENDENCE

The decision of the Liberian colony to regularize its status in keeping with existing international law was rather abrupt. Governor Joseph Jenkins Roberts argued that he had exhausted all possibilities to dissuade foreign powers from infringing on the commonwealth, without success. He finally announced why the declaration of independence was necessary: "Embarrassment we labor under with respect to the encroachments of foreigners, and the objections urged by Great Britain in regard to our sovereignty."[1]

The British, through its leadership in adjacent Sierra Leone, viewed Liberia and the American Colonization Society (ACS), as private entities, which did not have the legal right "to exercise sovereignty especially in the domain of levying and collecting customs duties."[2]

The Commonwealth government took the only course it had been advised to take: declaration of independence to gain international recognition. The ACS consented to relinquish its control at a time when the parent organization's financial burden was increasing and unbearable.

Harvard Law School Professor Simon Greenleaf drafted the proposed constitution from the United States. Although he never visited the Colony, Greenleaf was highly instrumental in pepping the Colony to declare independence. From that point, the decision to sever political ties with the American colonization Society was relatively hastened. An assembly was called to debate the document in Monrovia. The Convention appointed Samuel Benedict and Jacob Prout as president and secretary respectively.

---

[1] *The Liberian Constitution*, http://www.onliberia.org/con_1847.htm (accessed January 22, 2014).

[2] Ibid.

Hilary Teage wrote the Liberian Declaration of Independence in 1847 and announced to the world why it was imperative for the country to declare independence. He wrote:

> We, the representatives of the people of the commonwealth of Liberia, in convention assembled, invested with the authority of forming a new government, relying upon the aid and protection of the Great Arbiter of human events, do hereby in the name and on behalf of the people of this commonwealth, publish and declare the said commonwealth a free, sovereign, and independent state, by the name and title of the Republic of Liberia.

> While announcing to the nations of the world the new position which the people of this Republic have felt themselves called upon to assume, courtesy to their opinion seems to demand a brief accompanying statement of the causes which induced them, first to expatriate themselves from the land of their nativity and to form settlements on this barbarous coast, and now to organize their government by the assumption of a sovereign and independent character. Therefore, we respectfully ask their attention to the following facts:

*Liberian Flag: 1822-1847*

*Flag of Liberia: Since 1847*

*Joseph Jenkins Roberts (1809-1876): First President of Liberia*

We recognize in all men certain inalienable rights; among these are life, liberty, and the right to acquire, possess, enjoy, and defend property. By the practice and consent of men in all ages, some system or form of government is proved to be necessary to exercise, enjoy, and secure their rights, and every people have a right to institute a government, and to choose and adopt that system, or form of it, which in their opinion will most effectively accomplish these objects, and secure their happiness, which does not interfere with the just rights of others. The right, therefore, to institute government and powers necessary to conduct it is an inalienable right and cannot be resisted without the grossest injustice.

We, the people of the Republic of Liberia, were originally inhabitants of the United States of North America.

In some parts of that country we were debarred by law from all rights and privileges of man—in other parts, public sentiment, more powerful than law, frowned us down.

We were excluded from all participation in the government.

We were taxed without our consent.

We were compelled to contribute to the resources of a country which gave us no protection.

We were made a separate and distinct class, and against us every avenue of improvement was effectively closed. Strangers from other lands, of a color different from ours, were preferred before us.

We uttered our complaints, but they were unattended to, or only met by alleging the peculiar institutions of the country.

All hope of a favorable change in our country was thus wholly extinguished in our bosoms, and we looked with anxiety for some asylum from the deep degradation.

The western coast of Africa was the place selected by American benevolence and philanthropy for our future home. Removed beyond those influences which oppressed us in our native land, it was hoped we would be enabled to enjoy those rights and privileges and exercise and improve those faculties which the God of nature has given us in common with the rest of mankind.

Under the auspices of the American Colonization Society, we established ourselves here, on land, acquired by purchase from the lords of the soil.

In an original compact with this society, we, for important reasons, delegated to it certain political powers; while this institution stipulated that whenever the people should become capable of conducting the government, or whenever the people should desire it, this institution would resign the delegated power, peacefully withdraw its supervision, and leave the people to the government of themselves.

Under the auspices and guidance of this institution which has nobly and in perfect faith redeemed its pledge to the people, we have grown and prospered.

From time to time our number has been increased by immigration from America, and by accession from native tribes; and from time to time, as circumstances required it, we have extended our borders by the acquisition of land by honorable purchase from the natives of the country.

As our territory has extended and our population increased our commerce has also increased. The flags of most civilized nations of the earth float in our harbors, and their merchants are opening an honorable and profitable trade. Until recently, these visits have been of a uniformly harmonious character; but as they have become more frequent and to more numerous points of our extended coast, questions have arisen which, it is supposed, can be adjusted only by agreement between sovereign powers.

For years past, the American Colonization Society has virtually withdrawn from all direct and active part in the administration of the government, except in the appointment of the governor, who is also a colonist, for the apparent purpose of testing the ability of the people to conduct the affairs of government, and no complaint of crude legislation, nor of mismanagement, nor of mal-administration has yet been heard.

In view of these facts, this institution, the American Colonization Society, with that good faith which has uniformly marked all its dealings with us did by a set of resolutions in January, in the year of our Lord one thousand eight hundred and forty-six, dissolve all political connections with the people of this Republic, returned the power with which it was delegated, and left the people to the government of themselves.

The people of the Republic of Liberia, they, are of right, and in fact, a free, sovereign, and independent state, possessed of all the rights, powers, and functions of government.

In assuming the momentous responsibilities of the position they have taken, the people of this republic feel justified by the necessities of the case, and with this conviction they throw themselves with confidence upon the candid consideration of the civilization of the world.

Liberia is not the offspring of ambition, nor the tool of avaricious speculation.

No desire for territorial aggrandizement brought us to these shores; nor do we believe so sordid a motive entered into the high consideration of those who aided us in providing this asylum. Liberia is an asylum from the most grinding oppression.

In coming to the shores of Africa, we indulged the pleasing hope that we would be permitted to exercise and improve those faculties which impart to man his dignity; to nourish in our hearts the flame of honorable ambition; to cherish and indulge these aspirations which a beneficent Creator had implanted in every human heart, and to evince to all who despise, ridicule, and oppress our race that we possess with them a common nature; are with them susceptible of equal refinement, and capable to equal advancement in all that adorns and dignifies man. We were animated by the hope that here we should be at liberty to train up our children in the way that they should go;

to inspire them with the love of an honorable fame; to kindle within them the flame of a lofty philanthropy, and to form strongly within them the principles of humanity, virtue, and religion.

Amongst the strongest motives to leave our native land—to abandon forever the scenes of our childhood and to sever the most endeared connections—was the desire for a retreat where, free from the agitation of fear and molestation, we could approach in worship the God of our fathers.

Thus far our highest hopes have been realized. Liberia is already the happy home of thousands who were once the doomed victims of oppressions; and, if left unmolested to go on with her natural and spontaneous growth, if her movements be left free from the paralyzing intrigues of jealous ambition and unscrupulous avarice, she will throw open wider and yet a wider door for thousands who are now looking with an anxious eye for some land of rest.

Our courts of justices are open equally to the stranger and the citizen for the redress of grievances, for the remedy of injuries, and for the punishment of crime.

Our numerous and well-attended schools attest our efforts and our desire for the improvement of our children. Our churches for the worship of our Creator, everywhere to be seen, bear testimony to our acknowledgment of His providence.

The native African bowing down with us before the altar of the living God, declares that from us, feeble as we are, the light of Christianity has gone forth, while upon that curse of curses, the slave trade, a deadly blight has fallen, as far as our influence extends.

Therefore, in the name of humanity, virtue, and religion, in the name of the great God, our common Creator, we appeal to the nations of Christendom, and earnestly and respectfully ask of them that they will regard us with the sympathy and friendly considerations to which the peculiarities of our condition entitles us, and to that comity which marks the friendly intercourse of civilized and independent communities.

The Declaration of Independence was signed by twelve members of the Constitutional Convention in Monrovia, on July 5, 1847. The representatives included: Samuel Benedict, Hilary Teage, Elijah Johnson, John Naustehlau Lewis, Beverly R. Wilson and J.B. Gripon (Montserrado County); John Day, Amos Herring, Anthony William Gardiner and Ephriam Titler (Grand Bassa County); and Jacob W. Prout and Richard E. Murray (Sinoe County).[3]

Liberia declared Independence on July 26, 1847. Qualified voters approved the Constitution of the Commonwealth on September 27, 1847. Joseph Jenkins Roberts was elected first president of the new republic in October of 1847.

The Constitution stipulated that only Africans could become citizens, "if they adopted the Western culture and Christian beliefs of the American settlers."[4] From offset, citizenship was based on race, and non-Africans of Negro parentage were not to be admitted.

The question of citizenship became a contentious issue in the early days of the country. Some citizens wanted citizenship granted to Euramericans or white people. The Constitution Commission objected. It voted in favor of granting citizenship to persons of color or "Africans."[5] However, this stipulation led one Moorish Jew trader on the Liberian coast to claim a Liberian citizenship, because he considered himself an African, though he and his children looked white or European.[6] Many Liberians contended that the law needed a revision to exclude all white people from becoming citizens of Liberia. The fear was that some slave traders who had been in business in the region for a long time could claim citizenship as Africans and become a part of the Liberian society. Moreover, banning Europeans or whites from becoming citizens of Liberia at the time served a political interest of preserving the colony as a black experiment for democracy in Africa, without the dominance of white people.

Liberia became independent at a time when blacks were legally barred from obtaining citizenship in the United States. The Negro Republic made sure that whites could not gain citizenship in its territory. Consequently, the ambiguity in the constitution, "persons of color," was amended to read "Negroes or those of Negro decent."

Although the constitution was slavishly patterned after that of the United States, there were important distinctions. Slavery was banned

---

3  Charles Henry Huberich, *The Political and Legislative History of Liberia* (New York: Central Book Company, 1947).
4  Ibid.
5  Ibid, 159.
6  Ibid.

throughout Liberia. Only Negroes or those of Negro descent could become citizens.

At the time of independence, there were about 4500 Liberians who originated from the United States.[7] The first election was held on the first Tuesday of October 1847. Roberts defeated his rival Samuel Benedict and became president, with Nathaniel Brander as vice president.

Governor Roberts set up a committee of seven ladies to make the country's first national colors, the Lone Star. The flag was unfurled on August 24, 1847.[8] The flag became known as the *Lone Star*. The committee for creating the flag, included Susannah Waring Lewis (Chairwoman), Sarah Draper, Mary Hunter, Rachel Johnson, J. B. Russwurm, Matilda Spencer Newport, Collinette Teage.

Words to the "Lone Star" were written by Edwin J. Barclay in 1901. He was the18[th] President of Liberia.[9]

## The Lone Star

> When freedom raised her glowing form on Montserrado's verdant height,
> She set within the doom of night, 'midst low ring stars and thunderstorms the star of liberty—and seizing from the waking morn, its burnished shield of golden flame
> she lifted in her proud name and raise a people long forlorn
> to noble destiny
> **Refrain**
> The Lone Star forever! The Lone Star forever!
> O long may it float over land and over sea.
> Desert it, no never! Uphold it, forever!
> O shout for the Lone Star banner,
> All hail.

---

[7]   Yarema, 46.

[8]   Doris Banks Henries, *The Liberian Nation: A Sort History* (New York: Herman Jaffe, 1954), 198.

[9]   Liberia's eighteenth president, Daniel E. Howard, signed into law on Oct. 24, 1915, that August 24 be declare a national holiday to celebrate the "Lone Star."

## Pledge of Allegiance

Many Liberians, especially school children, can cite the Pledge of Allegiance to the Liberian Flag. It is quoted when the Flag is being hoisted, especial in schools and other public events. The words are: "I pledge allegiance to the flag of Liberia and to the Republic for which it stands, one nation indivisible, with liberty and justice for all."

The Pledge of Allegiance is similar to that of the United States. The major difference is the exclusion of the phrase "under God," which Congress added in 1954 for fear that the communists in the United States would transform the country to become a communist nation.[10] Liberia did not alter its Pledge to the Lone Star."

## Description of the Flag

The Liberian flag is called the Lone Star. It has eleven horizontal stripes, representing the eleven men who signed the Declaration of Independence and the Constitution. The blue squared field signifies the African continent. The five pointed white star in the blue field represents the nation as the first independent African republic on the continent. The red color symbolizes "courage or bravery;" the white, "purity or cleanliness," and the blue is the symbol for "trustworthiness or fidelity." Moreover, the Lone Star is modelled after the flag of the United States, "Old Glory."

## Description of the Seal

The "Coat of Arms" for Liberia is the official Seal. It contains a palm tree, signifying the land's natural resources. A plow and spade by the pam tree demonstrate how the nation would develop its sources through hard work. Within the Seal is a dove with an open scroll in its craws, which indicates the means of communication with the world and desire for peaceful coexistence with other nations. The

*The Coat of Arms*

---

[10]   http://www.ushistory.org/documents/pledge.htm (accessed April 18, 2014).

rising sun symbolizes the birth of the first African Republic in Africa. The sailing vessel represents the arriving of the immigrants. The motto is inscribed in the emblem above: "The Love of Liberty Brought Us Here," and below the emblem is the name of the country, "The Republic of Liberia."

The national motto has ignited controversies, especially among contemporary Liberian educators. Critics argue that the motto is not inclusive, because it seems to project an image of divisiveness between indigenous and settlers or those who came from the Americas in search of liberty. Many Liberians have argued, sometimes cynically, that the "Love of Liberty did not bring them to Liberia; it met them there." While that is easily said, it is difficult for most Liberian critics to answer the question, "If the Love of Liberty did not bring you to Liberia, what did?" The answer lies in the history of tribal people's migration to the coast.

Out of the major indigenous tribes in Liberia, with the exception of one, presumably, every other tribe migrated to the west coast from elsewhere in Africa.in search of liberty or trade opportunities. Almost every ethnic group that settled in the region did so through violent takeover of other tribal lands, as the chapter on *Peopling of the Grain Coast* clearly demonstrates. The Gola people are a typical example. After several battles in ancient Ghana, they lost their final battle and headed toward the west coast. On the Grain Coast, they nearly decimated the Dey people in the early 1800s, had it not been for the intervention of the settlers. The Gola and Vai ethnic groups had their own violent encounters, before an uneasy coexistence developed. The same can be said of most tribes in the region. No one had a free pass to the western coast of Africa. Settlement was achieved through violence.

## National Anthem

The National Anthem was written by Daniel B. Warner, third President of Liberia, and the music provided by a Liberian composer, Olmstead Lucas.[11]

> All hail, Liberia, hail! (All hail!), all hail, Liberia, hail! (All hail!)
> This glorious land of liberty, shall long be ours.
> Though new her name, green be her fame,
> And mighty be her powers, and mighty be her powers.

---

[11]   Johnston, 395.

In joy and gladness, with our hearts united,
We'll shout the freedom, of a race benighted.
Long live Liberia, happy land!
A home of glorious liberty, by God's command!
A home of glorious liberty, by God's command!

All hail, Liberia, hail! (All hail!), all hail, Liberia, hail! (All hail!)
In union strong success is sure, we cannot fail!
With God above, our rights to prove,
We will o'er all prevail, we will o'er all prevail!
With heart and hand our country's cause defending,
We'll meet the foe with valor unpretending.
Long live Liberia, happy land! A home of glorious liberty,
By God's command! A home of glorious liberty,
By God's command!

Several nations immediately recognized the first African Republic, except the United States. In high spirit, President Roberts travelled to England, where he was enthusiastically received. England offered the President a small gunboat.[12] Moreover, England recognized Liberia's ownership of the land between Cape Mount and Cape Palmas. The British government also informed Roberts that Liberia could have as many warships as needed to destroy slave centers around the Liberian settlements. France also recognized the Republic. In 1849, Portugal, Brazil, Sardinia, Austria, Denmark, Sweden, Norway, Hamburg, Brenem, Lubeck, and Haiti joined the bandwagon.

## Liberia College

When plans for a college were being formulated, Liberia had a coastline of about 350 miles from the Gallinas River, which was a part of Liberia at the time. The country also extended to about forty miles into the interior. Monrovia was the largest settlement in Montserrado. With its population of about 1300 inhabitants, it became the probable place to erect the first institution of higher education.

Liberia College was chartered in 1851, as a Liberian institution, but its plan was conceived and financially nurtured in Boston, Massachusetts. Two American Boards, the Trustees of Donations for Education in Liberia and the New York Colonization Society (a state branch of the ACS)

---

[12]    McPherson, *History of Liberia,* John Hopkins University Studies 9th Series, X, 34.

selected staff and provided all but a fraction of its support throughout the 19th century. Thus, while located on the west coast of Africa and under the aegis of the Liberian law, it was essentially an American college, the first of such American degree-granting college to be established abroad.[13]

> The college building cost $20,000, which was given by the Boston Board. Liberia gave 20 acres for the college and 1,000 acres of land in each of the four counties in Liberia. The first act of incorporation designated Clay Ashland as the proposed site In the matter of a site several suits were filed with the result that the college was located at Monrovia.

> Liberia College was opened in 1802 with a president 2 professors and 8 students with 8 more in preparation. The sources of its support until about 1890 were mainly the funds raised by the Boston board. In 1881, the Liberian legislature provided for the establishment of a preparatory school in each of the four counties. About 1890 the Republic assumed the responsibility of supporting the college principally.[14]

Joseph Jenkins Roberts, the first President of Liberia and the first President of Liberia College, was born in Virginia. He acquired broad education, even in the days of slavery. Professor Alexander Crummell had his education in New York and later graduated with a B.A. in literature from Queens College, Cambridge, London, in 1853. Another faculty member, Edwin Wilmot Blyden, a pure Negro from St. Thomas, acquired a fairly good education before immigrating to Liberia at age eighteen. In Liberia, his higher education was in classical studies under David A. Wilson, a conservative white American Presbyterian missionary.

Higher education in Liberia was hampered by many obstacles. Besides the hostile climate and diseases, racism had the most lasting effect.[15] For instance, there was great controversy over the site of the college between the Mulatto (headed by President Roberts) and the pure Negro (headed by Edward Wilmot Blyden). The former preferred Monrovia. The latter favored a site around the St. Paul River, to allow more indigenous people to gain access to the school.

---

[13]   Thomas Livingstone, Education and Race. A Biography Wilmot Blyden (San Francisco: The Glendesary Press) 1975.

[14]   United States. Bureau of Education, Report of the Commissioner of Education Made to the Secretary of . . . , Volume 1 (Washington: Government Printing Office, 1907), 126.

[15]   Bell Wiley, *Slaves No More*. Kentucky (The University Press of Kentucky, 1980).

Although politics and the caste question convulsed the country, the college continued to thrive. A significant number of educators saw it as necessary for development and as a symbol of prestige.

By the mid-1860, Blyden was considering introduction of Arabic and local languages in the College. He believed the liberalization of the curriculum would enable conversation and trade with the rural Muslim population. However, the missionaries shuddered, fearing that it would encourage the spread of Islam in the country. The elite also feared that the introduction of Arabic would be a threat to their power.

In 1951, the College took on a new name. It became known as the University of Liberia.

## U.S. Recognizes Liberia

Pressure mounted on the U.S. government to extend formal recognition to Liberia and Haiti. Henry Clay, one of the founding members of the ACS, wrote in October 18, 1851 thus, "I have thought for years that the independence of Liberia ought to be recognized by our government, and I have frequently urged it upon persons connected with the administration and I shall continue to do so if I have suitable opportunity."[16] The ACS and the Philadelphia Colonization Society were lobbying on behalf of Liberia. Newspapers and magazines took up the cause, pointing out that the time had come for Congress to recognize the African nation. One magazine declared: "It is high time that Congress should recognize Liberia as an independent self-sustaining government. Such a measure would be perfectly conformable to the principles, policy and direct interests of our country."[17]

For some Americans, the recognition of Haiti and Liberia was more than an act of benevolence. There were economic benefits for the three nations. In 1860, Haiti and Liberia ranked as America's 27th and 29th trading partners, respectively, out of 60 nations.[18]

A commercial agent at Cape Haytien alerted the United States government on June 5, 1854, thus:

---

16    The Journal of Negro History, Vol. 2, No. 4, Oct. 1917, 378.
17    The Journal of Negro History, 380.
18    *The Struggle for the Recognition of Haiti and Liberia as Independent Republics.* July 11, 2013. http://www.digilibraries.com/html_ebooks/120260/20752/www. digilibraries.com@20752@20752-h@20752-h-5.htm#Footnote_457_457.

By recognition of the Independence of Hayti, our commerce would be likely to advance still more. Our citizens trading there would enjoy more privileges, besides standing on a better footing. Many decided advantages might be obtained through treaty and our own government would exercise a wholesome influence over theirs, of which it stands much in need.[19]

In his first annual message of December 3, 1861, President Lincoln addressed the need to develop diplomatic relations with Haiti and Liberia. He emphasized the fact that there were "important commercial advantages" in recognizing the two Negro nations.[20]Meanwhile, in 1858, the Reverend John Seys of the Methodist Mission was appointed the United States agent for freedmen in Liberia, the U.S. government first consul to the country.[21]

Senator Charles Sumner[22] asked Congress on February 4, 1862, to appoint representatives to Haiti and Liberia, but the opposition argued otherwise. In the words of one:

If after such a measure should take effect, the Republic of Haiti and the Republic of Liberia were to send their Ministers Plenipotentiary or their Chargé d'Affaires to our government, they would have to be received by the President and by all the functionaries of the government upon the same terms of equality with similar representatives from other powers. If a full-blooded Negro were sent in that capacity from either of the two countries, by the laws of nations he could demand that he be received precisely on the same terms of equality with the white representative from the powers on the earth composed of white people.[23]

---

[19] Carter G. Woodson, Ed. *The Struggle of Liberia and Haiti For Recognition.*The Journal of Negro History, Volume 2 (PA: The Association For The Study Of The Negro Life And History, 1917), 378.

[20] Benjamin Quarles, *Lincoln and the Negro* (NY: Oxford University Press, 1962).

[21] Peter Duignan and L. H. Gann, *The United States and Africa: A History*(Cambridge: Cambridge University Press, 1984).

[22] Charles Sumner was a white abolitionist. He once delivered a speech on "Bleeding Kansas" on the Senate floor against slaveholders nearly, and it nearly caused him his life. Preston Brooks, Nephew of Butler, walked in Sumner's office and beat him with a cane until Sumner was unconscious. He stayed in doctor care for nearly four years. Southerners applauded Brooks and sent him more cans to be used, when necessary.

[23] Johnson, *83.*

Congress had difficulties reconciling the fact that the day would come when former slaves could become diplomatic and political partners in Washington. The expression of resistance was even more ruthless as declared by Saulsbury of Maryland:

> How fine it will look, after emancipating the slaves in this District, to welcome here at the White House an African, full-blooded, all gilded and belaced, dressed in court style, with wig and sword and tights and shoe-buckles and ribbons and spangles and many other adornments which African vanity will suggest; and if this bill should pass the Houses of Congress and become a law, I predict that in twelve months, some Negro will walk upon the floor of the Senate and carry his family into that which is apart for foreign Ministers. If that is agreeable to the tastes and feelings of the people of this country, it is not to mine.[24]

Nevertheless, the Bill passed in the Senate by thirty two to seven votes; eighty six to thirty seven in the House.[25] President Abraham Lincoln signed the historic document. Representatives from Haiti and Liberia were gracious at the occasion. The Liberian Commissioners, Alexander Crummell, Edward Blyden, and J.D. Johnson expressed their country's indebtedness to Senator Charles Sumner for pushing for the bill passage, despite major oppositions.

As the United States was progressing toward civil war over the peculiar institution of slavery, supporters and opponents of colonization had one last moment of reflection; an edgy silence and a deep sigh, before crossing over to stand on the right side of history on February 4, 1862. Even the AME Church could not hold out. Once, it became the first black institution to openly oppose the American Colonization Society by setting up twelve committees to obstruct the advancement of the ACS. It turned blacks against immigration to Liberia, but in 1862, 45 years later, a lot had changed politically and Liberia was no longer a colony. The Church praised the government, and added: "That, in the noble act of the United States Senate in passing a law recognizing the independence of Haiti and Liberia, we see the hand of God in a movement which we regard as ominous of good for the race."

In November of 1864, the two black republics signed treaties of friendship with the United States. Abraham Lincoln appointed Abraham

---

[24]   Ibid.

[25]   *African Repository*, 1863, XXXIX, 39.

Hanson, a native of the West Indies, as Consul General to Liberia.[26] In the same year, after forty eight years of operation, the American Colonization society legally seized operation and turned its properties over to Phelps-Stokes.

## Mysterious Death of Edward J. Roye

*Edward James Roye, 5th President of Liberia*
*January 3, 1870 – October 26, 1871*

Edward James Roye was born in the U.S. State of Ohio on February 3, 1815. His parents were Ibo from Nigeria.[27] Roye was one of the immigrants who arrived in the ACS Colony in 1846, while the country was inching toward independence. He became the first Negro, with pure African parentage, to become President of Liberia in 1870. Roye was removed from power in 1871. The circumstances surrounding his ouster remain imprecise, though it is generally believed that Roye was deposed in a coup d'état. It is not certain who carried out the assault, but he was found dead on February 12, 1872, after his deposition in October of 1871 and spending a few months in jail.

Although President Roye seemed to have been popular in the country for the fact that he won re-election for a second term of office, he angered many people and seemed to have given his political enemies the tools they needed to depose him. The President contracted an unpopular load from London to finance his domestic programs of railroad construction to connect rural Liberia with the coast for trade and commerce with the indigenous inhabitants. He proposed investment in education to benefit

---

[26]    *Principal Officers and Chiefs of Mission, by year: 1865.* http://history.state.gov/departmenthistory/people/by-year/1865 (accessed June 13, 2013).

[27]    President Edward J. Roye (1870-1871). http://www.liberiapastandpresent.org/EJRoye.htm (accessed October 3, 2013).

both Liberians and natives. But the terms of the loan was perceived by the Legislature to be too high and fraudulent. The government objected to the term of the loan. Meanwhile, Roye proposed raising the term of the presidency from two to four years, when he announced:

> In pursuance of a resolution passed at your last session, authorizing the president to cause an election to be held on the first Tuesday in May, 1870, to ascertain the opinion of the people constitutional amendment, I have to inform you that the said election was held, and according to the returns made to the Department of State of said election, the constitutional amendment was considered carried; and I have caused a proclamation to be issued to that effect.[28]

Roye was impeached by the Senate for allegedly violating "the constitution by issuing a proclamation falsely declaring the constitution to be so amended as to increase the presidential term to four instead of two years."[29]

How Roye died is still a mystery. Most historians have their own version of what happened. Most of the popular views have been summarized by Dr. Fred P.M. van der Kraaij, author of *The Open Door Policy of Liberia—An Economic History of Modern Liberia*.[30] He writes:

> According to some sources Roye escaped from prison but was drowned while trying to escape to a British ship. One author reports that the canoe in which Roye tried to make his escape capsized after which he drowned. The English money, which he had tied around his waist—thought to be the proceeds from the 1870 Loan—was taken from his body and stolen after his body was brought ashore (Huberich)[31]. Another author writes that the weight of the money around his waist was the cause of his drowning when he was swimming to a British ship (Banks Henries).[32]

---

[28] Teah Wulah, Back to Africa: A Liberian Tragedy (IN: Authorhouse, 2009), 362.

[29] Hanes Walton, Robert L. Stevenson, James B. Rosser, eds., Liberian Politics: The Portrait by African American Diplomat J. Milton Turner (Maryland: Lexington Books, 2002).

[30] President Edward J. Roye (1870-1871). http://www.liberiapastandpresent.org/EJRoye.htm

[31] Charles H., Huberich, *The Political and Legislative History of Liberia*, 2 volumes (New York, 1947).

[32] Henries, Banks, A. D., *Presidents of the First African Republic* (London, 1963).

According to other sources, Roye died in prison, after having been dragged half-naked through the streets of Monrovia after his attempt to escape from prison (Karnga, Cassell).[33] Cassell denies that Roye was drowned though he confirms that he carried money in a belt when he tried to escape. According to him, Roye was savagely beaten after being brought ashore and robbed of the money he carried in his belt.

After President Roye was ousted, Vice President James S. Smith, a True Whig, was sworn in as President. Under pressure, he was replaced by an Executive Committee, which governed the country until J.J. Roberts, a Republican) was sworn in as president again on January 1, 1872, without national election.

Nevertheless, the True Whig gained power in six years, when Anthony W. Gardiner became president in 1878. Since then, the True Whig (we hope in God) never lost another election until the toppling of the William R. Tolbert government on April 12, 1980, in a coup d'état.

---

[33]     Abayomi, Cassell, C., *Liberia: History of the First African Republic* (New York, 1970).

188

# CHAPTER XVII

# FINAL THOUGHTS:
# SLAVERY AND AFRICA'S
# CULPABILITY

On every continent and among all peoples exists historical evidence of the savagery of wars that had been waged against humanity throughout the ages. Equally appalling is the extent to which some historians will go to defend or ignore evidence of seismic brutality against indigents of the world.

Many blacks in the Americas have been ambivalent about their identity with Africa, and for a good reason. Most blacks have throbbing memories of the Negro experience in slavery. It is even more excruciating to consider the role their African ancestors played in organizing and profiting from the sales of Africans by African chiefs.

In 1859, Rev. Henry Highland Garnet, founder of the African Colonization Society, once addressed the following letter to abolitionists who opposed his scheme:

> I entreated you to tell your readers what your objections are to the civilization and Christianization of Africa. What objection has you to colored men in this country engaging in agriculture, lawful trade, and commerce in the land of my forefathers? What objection have you to an organization that shall endeavor to check and destroy the African slave trade, and that desires to co-operate with anti-slavery men and women of every grade in our own land, and to toil with them for the overthrow of American slavery?—Tell us, I pray you, tell us in your clear and manly style. 'Gird up thy loins, and answer thou me, if thou canst.[1]

---

[1]    Howard Brotz, *African-American Social and Political Thought, 1850-1920* (NJ: Transaction Publishers, 1992), 262.

Abolitionist Frederick Douglass' Response to Garnet:

> Among all the obstacles to the progress of civilization and of Christianity in Africa, there is not one so difficult to overcome as the African slave trade. No argument is needed to make this position evident . . . One of our chief considerations upon with the African Civilization Society is recommended to our favorable regard, is its tendency to break up the slave trade. We have looked at this recommendation, and find no reason to believe that any one man in Africa can do more for the abolition of that trade, while living in Africa, than while living in America. If we cannot make Virginia, with all her enlightenment and Christianity, believe that there are better uses for her energies than employing them in breeding slaves for the market, we see not how we can expect to make Guinea, with its ignorance and savage selfishness, adopt our notions of political economy. Depend upon it, the savage chiefs on the western coast of Africa, who for ages have been accustomed to selling their captives into bondage, and pocketing the ready cash for them, will not more readily see and accept our moral and economical ideas, than the slave-traders of Maryland and Virginia.[2]

Africans have had their share of woes and agonizing recollections of a brutal past from antiquity, as other continents. Historical inquiries bear this out. However, defenders of the African Innocence Project[3] see otherwise. They claim warlords and kidnappers were not aware of the brutal experience of enslavement away from Africa. The victims of European greed and atrocities, they argue, were the natives. Others argue that domestic slavery was benign and did not encourage violence as chattel slavery did. Indeed, this seems to have been the popular notion about slavery in Africa in the 19th century. Since then, historiographical inquiries present a different image of what really happened on the African frontier of slavery. It is not a pretty picture.

As Africa's participation in slavery is being discussed, it is worth noting that Africa did not originate the trans-Atlantic slave trade, nor was it a willing partner in the initial trade of its own natives. From the offset,

---

2    Ibid, 265.

3    This refers to the tendency to declare Africa as a victim or lesser player in the domestic and trans-Atlantic slave trade. Slavery in Africa is presented as a benign institution which did very little harm to its captives.

some African chiefs were lured by Europeans to become willing partners in the repulsive crime of servitude, but most natives fiercely resisted. They confronted traders as aggressively as they could. The resistance sometimes led to the kidnapping of European crewmen, burning of ships, setting watchmen over villages when most men were away, or offering other merchandise in exchange for captives.

Initially, European explorers went to Africa in search of ivory, elephant tusks, fish, palm oil, silver, indigo, cotton, silk, amber, spices, rice, wax and hides. That was before a major need for sugar arose in Europe. To keep up with rising demands, European merchants established huge sugar cane farms in the West Indies. After then, the need for cheap labor intensified. Eventually, African goods lost value, when slaves became the new medium to replenish cheap labor on plantations in the Americas.

However, before slavery was instituted as a dominant force, Africans were forceful in their earlier response against enslavement. An explorer called Alvise Ca'Damosto wrote about his own encounter in 1454, when nearly 150 men attacked his ship on the River Gambia. He stated:

> They (Gambians) had had news of our coming and of our trade with the negroes of Senegal [Senegal River], who, if they sought our friendship could not but be bad men, for they firmly believed that we Christians ate human flesh, and that we only bought negroes to eat them; that for their part they did not want our friendship on any terms, but sought to slaughter us all, and to make a gift of our possessions to their lord.[4]

The natives built high thick walls and dug trenches around vulnerable villages and sought to divert rivers. "They built ramparts and fortresses with deep ditches and planted venomous and thorny trees and bushes all around."

Abdel Kader Kane, the Muslim *almami* or leader of Futa Toro in northern Senegal mounted strong resistance against slave traders. He fought to release his tribesmen from kidnappers. In 1788, for instance, he ordered the search of a French convoy in Futa Toro and liberated ninety kidnapped Africans.[5] He sought to dissuade slave caravans from traversing his region.

---

[4] *African Resistance*, http://abolition.nypl.org/essays/african_resistance/2/ (access February 20, 2014).

[5] Sylviane A. Diouf, *Servants of Allah: African Muslims Enslaved in the Americas*, 15th Edition (NY: New York University Press, 1998).

After a kidnapping incident involving a Frenchman, Kane decried the criminal and dispatched the following letter to the French governor in St. Louise:

> We are warning you that all those who will come to our land to trade [in slaves] will be killed and massacred if you do not send our children back. Would not somebody who was very hungry abstain from eating if he had to eat something cooked with his blood? We absolutely do not want you to buy Muslims under any circumstances. I repeat that if your intention is to always buy Muslims you should stay home and not come to our country anymore. Because all those who will come can be assured that they will lose their life.[6]

African resistance to slavery softened overtime, as well equipped slave traders with advanced weapons became indomitable and ferocious. It is important to note that Europeans did not introduce slavery to Africa. Domestic slavery was well developed on the continent's three ancient empires of Ghana, Mali and Songhai, before Europeans established regular business routes to the continent in the 16th century for chattel slaves.

> The Arab slave trade predates the European slave trade in Africa. The Arab slave trade began in the 7th century and lasted more than 1000 years. Africans were taken from present-day Kenya, Tanzania, Sudan, Ethiopia, Somalia, Djibouti, and transported to Saudi Arabia, Iraq, Kuwait, Turkey, and other parts of the Arab world. The Arab slave trade stretched over three continents at its peak. African male slaves, who were often made eunuchs, were employed as servants, soldiers, or laborers by their Arab owners. An eunuch is a man who has been castrated and is incapable of reproduction; eunuchs usually guarded the Arab women. African female slaves were mostly purchased as concubines or house servants.[7]

While there is a tendency to romanticize domestic or trans-Sahara slavery, it is vital to point out that the treatment of slaves was uneven on the continent. Most slaves did backbreaking work in the salt and

---

[6]    Ibid, 47.

[7]    http://www.examiner.com/article/qaddafi-apologized-to-african-leaders-for-the-arab-slave-trade-africa (accessed May 4, 2012).

gold mines of West Africa. In agriculture, they irrigated fields, toiled on plantations to produce millet, sorghum, wheat and rice.[8] They carried goods and dignitaries over long distances on their heads or shoulders. The trips lasted from a few days to months, across the hot Sahara and Nubian Deserts. At the end of the journey, some porters or slaves were resold to other merchants, leaving families behind. Slaves were often enlisted in wars to fight for the protection of the warlords that captured them and burned down their villages. In those engagements, they risked being captured, killed, and sold again.

The masters controlled the sexual life of slaves. Some males were castrated and the women became sexual slaves.[9] Most castrated males died from diseases, but the price of the few who survived was higher than what it cost for a regular male.

Slave women were forced into marriages or concubinary relationships. The masters often made the arrangements and determined the nature of sexual relations with the captives. Professor Lovejoy made the following observation:

> The extent of coercion involved in slavery was sometimes obvious and sometimes disguised. The master could enforce his will because of his ability to punish slaves for the failure to comply with his orders or to perform their tasks satisfactorily. Whipping, confinement, deprivation of food, extra hard work and the ability to dispose of slaves through sale were common means of coercion. Physical punishment could lead to death, and even when there were legal and customary prohibitions on killing slaves, these were rarely enforced. Sacrifices of slaves at funerals and public ceremonies, which were common in some places, were also examples to the slaves. Such public displays were not usually a form of punishment for insubordination; in fact, they were sometimes conceived of as an honour, but most often slaves were purchased specifically for sacrifice.[10]

One of the most dreadful features of human servitude is the loss of the right to choose or make decisions for self or family members. Slave masters used women for reproduction and production. Females, including girls, were more likely to be objects of human sacrifice than men were. As

---

8 Lovejoy, 33.

9 James L. Watson, *Asian and African Systems of Slavery* (CA: University of California Press, 1980), 39.

10 Lovejoy, 4.

Jack Goody wrote in *Slaves in Time and Space*, "Apart from the appalling conditions of capture and of transfer to the market place, conditions which at times rivaled the horrors of the Atlantic-trade, they were kinless persons; their insecurity of life was often great. In that complex and sophisticated state of Ashanti, slaves fled the town when they heard the funeral drums for fear they would be slaughtered.[11] Lovejoy also contends that humans were sacrificed to religious deities:

> Slaves were also sacrificed to religious deities, at funerals and on other occasions; these practices too promoted social control. At Uburu, for example, a slave was ususally killed in deference to the supernatural protector of the salt lake and marked the opening of the salt season, while in the Niger delta, a slave could be offered to such river spirits as Duminea. The taking of titles, especially *ozo* titles, required the death of slaves too. The 400 title-holders at Asaba in 1881, for example, had each scarified a slave on assuming their titles; two more slaves were to be killed at the funerals of each of these men. At Calabar, the number funeral victims was much larger; hundreds of slaves were killed at several important funerals in the nineteenth century. In most places, however, one or two deaths was usually sufficient. The cheapening of human life symbolized in these practices was perhaps most gruesomely displayed at the house of skulls in Bonny and the shrine of Ibinukpabi at Aro Chukwu, which was lined with the heads of slaves.[12]

In Somali, slaves were acquired from markets primarily to perform objectionable tasks on the plantation premises. "They toiled under the control of and separately from their Somali patrons. In terms of legal considerations, Bantu slaves were also devalued. Additionally, Somali social mores strongly discouraged censure and looked down upon any kind of sexual contact with Bantu slaves. Freedom for these plantation slaves was also often acquired through escape."[13]

Though the variability of slaves' treatment in Africa was vast, a large number of captives experienced humane treatment during some time in their enslavement. Evidently, most slaves were not criminals or villains.

---

[11] Watson, 31.

[12] Lovejoy, 186

[13] Slavery in Somalia, http://www.absoluteastronomy.com/topics/African_slave_trade (accessed May 2, 2012).

They were ordinary people whose lives were changed abruptly by man stealers or headhunters. In a bizarre example, "The kings of Dahomey routinely slaughtered slaves in hundreds or thousands in sacrificial rituals, and the use of slaves as human sacrifices was also known in Cameroon."[14] Other states noted for brutal practices of enslavement were "Oyo, Benin, Igala, Kaabu, Asanteman, Dahomey, the Aro Confederacy and the Imbangalawar bands."

African slave catchers and sellers did not determine the conditions or supervise the treatment of captives away from Africa, but slavery was a business venture between Africans and European traders. Without the cooperation of African intermediaries, it is unlikely that the trans-Sahara or trans-Atlantic slave trade would have succeeded to the extent as it did.

The manner in which slaves were captured and arranged for the trek of no return to the coast or internal markets leaves no doubts that the African slave traders did not expect any humane treatment of their captives.

> Many slaves were obtained very far inland where they were collected in a coffle and marched to the coast. Two slaves were chained together around the leg and groups of four were secured by a rope. At times, a Y-shaped stick was fastened with the fork round the neck of the slave walking in front and the stem resting on the neck of the slave walking behind. Free Africans employed by the slave catchers guarded the coffle.[15]

The exaggerated benevolent accounts of domestic slavery may give the impression that the liberality of freedom was transcontinental. This distortion leads to the tendency to look at African slavery only through rose-colored glasses by suppressing the violence associated with it. Some historians have succeeded to do just that. *In Preparation for Slavery*, authors Salzberger and Taylor wrote:

> Slavery existed in Africa before the arrival of the Europeans; it was markedly different from the European institution of slavery. In Africa, slaves were captives taken in war or kidnapped in raids. They might win or earn their freedom. African slaves were not different from African masters, except by accident of fortune. They might be slaves for a time, and

---

[14]  Nicolas Argenti, *The Intestines of the State: Youth, Violence and Belated Histories in the Cameroon* (Grassfields: University of Chicago Press, 2007), 42.

[15]  http://www.guyana.org/features/guyanastory/chapter25.html (accessed May 2, 2012).

then free men and woman again. Their children were not slaves.[16]

In 1873, James Marshall, Chief Justice for the Gold Coast (Ghana) said, "I have not known any instance of domestic slaves leaving their owners for our castles, forts, or settlements . . . They are part and parcel of their families, to which they are so much attached as their own children." A Liberian environmental health professor, Dr. Syrulwa L. Soma, wrote in *Historical Resettlement of Liberia and Its Environmental Impact*, "Africa did not operate from a capitalistic context. Indigenous Africans could not have imagined the brutality of Europeans slavery."[17] Professor Soma added, "Africans trading African brothers and sisters into slavery did not do so of their own volition, succumbed to Europeans who ably employed the divide and rule tactic by choosing on ethnic group or another as their surrogates to whip up supplies of slaves." In this light, African cannot rightfully be held for slavery because they were the victims of European hoax."

## Dark Side of Domestic Slavery

The dark side of African slavery often overlooked is the violence associated domestic slavery. Slaves were obtained from tribal wars, kidnapping, raids, or pawns for debts or services. It was common for parents to pawn their children, especially young girls, to settle debts. The unredeemed women became concubines or wives of their new owners.

Strange as this may look, some relatives sold their kinsmen and women. "Communities tended to punish their criminals by selling them into slavery. Sometimes, parents sold their own children, coerced either by poverty and hunger, or in order to rid themselves of a ne'er-do-well.[18]

A slave trader who was in the habit of questioning captives how they were captured, wrote:

> On questioning them how they became slaves, I have only been told by one that her father sold her because he was in debt; several times I have been told that their elder brothers have

---

[16] Ronald P. Salzberger, Mary Turck, *Reparations for Slavery: A Reader* (MD: Rowman & Littlefield Publishers, 2004), 5.

[17] Syrulwa L. Soma, *Historical Resettlement of Liberiaand Its Environmental Impact* (MD: University Press of America, 1995), 7.

[18] Elizabeth Ischei, *A History of The Igbo People* (NY: St. Martin Press, 1976), 47.

sold them, but . . . the general reply I have received has been that they have been stolen when they had gone to fetch water from the river or the spring, as the case might be, or while they have been straying a little in the bush paths between their village and another.[19]

Of the 10-13 million slaves from Africa, it is estimated that 6-10 percent died at ports in Africa; 10-14 percent died in transit across the Atlantic.[20] Wars and raids often left the victims dead, and the captives were tied in a single file; pacing a few feet apart from each other, and escorted to the inland slave markets to the coast. The journey was hazardous, and many did not survive what could be many days of walking.

Raiding and kidnapping people at gunpoint became a common practice, especially among natives who made a business out of seizing others from neighboring tribes and selling them.[21] When the Europeans arrived, raiding intensified, as the slave traders became involved in the terrifying venture.

After invading villages for slaves, most of the women were retained for the domestic market and the men sold for destinations across the Atlantic.[22] "Slavery always was initiated through violence and it reduced the status of a person from a condition of freedom and citizenship to a condition of slavery."[23] Even in peonage, the victims did not give up their freedom and families voluntarily to move into a situation that greatly limited their capacity to control their labor or services and sex life.

## Africa's Liability

Although Africa's involvement in the trans-Atlantic slave trade was not voluntary initially, most chiefs and middlemen of the continent did benefit militarily and economically, wherever the trade was established. Therefore, Africa's culpability cannot be dismissed as a mere act of compulsion or crime of passion. It was a crime against humanity, and it

---

[19]   Ischei, 45.

[20]   Lovejoy, 63.

[21]   John Thornton, *Africa and Africans in the Making of the Atlantic World, 1400-1800*, 2nd edition (New York: Cambridge University Press, 1998). 310.

[22]   Watson, 13.

[23]   Paul Lovejoy, *Transformation into Slavery: A History of Slavery in Africa* (NY: *Cambridge Press, 2012)*, 3.

was not only criminals that were affected. Villages were burned and their inhabitants slaughtered, if they resisted capture.

African chiefs played a major role in all forms of slavery in Africa. This makes Africa culpable and should device means of compensating descendants of former slaves from Africa in the diaspora. It is time for Africa to set aside its version of "forty acres and a mule" for its victims of slavery.

Talks about reparation for wrongful enslavement of Africans are not new. The decision to compensate former slaves first took center stage after the Civil War in 1865. On January 16, 1865, General William Sherman moved fast to obtain approval from the War department to issue Special Field Order Number Fifteen to set aside strips of land for black settlements from confiscated Confederacy lands.[24] Nearly forty thousand black families benefitted from the plan before it was abandoned due to presidential veto from Andrew Jackson.

Under Republican radicalism for equality and social justice, Representative Thaddeus Stevens of Pennsylvania proposed a far-reaching bill in 1867 to amend for slavery. He called slaveholders "dethroned tyrants deprived of the luxuries of despotism." The Congressman suggested in a Reparations Bill for the African Slaves in the United States the following compensation scheme:

> Out of the lands thus seized and confiscated the slaves who have been liberated by the operations of the war and the amendment to the constitution . . . shall be distributed to them as follows, namely: to each male person who is the head of a family, forty acres; to each adult male, whether the head of a family of not, forty acres, to each widow who is the head of a family, forty acres.[25]

The civil rights movement was also vocal on the subject of reparation, but the United States government ignored the claims. However, the African World Reparations and Repatriation Truth Commission met in Accra, Ghana, in 1999 and discussed restitutions from western countries which benefitted from free African slave labor. The West was asked to "pay Africa $777 thousand billion within five years in restitution for

---

[24]   Angelyn Mitchell, *The Freedom to Remember: Narrative, Slavery, and Gender in Contemporary* (NJ: Rutgers University Press, 2002), 129.

[25]   By Ronald P. Salzberger, Mary Turck, *Reparations for Slavery: A Reader* (MD: Rowman & Littlefield Publishers, 2004).

enslaving Africans while colonizing the continent."[26] That was the first international conference on the subject. It also "called for all international debt owed by Africa to be "unconditionally cancelled.""

In March 2007, Archbishop of Canterbury, Dr. Rowan Williams, acknowledged the Church of England's role in the nefarious business of slavery. The Christian institution owned slaves in the Caribbean, and it freed them after the British government paid £13,000 for the loss of 665 slaves in 1833.[27] The Archbishop called for "paying reparations for its historical role in the slave trade."

On June 18, 2009, the United States Senate "unanimously passed a resolution apologizing for slavery and segregation in the United States."[28]However, the calls for the U.S. to pay up are unabated. The African Holocaust site suggests:

> The United States owes African-Americans over $100 trillion in reparations, based on 222,505,049 hours of forced labor between 1619 and 1865, with a compounded interest of 6%. Africans in America today have been enduring struggles of discrimination, lynchings, indentured servitude, high imprisonment rates from disproportionate bias sentencing, sold to the highest sugar cane and sharecropper plantation owners and the historical impact that slavery had on African American even today, that loss of wealth in inheritance, land, pay, history, culture, family names.[29]

Some African leaders see the need to close the shameful chapter on slavery by acknowledging Africa's culpability. The presidents of Ghana and Benin had already apologized. Benin president Matthieu Kerekou said intertribal hostility over the slave trade still exists in his country. Many of his people have never seen descendants of their forebears who were shipped off to the Americas. The late Libyan leader Muammar Qaddafi apologized on behalf of Arab nations for their involvement in the African slave trade at the Second Afro-Arab summit in Sirte, Libya, when he said:

26    *World: Africa Trillions Semanded in Slavery Reparations*, http://news.bbc.co.uk/2/hi/africa/ 424984.stm (access April 12, 2012).

27    Mark Oliver and Agencies, March 26, 2007, *Archbishop urges church to consider slavery reparations*, http://www.guardian.co.uk/ world/ 2007/mar/26/religion.race (accessed April 22, 2012).

28    http://www.nationalcenter.org/P21PR-Reparations_062209.html (accessed April 23, 20120).

29    http://www.africanholocaust.net/html_ah/holocaustspecial.htm#african (accessed May 2, 2012).

I regret the behavior of the Arabs . . . They brought African children to North Africa, they made them slaves, they sold them like animals, and they took them as slaves and traded them in a shameful way. I regret and I am ashamed when we remember these practices. I apologize for this.[30]

---

[30]   Libya: Kadhafi apologizes for slave trade—AfricaNews.com (accessed May 2, 2012).

# Select Bibliography

Adams, Francis D., and Barry Sanders. *Alienable Rights: The Exclusion of African Americans in a White Man's Land*. New York: HarperCollins Publishers, 2003.

Adams Oloo, *The Quest for Cooperation in the Nile Water Conflicts: The Case of Eritrea*. 8 May 2013.

Adams, Francis D., and Barry Sanders. *Alienable Rights: The Exclusion of African Americans in a White Man's Land*. New York: HarperCollins Publishers, 2003.

*Address of the Board of Managers of the American Colonization Society to Auxiliary Society and the People of the United States*. Pennsylvania: Davis and Force, 1820.

*African Repository*, Vol. XLIII, 1872.

Alexander, Leslie M. and Walter C. Rucker, Eds. *Encyclopedia of African American History 3 Volume*. CA: ABC-CLIO, LLC, 2010.

Aptheker, Herbert. *American Negro Slave Revolts*, new edition. New York: International Publishers, 1974.

Archives of the Ministry of Foreign Affairs, Monrovia. *Treaty of Peace and Amity between the Colony of Liberia and the Kings and Chiefs of the Dey Country* (n.d.), quoted in Bronwen Everill, "Those That Aare Well off Do Have The Natives as Slaves: Humanitarian 'Compromises' With Slavery in Sierra Leone and Liberia." JOUHS, 7 (Special Issue—Colloquium 2009).

Argenti, Nicolas. *The Intestines of the State: Youth, Violence and Belated Histories in the Cameroon*. Grassfields: University of Chicago Press, 2007.

Armistead, Wilson. *A Tribute for the Negro: Being a Vindication of the Moral, Intellectual, and Religious Capabilities.* Manchester: William Irwin, 1848.

Ashmun, Jehudi. *History of the American Colony in Liberia from December 1821 to 1823.* Washington City: Way and Gidean, 1826.

Bailey, Julius H. *Race Patriotism: Protest and Print Culture in the A.M.E. Church.* Knoxville: University of Tennessee Press, 2012.

Baron Henry Brougham Brougham and Vaux, *Historical Sketches of Statesmen Who Flourished In The Time of George III* (London and Glasgow: Richard Griffin and Company, 1861), 284.

Barton, David. *Original Intent: The Courts, the Constitution, and Religion.* TX: Wallbuilder, 2008.

Bateman, Newton et al. *Historical Encyclopedia of Illinois.* Chicago, IL: Munsell Publishing Company, 1908.

Bayard, Samuel J. *A sketch of the life of Com. Robert F. Stockton: with an appendix.* New York: Derby and Jackson, 1856.

Bedini, Silvio. *The Life of Benjamin Banneker: The First African-American Man of Science.* The Maryland Historical Society, 1999).

Bellman, Bery. *The Language of Secrecy.* NJ: Rutgers University Press, 1984.

Bernal, Martin. "Geography of a Life." *Xlibris Corporation.* Jul 3, 2012.

Beyan, Amos. *African American Settlements in West Africa.* New York: Palgrave Macmillan, 2005.

Blake, W. O. *The History of Slavery and the Slave Trade; Ancient and Modern. The Forms of Slavery that Prevailed in Ancient Nations, Particularly in Greece and Rome. The African Slave Trade and the Political History of Slavery in the United States.* Ohio: J. & H. Miller, 1857.

Boyd, John. *Christopher Columbus, His Life, His Work, His Remains.* NY: Putnam's Sons, 1903.

Brawley, Benjamin Griffith. *A social history of the American Negro*. NY: McMillian Company, 1921.

Brooks, Elbridge Streeter. *The True Story of George Washington: Called The Father Of His Country*. Lothrop Publishing, 1895.

Brown, Christopher L. *Moral Capital: Foundations of British Abolitionism*. NC: University of North America Press, 2006.

Chadwick, Bruce. *The Forging of A Revolutionary Leader and the Making of the Presidency: George Washington*. Ill: Sourcebooks, 2004.

Crossley, Pamela Daniel R. Headrick, Steven Hirsch, Lyman Johnson, *The Earth and Its Peoples: A Global History to 1550*. MA: Houghton Mifflin, 2009.

Davis, David B. *Inhuman Bondage: The Rise and Fall of Slavery in the New World*. New York: Oxford Press, 2006.

Davis, David B. *The Problem of Slavery in Western Society*. New York: Cornell University Press, 1966.

Deburg, William V. *Slavery and Race in American Popular Culture*. Madison: The University of Wisconsin, 1984.

Delany, Martin R. and Robert Steven Levine. *Martin R. Delany: A Documentary Reader*. NC: UNC Press, 2003.

Document: Edward Coles to James Madison, January 8, 1832, folder 30, box 1, E. *Coles Papers*, Princeton University Library.

Donald Yacovone, *Freedom's Journal: African American Voices of the Civil War*, (Chicago: Lawrence Hill, 2004), 31.

Douglas Brooke Wheelton Sladen, Ethel M. Stevens, Joseph I. Spadafora Whitaker, *Hanno and Tunis: the Old and New Gates of The Orient*. (London: Hutchinson and Company, 1906).

Duignan, P., and L. H. Gann, *The United States and Africa: A History*. Cambridge: Cambridge University Press, 1984.

Dunn D. E., and Svend E. Holsoe. *Historical Dictionary*. NJ: The Scarecrow Press, 1985.

E Lovejoy, Paul. *Transformations in slavery: a history of slavery in Africa*. UK: Cambridge University Press, 2000.

Evangelist Edwards' father, the revered Rev. Jonathan Edwards, Sr. of the Great Awakening, owned slaves and defended slavery. Edwards, Jr. opposed slavery and often preached against the dehumanization of blacks.

Fitzpatrick, John C. ed. *George Washington, The Writings of George Washington*. Washington, D. C.: United States Government Printing Office, 1936.

*Focus on the slave trade*. 28 May 2013). http://news.bbc.co.uk/2/hi/africa/1523100.stm.

Foote, Andrew H. *African and the American flag*. New York: D. Appleton & Company, 1854.

Forster, Kristen. *Moral Visions and Material Ambition: Philadelphia Struggles to Define the Republic 1776-1836*. Lexington Books, 2004.

Franklin Waters, Thomas. *Ipswich in the Massachusetts Bay Colony, Vol. 2*. Boston: Ipswich Historical Society, 1917.

Franklin, John H. *The Free Negro in North Carolina*. NC: University of North Carolina Press, 1943.

Gabriel Haslip-Viera, Bernard Ortiz de Montellano, and Warren Barbor. "CA Forum on Anthropology in Public: Robbing Native American Cultures: Van Sertima's Afrocentricity and the Omecs." *Current Anthropology*, Vol. 38, No. 3 (June, 1997), 419-422.

Gershoni, Yekutiel. *Black Colonization: The Americo-Liberian Scrambles for the Hinterland*. London: Westview Press, 1985.

Glazier, Stephen D. *Encyclopedia of African and African-American Religions*. NY: Routlege, 2001.

Grizzard, Frank E. *George! A Guide to All Things Washington*. Mariner Publishing, 2005.

Guelzo, Allen C. *Lincoln's Emancipation Proclamation: The end of Slavery in America*. NY: Simmon & Schuster, 2004.

Gurley Ralph, R. *Life of Jehudi Ashmun, Late Colonial Agent of Liberia*. Washington: James C. Dunn, 1835.

Hale, Sarah J. *Liberia of Mr.* Peyton's Experiments. New York: Harper & Brothers, 1853.

Hammond, Scott J. et al, ed. *Classics of American Political and Constitutional Thought: Origins Through The Civil War*. ID: Hackett Publishing Company, 2007.

Hashaw, Tim. *"The First Africans: A group of enslaved Africans changed Jamestown and the future of a nation,"*, in *USNews & World*

Henries, Doris B. *The Liberian Nation: A Sort History*. New York: Herman Jaffe, 1954.

Higginbotham, Don. *George Washington Reconsidered*. VA: University Press of Virginia, 2001.

Higginbotham, Don. *George Washington Reconsidered*. Virginia: The University of Virginia, 2001.

Hirschfeld, Fritz. *George Washington And Slavery: A Documentary Portray*. Missouri: University of Missouri Press, 1997.

Holen, Claude H. *African Americans in slavery, Civil War, and Reconstruction*. McFarland & Company, 2001.

Holen, Claude H., *African Americans in slavery, Civil War, and Reconstruction*, McFarland & Company, 2001.

Holland, Jesse J. *Discovering African-American History In and Around Washington, D.C.* Connecticut: The Globe Pequet Press, 2007.

Holsoe, S. E. *The Condo Confederation in Western Liberia*. Liberia Historical Review, III, 1 (1966).

Howard Brotz, *African-American Social and Political Thought, 1850-1920* (NJ: Transaction Publishers, 1992), 262.

Idowu, Amos A. *Effects of Female Genital-Mutilation on Human Rights of Women and Female Children: The Nigerian Situation*, Research Journal of International Studies, Issue 8 (November, 2008).

Ifayomi, Paul. *Grant, Blue Skies for Afrikans*. United Kingdom: Navig8or Press, 2005.

Imhotep, David. *The First Americans Were Africans: Documented Evidence*. IN: Authorship. 2012.

Irving, Washington. *A History of the Life and Voyages of Christopher Columbus*, Vol. 2. NY: G & C CARVILL, 1828.

Ischei, Elizabeth. *A History of The Igbo People*. NY: St. Martin Press, 1976.

Isichei, Elizabeth. *Igbo Worlds: An Anthology of Oral Histories and Historical Descriptions*. Philadelphia: ISHI, 1978.

Jackson, Gerald—2005—Preview "Robbing Native American cultures Van Sertima's Afrocentricity and the Olmecs." *Current Anthropology*, 38, (3), 419-431. 358 (October 26, 1999).

James Fairhead, Time Geysbeek, Svend E. Holsoe, Melissa Leach, *African American Exploration in West Africa: Four-Century Diaries* (Indiana: Indiana University Press, 2003).

Jay, William. *A view of the action of the federal government, in behalf of slaver*. New York: J.S. Taylor, 1839.

*Jefferson Writings* (1903), Vol. VIII, 241-242, to Benjamin Banneker on August 30, 1791.

Jefferson, Thomas and William Peden. ed. *Notes on the State of Virginia*. NC: University of North Carolina Press, 1955.

Jefferson, Thomas. *Notes on the State of Virginia*, 2nd ed. New York: M. L. & W. A. Davis, 1794. 240-242, Query XVIII.

Jeffrey A. Segal and Harold J. Spaeth, *The Supreme Court and the Attitudinal Model Revisited*. UK: Cambridge University Press, 2002.

Johnson, Clint.*The politically incorrect guide to the South: and why it will rise again*. Washington: Regnery Publishing, 2006.

Johnson, Kevin. *Mixed Race America and the Law*. NY: New York University Press, 2003.

Johnson, Tarnue C. *Education and Social Change in Liberia: New Perspectives for the 21st Century*. Indianna: Authorhouse, 2004.

Joseph Blake to R. R. Gurley, A.C.S., March 9, and May 13, 1835, *American Colonization Society Papers*, Library of Congress, Reel 153. Blake never received the redress he petitioned for, and left Liberia for Sierra Leone in 1837.

Joseph J. Roberts to President, *American Colonization Society*, Jan. 24, 1845 in Maryland Colonization Journal 2/21 (March 1845) "Slave Trading," 334-335.

*Journals of the Continental Congress*, Volume XXVI, pp. 118-119, Monday, March 1, 1784.

Kalra, Paul. *From Slave To Untouchable: Lincoln's Solution*. CA: Antenna Publishing, 2011.

Kapferer, Bruce. Biorm E. Bertelsen. *Crisis of State: War and Social Upheavals*. Ny: Berghalm Books, 2009.

Kenneth Barnes, *Journey of Hope: The Back-to-Africa Movement in Arkansas in the Late 1800s*. (NC: UNC Press, 2004), 154.

Ketcham, Ralph. *James Madison, A Biography*. Virginia: The University Press of Virginia, 1990.

Kete A. Molefi.*The History of Africa: The Quest for Eternal Harmony*. NY: Routledge, 200.

Ledgin, Norm. *Diagnosing Jefferson: Evidence of a Condition That Guided His Beliefs, Behavior and Personal Associations*. Arlington: future Horizon, 2000.

Léon Dénius Pamphile, *Haitians and African Americans: a Heritage of Tragedy and Hope* (Gainesville: University Press of Florida, 2001).

Leslie Alexander, *African or American? Black Identity and Political Activism* (NC: University of North Carolina Press, 2004).

Levy, Debbie. *James Monroe*. MN. Lerner Publications Company, 2005.

Levy, Patricia and Michael Spilling. *Cultures of the world:* Liberia. Cavendish, Marshall Corporation, 2008.

Leyman, Michael and Elliott R. Barkan. *U.S. Immigration and Naturalization Laws and Issues: A Documentary History*. CT: Greenwood Publishing Group, 1999.

Liebenow, J. Gus. *The Evolution of Privilege*. NY: Cornell University Press, 1969.

Litwack, Leon F. *Been in the Storm So Long: The Aftermath of Slavery*. NY: Random House, 1980.

Loewen, James W. and Edward H. Sebesta. *The Confederate and Neo-Confederate Reader: The Great Truth About the Lost Cause*. MS: University Press of Mississippi, 2010.

Lossing, Benson J. *Emminent Americans Comprising Brief Biographies of Leading Statesmen, Patriots, Orators, and Other Men and Women Who Have Made the American History* Vol. II. NY: American Publishers Corporation, 1890.

Lovejoy, Paul. *Transformation Into Slavery: A History of Slavery in Africa*. NY: Cambridge Press, 2012.

Lynch, Hollis. *Edward Blyden: Pan-Negro Patriot: 1832-1912*. Oxford: Oxford University Press, 1967.

M. Stanley, Henry. *Through the Dark Continent: Or, the Sources of the Nile, around the Great Lakes of Equatorial Africa and down the Livingstone River to the Atlantic Ocean*. NY: Harper and Brothers Publishers, 1878.

Malcomson, Scott L. *One Drop of Blood: The American Misadventure of Race.* NY: Farrar, Straus, and Girous, 2000.

Malone, Ann P. *Sweet Chariot.* NC: The University of North Carolina Press, 1992.

Mancall, Peter C. *The Atlantic World and Virginia, 1550-1624.* NC: University of North Carolina Press, 2007.

*Mandinka (Mandidng) Voyages and Exploration. 10* March 2013. http://historyofislam.com /contents/the-classical-period/ the-african-and-muslim-discovery-of-america-before-columbus.

Mann, Charles C. *1493: Uncovering the New World Columbus Created.* NY: Alfred A. Knopf, 2011.

Marder, William *Indians in the Americas: The Unknown Story.* CA: Boo k Tree, 2005.

Marshall, John and Bushrod Washington. *Life of George Washington: Commander in Chief of the American Forces and First President of the United States.* PA: C.P. Wayne, 1806.

McColley, Robert in. *Dictionary of Afro-American Slavery*, Randall M. Miller and John David Smith, eds. CT: Greenwood Press, 1988.

McCullough, David. *John Adams.* NY: Simon & Schuster, 2001.

McMaster, John Bach. *A History of the United States, From Revolution to Civil War.* New York: D. Appleton and Company, 1922.

McPherson, J.H.T. *History of Liberia,* John Hopkins University Studies 9th Series, X, 34.

Michele Mitchel, *Righteous propagation: African Americans and the politics of racial destiny* (NC: University of North Carolina Press, 2004), 23.

Miller, John C., *This New Man, the American: Beginnings of the American People.* NY: Oxford University Press, 1974.

Miller, Randall M. and John David Smith, *Dictionary of Afro-American Slavery*.CT: Greewood Press, 1997.

Miller, Randall. *Dear Master: Letters From a Slave Family*. GA: University of Georgia Press, 1990.

Mitchell, Angelyn. *The Freedom to Remember: Narrative, Slavery, and Gender in Contemporary*. NJ: Rutgers University Press, 2002.

Morgan, Kenneth. *Slavery and the British Empire*. Oxford: Oxford University Press, 2007.

Moses, Wilson J. *Classic Black Nationalism: From American Revolution to Marcus Garvey*. NY: New York University Press, 1996.

Moses, Wilson J. *Classical Black Nationalism: From the American Revolution to Marcus Garvey*. NY: New York University Press, 1996.

Newcomb, Harvey. *Cyclopedia of Missions: Containing Comprehensive New of Missionary Operations Throughout the World*. NY: Charles Scribner, 1856.

Niles, Grace G. *The Hoosac Valley—Its Legends and Its History*. MD: Heritage Books, 1997.

Nowlan, Robert A. *The American Presidents, Washington to Tyler: What They Said*, What was Said About Them, with Full Source Notes NC: Farland and Company, 2002.

O. Gabriel, Kingsley. *African Contributions to Civilizations*. MD: Black Classic Press, 1999.

Olukoju, Ayodeji. *Culture and Customs of Liberia*. CT: Greenwood Press, 2006.

Papenfuse, Eric R. *The Evils Of Necessary: Robert Goodloe Harper and the Moral Dilemma of Slavery*. Philadelphia: American Philosophical Society, 1997.

Paul F. Paskoff and Daniel J. Wilson, ed. *The Cause of the South: Selections from De Bow's Review, 1846-1867*. Louisiana: Louisiana State University Press, 1982.

Paul Kalra, *Slave to Untouchable: Lincoln's Solution*. CA: Antenna Publishing Company, 2011.

Pinkney, Alphonso. *Red Black and Green: Black Nationalism in the United States*. London: Syndics Cambridge University Press, 1976.

Putney, Martha S. *Blacks in the United states Army*. NC: McFarland, 2003.

Quarles, Benjamin. *Lincoln and the Negro*. NY: Oxford University Press, 1962.

Ress, David. *Governor Edward Coles and the Vote to Forbid Slavery in Illinois: 1823-1824*. NC: McFarland & Company, 2006.

Sabine R. Huebner (2009), *Female Circumcision as a Rite de Passage in Egypt—Continuity Through the Millennia?* Journal of Egyptian History, Volume 2, Numbers 1-2, 2009, 149-171(23).

Salzberger, Ronald P., and Mary Turck, *Reparations for Slavery: A Reader*. MD: Rowman & Littlefield Publishers, 2004.

Schafer, Judith K. *Becoming Free, Remaining Free: Manumission and Enslavement in New Orleans: 1846-1862*. Louisiana: Louisiana University Press, 2003.

Schultz, Kevin. *America Unbound: A U. S. History*. Clark Baxter and Susanne Jeans, 2010.

Schwarz, Frederic D. *1831: "Nat Turner's Rebellion,"* *American Heritage*, August/September 2006.

Schwarz, Philip J. *Slave Laws in Virginia*. Georgia: University of Georgia Press, 1996.

Sidbury, James. *Becoming African In America: The African American*. New York: Oxford University Press, 2007.

Sir Johnston, Harry H. *The Negro in the New World*. New York: Macmillan Company, 1910.

Sir Johnston, Harry. *Liberia*Vol. 1. NY: Dodd, Mead & Company.

Sirleaf, Ellen J. *The Child Will Be Great: Memoir of a Remarkable Life by Africa's First Woman President*. NY: HarperCollins Publishers, 2009.

Soma, Syrulwa L. *Historical Resettlement of Liberia and Its Environmental Impact*. MD: University Press of America, 1995.

Starr, Frederick. *Liberia: Description, History, Problems*. Chicago, 1913.

Steady, Filomina C. *Women And Collective Action in Africa*. NY: Palgrave & Macmillan, 2006.

Stroud, George M. *A Sketch of the Laws Relating to Slavery in the Several States of the United States of America*. Philadelphia: Henry Longstreth, 1856.

T. Jefferson to Edward Coles, Aug. 25, 1814, Ford, ed., *Works of Thomas Jefferson*, XI, 416.

Taylor, Nikki. *Reconsidering the 'Forced' Exodus of 1829: Free Black Emigration from Cincinnati, Ohio to Wilberforce, Canada*. The Journal of African American History No. 87 (2002, 288).

*The African Repository and Colonial Journal*, Volume 45, 1869, 370.

*The African Repository and Colonial Journal*, Vol. 2, No. 4, June 1826.

*The African Repository and Colonial Journal*, Vol. XV. Washington: American Colonization Society, 1839.

The African repository, Volume 9, No. 1, *American Colonization Society*. Washington DC: James C, Dunn, 1834.

The coastline from Sierra Leone and Ivory Coast was called Malagueta Coast or Pepper Coast. The Malaueta Pepper was used for spices. "Grains of Paradise" became a preferred name for the English and Dutch explorers for the same product.

The Journal of Negro History, Vol. 2, No. 4, Oct. 1917.

*The Late Hilary Teage of Liberia*, African Repository (October 1853).

*The Liberian Repository and Colonial Journal*, Vols. LVII, LVIII, LIX. Washington D.C.: American Colonization Society 1883.

*The Seventh Annual Report of The American Society For Colonizing the Free People of Colour Of The United States With An Appendix.* Washington, DC: Davis and Force Franklin's Head, 1824.

This refers to the tendency to declare Africa as a victim or lesser player in the domestic and trans-Atlantic slave trade. Slavery in Africa is presented as a benign institution which did very little harm to its captives.

Thomas Jefferson to Edward Coles, August 25, 1814, *E. Coles Papers,* Princeton University Library.

Thornton, John. *Africa and Africans in the Making of the Atlantic World, 1400*-1800, 2$^{nd}$ edition. New York: Cambridge University Press, 1998.

Sertima, Ivan. "African presence in early America," *Journal of African Civilizations,* Vol. 8, Issue 2 (1992), 80.

Walters, Joseph J., Gareth Griffiths and John Victor. *Singler Guanya Pau: A Story of an African Princess.* Broadview Press, 2004.

Watkins, Samuel R. *Liberia Communication.* Indiana: Authorhouse, 2007.

Watson, James L. *Asian and African Systems of Slavery* (CA: University of California Press, 1980), 39.

White, Deborah G. *Ar'n't I a Woman?: Female Slaves in the Plantation South* (Revised Edition). NY: Norton & Company, 1999.

White, Deborah G., *Ar'n't I a Woman?: Female Slaves in the Plantation South* (Revised Edition). NY: Norton & Company, 1999.

Whittaker, Sabas. *Africans in the Americas Our Journey Throughout the World.* NE: iUniverse, 2003.

Wiencek, Henry. *Imperfect God: George Washington, His Slaves, and the Creation of America.* New York: Farrar, Straus and Girous, 2004.

Wood, Gordon. *The American Revolution: A History.* New York: Modern Library, 2002.

Woodson, Carter G. Ed. *The Struggle of Liberia and Haiti For Recognition.* The Journal of Negro History, Volume 2. PA: The Association For The Study Of The Negro Life And History, 1917.

Wulah, M. Teah. *Back to Africa: A Liberian Tragedy.* In: Authorhouse, 2009.

# Select Index

## A

Abubakari II, King 4
Africa 1, 2, 10, 87, 98, 100, 104, 123, 138, 154, 208
African Methodist Episcopal Church 20, 71
Alexandria, Egypt 10
Allen, Richard 20
Allen, Richard 103
Almoravids 117
American Colonization Society xvi, 78, 83, 85, 99, 102, 106, 121, 146
Americo-Liberians 154
Angola 12, 105
Antebellum America 27
Ashmun, Jehudi 132, 139
Ayres, Eli 126, 130, 143

## B

Bacon, Samuel 85, 87
Banneker, Benjamin 36
Bartolomé de las Casas 1, 8
Barton, David 26
Bassa 112, 113, 118, 129, 150, 151, 158
Benjamin Rush 19, 21, 63, 67
Beyan, Amos 123
Blanco, Pedro 115
Blyden, Edward Wilmot 163, 167
Brazil 4, 6, 181
Brown, John 71, 96, 97
Bryant, Linda

Blacks relative of George Washington 57
Buchanan, Thomas 151, 164
Bukele, Momolu Duwalu 118
Burgess, Ebenezer 98, 120

## C

cannibalism 156
Carey, Lott 132, 136, 138, 139, 144, 146
Caribs 6
Cartwright, Samuel 23
Cavalla River 119
Celia's Trial 54
Chares 6
circumcision 158, 159, 161
Clay, Henry 78, 79, 183
clitoridectomy 159
Coker, Daniel 86, 87
Coles, Edward 38, 40, 108
Colonization 96, 108, 189
Columbus, Christopher 1, 2, 8, 10
Constitutional Convention 29, 41, 42
Criticism of the ACS 88
Cuffe, Paul 76, 88, 124
Custis, Martha 28, 57, 58

## D

Declaration of Independence 16, 33, 61, 66, 172
Delany, Martin 102, 108
Delany, Martin R. 104, 105
Douglass, Frederick 52, 96, 104, 190
Dred Scott Case

Controversy Over Black
Citizenship 22

## E

Edward J. Roye 186
Edwards, Jonathan 68
Egypt xiv, 2, 10
Emigration 79, 94, 99, 102

## F

Female Genital Mutilation or Cutting
(FGM/C), 159
Finley, Robert 77, 78, 151
Forten, James 88, 103
Freedmen 70, 79
Fugitive Act of 1793 28

## G

Gallinas 114, 115, 168, 169
Garrison, William Lloyd 94
Gatumba 135
Gatumba, Chief 155
Gbandi 117, 118, 158
Gehtumben, Chief 130
Ghana 10, 116, 117, 192, 196
Gio 118, 119, 155
Gola 105, 115, 118, 130, 155, 158, 159,
166
*Grain Coast* 112, 117, 119
Gray, Bob 143, 150
Gray, Catherine D. 137
Grebo 118, 149, 150
Grégoire, Henri-Baptiste 35
guanín 1
*Gurley Constitution* 138, 146
Gurley, Ralph 96, 107, 136

## H

Haiti 28, 70, 102, 103, 120, 181, 184
Haitian Revolution 68
Hanno of Carthage 111
Harper, Robert Goodloe 69

Hawkins, John 114
*Haytian Emigration Society* 103
Hemings, Sally 60
Hispaniola 1, 2
Hopkins, Samuel 98
Hueyapan, Veracruz 7
Hulsius, Levinus 113

## I

Immigration 22
Indentured servants 11, 13, 18
Irving, Washington 2

## J

Jairazbhoy, R.A. Jairazbhoy
Indian historian 5
Jame, Mauren 10
Jamestown 1, 12, 14, 22
Jefferson, Thomas 15, 25, 33, 38
Johnson, Elijah 131, 132
Jones, Absalom 20

## K

Karnga, Abayomi 117
Kerekou, Matthieu 199
King Boatswain 130, 148
King John II of Portugal 1
King Musa 4
King Peter 113, 127, 128, 129
Kissi 115, 118, 158
Kizell, John 121, 122, 123, 124, 125
Kpelle 118, 158
Krahn 118
Kru 113, 115, 158

## L

Lafayette, Marquis de 30
La Isabela's 15th-century graveyard 3
Laurens, Henry 27
Liberia xv, 85, 100, 116, 131, 138, 139,
147, 169, 170, 183, 184
Liberia College 181

Lone Star 178
Lorma 115, 117, 118

# M

Madison, James 39, 62, 75, 78, 93
*Malagueta Pepper Coast* 112
Mali 4, 10, 116, 118, 119, 192
Mandingos 119
Massachusetts 14, 15, 70
Mechlin, Joseph 141
Mesurado 112, 113, 125, 132
Mexico 5, 6, 7, 167
Mills-Burgess Report 124, 125
Mills, John S. 125
Mills, Samuel J. 98
Monroe, James 70, 83, 107, 126, 166
Monrovia 132, 146
Montpelier Plantation 40
Morocco 11
motto 70, 180
Mount Vernon 28, 31, 91
Mulattoes 14, 26, 59, 122, 163, 164

# N

National Anthem 180
Negro diseases 22
*Negrohead Run* 40
New Jersey 18, 77
Nile 2
*Northwest Territory Act* of 1789 28

# P

Pedro de Cintra 112, 116
Philadelphia 19, 20, 31, 88, 146, 194, 206
*Popol Vuh.*
  And \ 6
Poro and Sande 156, 158, 159, 162
Price, Douglas 3
*Prince Regent* 134
Prosser, Gabriel 70

# Q

Qaddafi, Muammar 199
Quaker 15, 67, 93, 95

# R

Randolph, John 18, 39, 78, 79, 94, 108
Recaptives 119, 151
Remisch, Herr
  Viennese and Egyptologist 5
Revolutionary Fathers 16, 24, 56
Revolutionary War 16, 24, 28, 30, 98, 122
Richard Allen 88, 91
Roberts, Joseph J. 151
Rolfe, John 12
Rush, Benjamin 33
Russwurm, John Brown 96

# S

Sally Hemings 60
Saltonstall, Richard 15
scarification 159
Schroeder, Hannes 3
Sierra Leone 88, 98, 121, 122, 123, 124,
  141, 151
Songhay 10
South Carolina 18, 68, 115, 122
Stanley, Henry 8
Stockton, Robert F. 126

# T

Taney, Roger B. 22
Tarzan xiii, xiv
Teage, Hilary 143, 172
Thanksgiving Day 134
The *Alligator,* 126
The American Colonization Society xv,
  73, 77, 79, 85, 96, 141, 143
The *Elizabeth* 87, 125
The Jefferson Bible 63
The Life and Morals of Jesus of
  Nazareth 63

The *Nautilus* 125, 132
The *Strong* 132
three-fifths ratio 43
Timbuktu xiv, 10
Tribes 114, 115, 155, 158, 159
Turner, Nat 71

## V

Vai Script 113, 115, 118, 130, 158
Vesey, Denmark 71
Virginia 1, 12, 13, 22, 25, 34, 74, 95

## W

Walker, John 62, 65, 66
Washington, George 16, 28, 56, 57, 58, 59
West Africa 111
West Ford 57, 58, 59, 91
Wiener, Leo 8
Wiercinski, Andrzej
    Discovered colossal head at Olmec
      sites 7
Wiltherger, Christian 131
Woodson, Carter 8
WPA (Works Progress Administration)
    Slave Narrative Project 45